D0338528

365 Recipes

Delicious meals for every day

Editorial and texts Silke Propp-Frey, Wolfgang Zahner
Art direction Hans-Jürgen Polster
Photography Matthias Haupt
Recipes Cornelia Dümling, Anne Haupt
Marion Heidegger, Oliver Trific
Styling Isabel de la Fuente, Meike Graf, Anke Grelik
Michaela Suchy, Tanja Wegener
Layout Christina Ackermann, Anja Jung
Picture editing MWW Repro GmbH
Proofreading German original Daniela Karpinski
Project manager Dr. Frank Stahmer

Special edition by Naumann & Göbel Verlagsgesellschaft mbH,
a subsidiary of VEMAG Verlags- und Medien Aktiengesellschaft, Cologne
www.vemag-medien.de
All rights Gruner + Jahr AG & Co, Hamburg
Translation from German: Rosetta Translations, London
Proofreading American version: Christopher Morley
Complete production: Naumann & Göbel Verlagsgesellschaft mbH, Cologne
Printed in Germany
All rights reserved
ISBN 978-3-625-01001-2

365 DAYS AND JUST AS MANY RECIPES

IT'S AN AGE-OLD QUESTION: WHAT SHALL I COOK TODAY? This recipe book will provide you with plenty of ideas. It contains 365 delicious recipes, one for every day of the year. The simple instructions are easy to follow and the results are sure to please. Arranged by the months of the calendar, some of the recipes are based on seasonal ingredients while many others can be made all year round. You will certainly find some special favorites among them that you will enjoy again and again. Every recipe is accompanied by detailed nutritional information and guidance as to how long it takes to prepare. All in all, this book will help you answer one of the questions most often asked at home: "What shall I cook today?"

CONTENTS

JANUARY – PAGE 12 ONWARDS

FEBRUARY –

PAGE 52 ONWARDS

MARCH – PAGE 86 ONWARDS

CONTENTS

CONTENTS

CONTENTS

Good resolutions for the New Year

People make so many resolutions for the New Year! Giving up smoking, exercising more, or going on that diet. But we suggest you relax. We do not want to force you to diet, instead we offer you something you will really enjoy. Our dishes are both healthy and well-balanced. Have a happy and tasty New Year!

Smoked Loin of Pork

Because it makes roasting the loin of pork so much easier, and because the roast remains so juicy, a roasting bag is a real boon in the kitchen.

Serves 4:

14 oz thin carrots

7 oz onions

14 oz small potatoes

4 tbsp oil

7 oz sauerkraut

salt

pepper

2 tsp ground caraway seeds

2 lb 3 oz smoked loin of pork (boneless)

2 bay leaves

½ bunch parsley

⅝ cup vegetable stock

1 Peel the carrots, halve them lengthways and cut them into pieces diagonally. Cut the onions into slices. Peel the potatoes and fry them in hot oil in a large pan, turning them regularly. After 7 minutes, add the carrots and onions. Stir in the sauerkraut and season with salt, pepper, and caraway.

2 Prepare a roasting bag (about 16 in long) according to the instructions on the package and place on a cookie sheet. Put the vegetable mixture inside the bag. Sprinkle a generous amount of pepper on the smoked loin of pork and then place it on top of the vegetables. Add the bay leaves and half the parsley, then pour in the vegetable stock. Close the roasting bag according to the instructions on the package and cut a few slits in it.

3 Preheat the oven to 390 degrees. Put the cookie sheet with the loin of pork on the lowest shelf and cook for 40 minutes. Arrange on a dish, sprinkle with the rest of the parsley and serve.

Preparation time: 60 minutes.
Per serving: 50 g P, 21 g F, 21 g C = 480 kcal (2013 kJ).

ROASTING BAG METHOD:
Even simpler: all the ingredients are placed in the roasting bag with the loin of pork. Close the bag, cook in the oven and relax until the roast is ready.

Corn salad with Apple Vinaigrette

Spruce up your favorite salad with a delicious fruity apple dressing and crunchy roast sunflower seeds.

Serves 2: 1 Core a red **apple** and cut one half into small cubes, leaving the skin on. Dice one **onion** finely. Mix together 3 tbsp of **oil**, 3 tbsp of **grape seed oil**, and 2 tbsp of **cider vinegar**, then add the diced apple and onion. Season with salt, pepper, and a little **sugar**. **2** Roast 1 tbsp of **sunflower seeds** in a pan without fat. Wash and prepare 4½ oz of **corn salad**, spin until dry and arrange on two plates. Drizzle the vinaigrette over the top, then sprinkle with the sunflower seeds and freshly ground **pepper**.

Preparation time: 20 minutes. **Per serving:** 2 g P, 33 g F, 9 g C = 338 kcal (1416 kJ).

Vol-au-vent with Chicken Ragout

A light and very satisfying delicacy: a classic chicken ragout in a delicate puff pastry.

Serves 2: 1 Season 2 **chicken fillets** (5 oz each) with salt and pepper. Bring 2¼ cups **chicken stock** to the boil with 1 **bay leaf**. Add the chicken breasts, cover and simmer over medium heat for 15–18 minutes. Remove the chicken breasts and put to one side. Pour the stock through a strainer. **2** Clean and slice 3½ oz **mushrooms**. Cut 1 **onion** into small cubes, peel 3½ oz **carrots** and cut into cubes of ⅛ in. Melt 2 tbsp of **butter** in a pan, add all the vegetables and braise lightly. Stir in 6 tbsp of **white wine**, then add 1 cup of the chicken stock saved from earlier, and ½ cup of **whipping cream**. Cook for 5 minutes. **3** Bake 4 frozen **vol-au-vent shells** (1 oz each) following the instructions on the packet. Stir 2 tbsp of **classic roux mixture** into the pan with the vegetables and cream, and bring to the boil again. Cut the chicken into small pieces and add to the vegetable mixture together with 3½ oz **frozen peas**. Heat the mixture through and season with salt, pepper, **nutmeg**, and 1–2 tsp **lemon juice**. Spoon the mixture into the prepared vol-au-vent shells, then sprinkle 4 tbsp of minced parsley on top.

Preparation time: 40 minutes.
Per serving: 48 g P, 43 g F, 36 g C = 730 kcal (3049 kJ).

Sweet and Sour Pork

There is no need to go out to a Chinese restaurant when you can prepare your favorite dish very quickly and easily at home.

Serves 2 portions: 1 Cut 10 ½ oz of **escalope of pork** into strips ⅜ in wide. Stir together 3 tbsp **soy sauce** and 2 tbsp **white wine vinegar**. Sprinkle half over the meat and leave to marinate. Wash and prepare 1 **red bell pepper** and cut into thin strips. Slice 1 **onion** into thin strips. Cut open 1 red **chili pepper**, de-seed and mince. **2** Drain 1 can of **pineapple** slices (8 ½ oz drained weight), reserving 5 tbsp of the juice. Cut the pineapple slices into pieces. **3** Pat the meat dry and fry briskly in 2 tbsp hot **oil** until brown all over. Remove the meat and lightly braise the onion, chili pepper, pineapple pieces, and red bell pepper in the same pan. **4** Add the remaining soy sauce mixture, ⅝ cup **vegetable stock**, 3 tbsp **ketchup**, 1 tsp **honey**, and the pineapple juice. Simmer uncovered for 5 minutes. You can also thicken the sauce with gravy browning if necessary. Add the meat, heat briefly and season again to taste. Sprinkle with 2 tbsp minced **parsley**. This dish should be served with rice.

* **Preparation time:** 40 minutes. Per serving: 38 g P, 14 g F, 39 g C = 440 kcal (1849 kJ).

"Poor Knight"

You must be joking: those old knights amassed vast wealth.
But then again, who wants white bread when you can have stollen!

Serves 4:

3 ½ oz cranberry compote

½ cup orange juice

2 pinches ground cinnamon

2 eggs (medium)

⅝ cup milk

1 ½ tsp vanilla sugar

salt

8 slices stollen (1 ½ oz each)

4 scoops vanilla ice cream

1 Stir together the cranberry compote, orange juice, and cinnamon in a small pan, bring to the boil and simmer for 3–4 minutes. Put to one side.

2 Whip the eggs, milk, vanilla sugar, and a pinch of salt briskly together. Turn the slices of stollen several times in the egg and milk mixture until it is completely soaked.

3 Heat the clarified butter in a pan and fry the stollen slices over medium heat for 3–4 minutes on each side. Remove from the pan and drain briefly on kitchen paper.

4 Serve with vanilla ice cream and the cranberry compote mixture.

* **Preparation time:** 25 minutes.
  Per serving: 12 g P, 32 g F, 63 g C = 589 kcal (2470 kJ).

JUICY KNIGHT:
Stollen is richer than white bread, which is usually used to make "Poor Knight". Therefore, you should turn the slices several times, allowing them to get fully soaked.

Horseradish and Cream Soup

If you like horseradish (and who doesn't?), then this spicy soup will make a perfect appetizer.

Serves 4: 1 Peel 1 lb 2 oz floury **potatoes** and cut into cubes together with 1 **onion**, also cut into cubes. Lightly fry these in 2 tbsp **butter**, add 4 ½ cups **vegetable stock** (made from a bouillon cube or powder), bring to the boil, cover and cook over medium heat for 20 minutes. Peel 7 oz **carrots** and grate or cut into thin strips. Cook in boiling salted water for 3 minutes. Drain, quench with cold water and drain again. **2** Puree the soup finely and heat up again with **whipping cream**. Season with 4–5 tsp **horseradish** (from a jar), salt, pepper, 1 pinch **sugar**, and 1–2 tsp **lemon juice**. Reheat the carrots in the soup. Sprinkle some **cress** over the soup as garnish.

Preparation time: 35 minutes. **Per serving:** 5 g P, 18 g F, 22 g C = 270 kcal (1129 kJ).

Pollock in Mustard Sauce

A marriage made in heaven: the crisply fried fish fillets are served with a smooth mustard sauce, which makes a perfect accompaniment.

Serves 2: 1 Add ½ cup of **vegetable stock** to ½ cup **whipping cream**, bring to the boil and simmer for 3 minutes in a pan without a lid. You may also thicken this mixture with 1 tsp **cornstarch**, if required. Stir in 2–3 tbsp **mustard** with seeds. Season with salt, pepper, 1 pinch **sugar**, and 1–2 tsp **lemon juice** and keep warm. Season two **pollock fillets** (5 oz each) with salt, pepper, and 1–2 tsp lemon juice. **2** Coat the pieces of fish first in 4 tbsp **flour**, then in 1 **egg** and finally in 6 tbsp **breadcrumbs**. Heat 2 tbsp **oil** and 2 tbsp **butter** together in a non-stick pan. Fry the fillets for 3–4 minutes on each side until golden brown. Remove the leaves from 6 stems of **dill**, mince them and add to the sauce. Serve the fish and sauce with a **lemon quarter** to garnish.

* **Preparation time:** 30 minutes. **Per serving:** 36 g P, 38 g F, 30 g C = 604 kcal (2530 kJ).

Fish Cakes

*After trying this delicious fish cake and potato combination,
your children (and you) may never want to eat fish sticks again.*

Serves 4:

1 ¼ lb pollock fillet

2 eggs (medium, separated)

3 tbsp breadcrumbs

2 tsp prepared mustard

5 oz crème fraîche

6 tbsp milk

2 tsp hot mustard

1 tbsp dill (minced)

salt

pepper

sugar

6 tbsp potato flakes (e.g. instant mashed potatoes)

2 tbsp oil

1 Cut the pollock fillet into small pieces and process in a small grinder or food processor. In a bowl, mix together the fish, egg whites, breadcrumbs, and 1 tsp prepared mustard. Shape this mixture into 16 small fish cakes and put them into the freezer for 10 minutes.

2 Mix together 5 oz crème fraîche, 5 tbsp milk, 2 tsp hot mustard, 1 tsp prepared mustard, and dill. Season with salt, pepper, and a little sugar to make the sauce.

3 Stir 1 tbsp milk into the egg yolks, dip the fish cakes into this egg mixture, then coat with potato flakes. Fry in hot oil in a non-stick pan over medium heat for 3–4 minutes on each side until golden brown. Serve with the sauce and French fries.

Preparation time: 50 minutes.
Per serving: 35 g P, 22 g F, 20 g C = 418 kcal (1752 kJ).

FOR A GOLDEN CRUST:
The trick is to first coat the fish cakes in the egg mixture, then coat with potato flakes. The result is a marvelously crisp coating.

Rigatoni with Smoked Loin of Pork

Smoked loin of pork and sauerkraut is a classic combination, and the rigatoni make a delicious addition.

Serves 2: 1 Finely dice 2 **onions**. Cut 7 oz of **loin of pork** into cubes and fry the meat in a pan in 1 tablespoon of **oil** until golden brown. Remove the cubes of pork and braise the diced onion lightly in the pan. Sprinkle 1 tsp of **sweet paprika powder** over the onions. **2** Add 1 can of **sauerkraut** (10 oz drained weight), 1 tbsp **sugar**, and 1 tbsp **vinegar** to the pan. Cook for 5 minutes over medium heat, stirring continuously. Return the cubed pork to the pan and cook for another 3 minutes. **3** In a second pan, heat 2 tbsp butter until foaming and stir in 14 oz of **rigatoni**. Sprinkle 1 tbsp of minced **parsley** over the rigatoni. **4** Mix together the rigatoni and the sauerkraut mixture and serve with **sour cream**.

* **Preparation time:** 25 minutes.
  Per serving: 29 g P, 25 g F, 75 g C = 646 kcal (2720 kJ).

Mango-banana Shake

Very, very creamy and smooth: the best remedy for the winter blues!

Serves 2: 1 In a blender, puree 1 <u>**banana**</u> and 9 oz of the <u>**flesh of some mangoes**</u> with 5 oz <u>**low-fat yoghurt**</u>, 1 cup of <u>**milk**</u>, 1 tsp <u>**ground cinnamon**</u>, and ½ tsp ground <u>**ginger**</u>. **2** Beat ½ cup <u>**whipping cream**</u> until semi-thick. Pour the milk shake into two cooled glasses, top with whipped cream, sprinkle with cinnamon and serve.

Preparation time: 10 minutes.
Per serving: 10 g P, 20 g F, 36 g C = 370 kcal (1553 kJ).

Cashew Rice

Rice for every occasion. Grainy and light, the scallions add a fresh taste while the roast cashew nuts give it a crisp, crunchy texture.

Serves 2: 1 Mince 1 **onion** and fry in 2 tbsp **butter** until transparent. Now add ¾ cup **long-grain rice**, stir and fry for 30 seconds, then add 1 ½ cups water. Season with salt and bring to the boil. Allow to boil fiercely for 1 minute, then reduce the heat and simmer for 20 minutes over low heat. **2** Dry roast 1 ¾ oz **cashew nuts** in a pan and mince coarsely. **3** Wash and prepare 2 **scallions** and cut into fine rings. Fry in 2 tbsp butter, season with salt and pepper, and stir into the rice.

* **Preparation time:** 30 minutes. **Per serving:** 10 g P, 34 g F, 70 g C = 623 kcal (2609 kJ).

Crêpes with Pear Compote

This delicious dish combines two favorite desserts: a lovely pear compote and delicate crêpes.

Serves 4: 1 Peel, quarter and de-seed 1 lb 2 oz **pears**, then slice length-ways. Bring to the boil ½ cup **caramel sauce** (from a bottle), together with the grated zest of an **(untreated) orange**, ⅝ cup of **orange juice** and the pulp of 1 **vanilla bean** in a wide-bottomed saucepan. Mix together 1 tsp **cornstarch** and 1 tbsp **orange liqueur** until smooth, then add to the orange-caramel mixture. **2** Now add the slices of pear, cover and cook over medium heat for 5–6 minutes. Spread 4 **crêpes** (2 oz each, from the frozen food section) with 2 tbsp of melted **butter**. Stack on top of each other on a cookie sheet. Preheat the oven to 300 degrees and bake for 10 minutes on the middle shelf from the bottom (in a fan oven: 7 minutes at 265 degrees). Stuff the crêpes with the pear compote. Sprinkle each crêpe with 1 tbsp **confectioners' sugar** and minced **pistachio nuts** before serving.

* **Preparation time: 25 minutes. Per serving: 7 g P, 11 g F, 47 g C = 323 kcal (1349 kJ).**

Potato and Ceps Gratin

You can quickly transform a simple potato gratin into a sophisticated dish by adding ceps and Gruyere

Serves 2:

½ cup whipping cream

⅝ cup milk

⅓ oz dried ceps

1 clove garlic

1 lb 9 oz potatoes

salt

pepper

nutmeg

1¾ oz grated Gruyère, Emmental or other semi-hard cheese

1 Heat the whipping cream and milk. Rinse the ceps with cold water and add to the hot cream-milk mixture. Remove the pan from the heat and leave to stand for 10 minutes. Using a skimming ladle, remove the ceps from the cream-milk mixture and mince. Also mince the clove of garlic.

2 Peel the potatoes and cut into thin slices ⅒-in thick. Now add the potatoes, minced ceps, and garlic to the milk and cook for about 10 minutes over medium heat. Stir several times to prevent the potatoes from sticking. Season generously with salt, pepper, and nutmeg.

3 Arrange the slices of potatoes in a greased gratin dish (9½ x 6 in). Sprinkle cheese on top. Bake in the oven, preheated to 390 degrees (fan oven 350 degrees), on the middle shelf for about 15 minutes. Leave to cool for 10 minutes in the oven after turning it off, then serve.

Preparation time: 40 minutes.
Per serving: 17 g P, 29 g F, 39 g C = 490 kcal (2058 kJ).

DRIED CEPS:
In the past, dried ceps were only available in delicatessens but today they are also available at reasonable prices in supermarkets.

Top Round with Mushrooms

Pleasantly juicy because it is cooked in one large piece and sliced just before serving.

Serves 2:1 Cut 3½ oz **onions** into thin strips. Wash and prepare 10½ oz **oyster mushrooms** and cut in half if too large. Wash and prepare 3½ oz **arugula** and mince coarsely. Season the piece of **beef top round** (about 10½ oz) with salt and pepper. Fry briskly in 2 tbsp hot **oil** in a non-stick pan for 1 minute on each side. **2** Place the meat in an oven-proof dish and cook in the oven, preheated to 355 degrees, on the second shelf from the bottom for 8–10 minutes, depending on how well-cooked you like it. (Cooking in a fan-assisted oven is not recommended). **3** Add 5 tbsp **white wine** and ⅞ cup **beef stock** and cook without a lid for 5 minutes. Thicken with ½ tbsp **cornstarch** as needed. Season with salt, pepper, and **nutmeg**. Allow the meat to stand briefly. Add the arugula to the mushrooms and serve with the sliced meat.

* **Preparation time:** 40 minutes. **Per serving:** 37 g P, 27 g F, 27 g C = 480 kcal (2012 kJ).

Gratinéed Grapefruit

Stunningly simple and amazingly delicious: hot grapefruit with brown sugar and lemon cream with coriander.

Serves 2: 1 Cut 1 **pink grapefruit** in half and cut all round so that the flesh is detached from the zest and is only attached in the middle. Dab the cut surface dry and place in the refrigerator for 15 minutes. **2** Stir together 2 tbsp cream with ½ tsp **grated lemon zest (untreated)**, 1 tsp **lemon juice**, 2 pinches ground **coriander**, and 2 tsp **sugar** until smooth. Cover and put in a cool place. **3** Take the grapefruit halves out of the refrigerator and sprinkle 2 tbsp **brown sugar** on top. Place on a cookie sheet and allow to caramelize on the top shelf under the preheated oven broiler. Keep a close eye on the broiler to make sure that the sugar doesn't burn! Serve with the lemon-flavored cream.

* **Preparation time: 20 minutes. Per serving: 1 g P, 6 g F, 54 g C = 283 kcal (1185 kJ).**

Winter Stew

There is nothing more warming than a tasty stew, made with good winter vegetables and delicious cooked sausage.

Serves 2:

10 oz yellow turnips

10 oz potatoes

1 bunch soup vegetables (carrots, leeks, parsnips, cabbage)

5 oz onions

2 tbsp butter

salt

pepper

nutmeg

4 ½ cups vegetable stock

1 bay leaf

14 oz cooked sausages

2 tbsp marjoram or parsley (coarsely minced)

1 Wash and prepare the yellow turnips, potatoes, and soup vegetables. Peel if necessary and cut everything into cubes of about ¾ in. Dice the onions. Braise lightly with the other vegetables in the melted butter in a casserole. Season generously with salt, pepper, and nutmeg.

2 Add the vegetable stock, bay leaf and sliced-cooked sausage, bring to the boil, cover, and simmer for 25–30 minutes. Remove the bay leaf and sprinkle marjoram or parsley on top.

Preparation time: 45 minutes.
Per serving: 25 g P, 39 g F, 37 g C = 607 kcal (2534 kJ).

CONSISTENCY
To ensure that all the vegetables are cooked at the same time, they should all be cut, as far as possible, into pieces of about the same size. For instance: first into slices, then into strips, then into cubes.

Quick Coq-au-Vin in White Wine

*Probably the quickest way to prepare chicken for
Sunday lunch and one of the most delicious.*

Serves 4: 1 Cut 2 **onions** into thin slices. Wash and prepare 9 oz **mushrooms** and cut in half. Cut 2 **chicken legs** in pieces at the joint (about 10 oz
each) and cut 2 **chicken breasts** (9 oz each) diagonally. Fry 2 oz **diced
bacon** in 2 tbsp oil in a pan until crisp, then remove from the pan. Fry
the chicken in the fatty cooking juices, then season with salt and pepper.
2 Add the onions and mushrooms and fry briefly. Prepare ⅞ cup **white
wine** and ⅞ cup **chicken stock** and add half to the onions and mushrooms.
Return the bacon to the pan. Cover and cook in the oven, preheated to
390 degrees (fan oven 355 degrees) on the second shelf from the bottom
for 35 minutes. After 20 minutes add the rest of the wine and chicken stock
and continue to cook without the lid until ready. **3** If necessary season
again with salt, pepper, and **nutmeg**, and sprinkle 4 tbsp **parsley** on top.

* **Preparation time: 50 minutes. Per serving: 40 g P, 30 g F, 1 g C = 484 kcal (2023 kJ).**

Rigatoni with Browned Butter

Butter, melted until brown, makes a perfect seasoning for winter dishes. You should try it!

Serves 2: 1 Cut 2 **tomatoes** into quarters, remove the seeds and mince. Wash and dry 2 oz **arugula**. **2** Cook 9 oz **rigatoni** according to the instructions on the packet. **3** Three minutes before the end of the cooking time, melt the **butter** in a pan and let it turn brown over medium heat, then add the tomatoes. **4** Add 2 tbsp **white balsamic vinegar** and season generously with pepper. Drain the pasta and stir it in the tomatoes together with the arugula. Sprinkle grated **Parmesan** on top.

* Preparation time: 20 minutes.
  Per serving: 17 g P, 24 g F, 93 g C = 662 kcal (2776 kJ).

Pasta Soup

Very quick, very easy, yet rather sophisticated, with a great seasoning made from lemon, garlic, and parsley.

Serves 2:

1 onion

1 clove garlic

3 ½ oz leeks

7 oz green asparagus

3 tbsp olive oil

2 ¼ cups vegetable stock

1 bay leaf

½ bunch parsley

2 oz soup pasta shapes, e.g. star pasta

salt

3 ½ oz frozen peas

1–2 tbsp lemon juice

pepper

sugar

3 oz shrimp

1 Mince the onion and clove of garlic. Wash and prepare the leeks, then mince. Peel the lower third of the asparagus stem, then cut off the woody ends. Cut the stems diagonally into thin slices. Fry the onion, garlic, and leeks in 2 tbsp olive oil until transparent. Add the stock, bay leaf, and 2 sprigs of parsley, cover, and simmer for 10 minutes over medium heat.

2 Cook the pasta in salted boiling water, following the instructions on the packet. Drain and run cold water through it. Add the asparagus and peas to the stock mixture and simmer for another 5 minutes. Season the soup with lemon juice, salt, pepper, and 1 pinch sugar. Heat the shrimp briefly in the soup. Sprinkle the rest of the minced parsley or gremolata (see below) over the soup.

Preparation time: 30 minutes.
Per serving: 19 g P, 17 g F, 34 g C =370 kcal (1550 kJ).

GREMOLATA SEASONING
Mix together the grated zest of 1 lemon with 1 minced clove of garlic and 6 tbsp minced parsley, then sprinkle over the soup.

Curd Rissoles

Meatless rissoles that are every bit as delicious as traditional ones.

Serves 2: 1 Mix together 9 oz **<u>low-fat curd</u>** with 1 medium egg,
1 crushed **<u>clove of garlic</u>**, salt, pepper, and a little **<u>nutmeg</u>**. Stir 2 oz
<u>breadcrumbs</u>, ¾ oz minced **<u>sun-dried tomatoes</u>**, and 1 pinch dried
<u>thyme</u> into the mixture, then leave it to stand for 20 minutes.
2 Shape the mixture into 8 rissoles and fry them in plenty of **<u>olive oil</u>**
or **<u>clarified butter</u>** for 4 minutes on each side over medium heat.

* **Preparation time:** 20 minutes (plus standing time).
Per serving: 23 g P, 20 g F, 25 g C = 375 kcal (1572 kJ).

Pureed Peas with Cress

We need color in winter! And here it is. The greenest and most delicious pea puree of the season.

Serves 2: 1 Put 10 oz **frozen peas** in a pan together with 2 tbsp **butter** and ½ cup **whipping cream**. Season with salt, pepper, and **sugar**. Cover, bring to the boil and cook for 6 minutes over medium heat. **2** Puree the peas finely in a blender. Bring back to the boil in a pan and thicken with 1–2 tbsp **instant mashed potato powder**. Adjust the seasoning if necessary. Cut some **cress** and sprinkle on top.

Preparation time: 20 minutes. **Per serving:** 13 g P, 28 g F, 27 g C = 411 kcal (1724 kJ).

Shrimp Rissoles

Mouth-watering and very refined, but as easy to make as traditional meat rissoles, these shrimp rissoles make an ideal appetizer.

Serves 2–4: 1 Process 14 oz **shrimp** in a small vegetable mill. Stir in 1 **minced scallion**, 1 crushed **clove of garlic**, ¾ oz grated **ginger**, 1 tsp **soy sauce**, and 1 tsp **lemon juice**. Season with salt and pepper. **2** With moistened hands, shape this mixture into 8 rissoles. Fry in 1–2 tbsp oil over medium heat for 3–4 minutes on each side.

* **Preparation time:** 30 minutes.
  Per serving (based on 4 servings): 21 g P, 4 g F, 2 g C = 133 kcal (554 kJ).

Spicy Semolina Gratin

In Italy maize semolina, that is polenta, is often used as a side dish. Here we are using wheat-based semolina which is also perfect for this dish.

Serves 4: 1 Pour 2¼ cups **milk** into a pan and add ¾ cup **wheat semolina** and ½ tsp **salt**. Stir briskly with a whisk and bring to the boil, stirring occasionally. Reduce the heat and simmer for 5 minutes while stirring. Remove from the heat, cover and leave to draw for 10 minutes.
2 Grease 4 gratin dishes (4¾ x 3¼ in). **3** Stir ⅓ cup grated **Parmesan** and 1½ tbsp **butter** into the semolina mixture. Season generously with **salt**, **pepper**, and **nutmeg**. Beat 1 egg white until stiff with a hand-held mixer and fold into the semolina. Put this mixture into the 4 gratin dishes and sprinkle 1 tbsp grated Parmesan over each one.
4 Place on a cookie sheet on the top shelf of the oven, preheated to 390 degrees (fan oven 355 degrees) and brown lightly for 5–7 minutes. The cheese should be melted and lightly brown.

* **Preparation time:** 30 minutes. **Per serving:** 16 g P, 19 g F, 28 g C = 345 kcal (1446 kJ).

Lemon Waffles

Pure pleasure after a long walk in the winter: freshly made waffles, still warm, served with a colorful fruit salad.

Serves 4–6:

3 oranges and 3 clementines

2 kiwi fruit

7 tbsp lemon juice

1 cup confectioners' sugar

⅞ cup butter or margarine

1 ½ tsp vanilla sugar

2 tsp zest of lemon (untreated)

salt

4 medium eggs

1 cup flour

¾ cup cornstarch

1 tsp baking powder

4 tbsp whipped cream

oil for the waffle iron

1 Peel the oranges and clementines, and remove all trace of white pith. Remove the membrane round each segment, catching the juice as you do so. Squeeze the residue to remove any remaining juice. Peel the kiwi fruit, cut in half lengthways, and cut into thin slices. Stir 3 tbsp confectioners' sugar into 4 tbsp of the juice you have collected and 2 tbsp lemon juice, and pour over the fruit.

2 Beat the softened butter or margarine, ⅔ cup confectioners' sugar, vanilla sugar, lemon zest, and 1 pinch of salt for 5 minutes until you obtain a very creamy mixture, using a hand-held mixer. Stir in the eggs, one by one, for ½ minute each. Sift the flour, cornstarch, and baking powder and stir in the whipping cream and 5 tbsp lemon juice. Preheat the waffle iron, grease with oil, and make about 10 square golden brown waffles (or 6–7 more generous waffles). Serve with fruit salad and perhaps even whipped cream.

* **Preparation time:** 30 minutes.
Per serving (out of 6 servings): 9 g P, 39 g F, 74 g C = 683 kcal (2860 kJ).

PERFECT ORANGE SEGMENTS
1. Cut off the top and bottom of the orange, using a sharp knife.
2. Cut off the zest from top to bottom, making sure that you remove all the white pith at the same time.
3. Remove the membranes surrounding each segment.

Potato Salad with Arugula

Potato salad is a beautiful dish and arugula is also delicious. The combination of the two is irresistible.

Serves 2: 1 Wash 12 oz **waxy potatoes** in salted water. Now peel the **potatoes**, cut into thin slices and arrange in a bowl. **2** Mince 2 **red onions**. Bring to the boil ⅝ cup **vegetable stock** (from a bouillon cube) with 1 tbsp **oil**, 2 tbsp **white wine vinegar**, a little salt, and **sugar**. Pour hot over the sliced potatoes and mix thoroughly. **3** Shortly before serving, wash and dry the **arugula**. Cut into bite-sized pieces and stir into the potato salad. Sprinkle with freshly ground pepper. You can also use minced dried tomatoes instead of the onions.

* **Preparation time:** 40 minutes.
  Per serving: 4 g P, 5 g F, 26 g C = 177 kcal (743 kJ).

Lamb Chops with Curd

A sensational combination: sharp, spicy chops, served with creamy, mild mint-flavored curd.

Serves 2: 1 Press 1 **clove of garlic** and stir into 1 tbsp **olive oil**, the grated zest of ½ **lemon (untreated)**, and ¼ tsp crushed **chili peppers**. Stir in 7 oz **low-fat curd**, 7 tbsp **sour cream**, and 4 tbsp minced **mint**. Season with salt, pepper, and 1–2 tsp **lemon juice**. **2** Season 4 **lamb chops** (about 3 oz each) with salt and pepper. Heat 2 tbsp olive oil. Add the meat and fry briskly for 3 minutes on each side, drizzle some spiced oil over the chops, and fry for one more minute. Serve with the curd.

* **Preparation time:** 20 minutes. **Per serving:** 34 g P, 34 g F, 7 g C = 476 kcal (1995 kJ).

Pasta with Savoy Cabbage in a Cream Sauce

A good accompaniment to pasta is a rich, creamy sauce. Here it is, made with Savoy cabbage, bacon, béchamel, and whipping cream.

Serves 2: 1 Mince 3½ oz **bacon**. Mince 2 **onions**. Wash and prepare 10 oz of **Savoy cabbage**, cut into thin strips. **2** Fry the onions and bacon together in 1 tbsp **oil**. Add the Savoy cabbage and cook for another 2 minutes. Now stir in ⅞ cup **béchamel sauce** (made from a packet mixture), and ½ cup **whipping cream**. Cover and cook over medium heat for 6–7 minutes. Season with salt and pepper, and freshly grated **nutmeg**. **3** Cook 9 oz **pasta** in salted water following the instructions on the packet. Pour out the water and drain. Fry in 2 tbsp **butter** and serve with the Savoy cabbage in the cream sauce.

Preparation time: 35 minutes. Per serving: 32 g P, 70 g F, 97 g C = 1142 kcal (4794 kJ).

Duck Breast à l'Orange

An extremely simplified but also improved variation of the famous classic recipe. Try it!

Serves 4: 1 Mince 1 **onion** and crush 2 tsp **green peppercorns**. Peel 2 **oranges**, making sure that you remove all the white pith at the same time. Cut into slices and then halve them. Squeeze ⅝ cup juice from 1–2 oranges. Score the skin of 2 **Barbary duck breasts** (about 10 oz each) cross-ways. Season the flesh with salt and pepper. **2** Heat a pan and place the duck breasts with the skin facing downward. Fry briskly for 2 minutes, then turn and fry for a further 2 minutes. Now place in an oven-proof dish with the skin facing upward. Continue cooking in the oven, preheated to 375 degrees (fan oven 170 degrees), on the second shelf from the bottom, for 12–14 minutes. **3** Lightly braise the onion and green peppercorns in the duck cooking fat. Add 4 tbsp **cognac**, the orange juice, and ⅞ cup **chicken stock**. Cook uncovered for 5–8 minutes. If necessary you can thicken the sauce with 1 tbsp **dark gravy thickener**. Add the oranges, season with salt, pepper, and **sugar**. Allow the duck breast to rest for a short while, then serve with the sauce, and sprinkle **thyme** on top if you like.

* **Preparation time:** 40 minutes. **Per serving:** 29 g P, 26 g F, 10 g C = 397 kcal (1674 kJ).

Apple Clafoutis

Light and aromatic with a hint of marzipan: this apple gratin always creates a sensation, whether made in a cup or large dish.

Serves 4: 1 Peel 2 small sour **apples**. Cut them into quarters, remove the core, and cut into slices. Immediately stir 2 tbsp **lemon juice** into the sliced apples. Crumble up 3 ½ oz **marzipan** and purée with ⅝ cup **milk**. Beat 3 medium **egg yolks** together with 2 tbsp **sugar**, using a hand-held mixer, for 5 minutes until the mixture becomes creamy. Stir in 4 tbsp **flour** and 3 tbsp **cornstarch** into the marzipan, milk, and egg mixture. **2** Add a pinch of salt to 3 medium **egg whites** and beat until stiff, add 1 ½ tbsp **sugar**, and continue whisking for 1 minute. Fold into the pastry mixture. Grease four oven-proof cups (1 cup each or an oven-proof dish, about 8 x 8 in) and pour the pastry mixture into the cups or dish. Arrange the sliced apples and ¼ cup **slivered almonds** on top. **3** Place in the oven, preheated to 375 degrees (fan oven 170 degrees), on the second shelf from the bottom for 25–30 minutes. Sprinkle 1 tbsp **confectioners' sugar** on top.

Preparation time: 50 minutes.
Per serving: 12 g P, 18 g F,
45 g C = 393 kcal (1650 kJ).

Filbert and Orange Broccoli

The fresh aroma of the oranges balances the earthy flavor of the broccoli while the filberts add an additional crunchiness to the texture.

Serves 2: 1 Divide generous 1 lb **broccoli** into rosettes, peel the stems, and cut into ⅜-in cubes. Coarsely mince 1 oz **filbert kernels**. **2** Using a peeler, peel off the rind of 1 untreated **orange**, and cut it into thin strips. Then peel the orange removing all the white pith. Separate the orange into segments and remove the membranes. Collect the juice. **3** Cook the broccoli in salted boiling water for 4 minutes. 1 minute before the end of the cooking time, add the orange zest. **4** Meanwhile, foam up 2 tbsp **butter** in a pan, add the filberts and brown briefly. Stir in the orange juice and orange segments. Drain the broccoli and stir into the butter mixture. Season with salt and pepper.

* **Preparation time:** 35 minutes.
  Per serving: 6 g P, 29 g F, 9 g C = 317 kcal (1327 kJ).

Lamb Shanks

Braised in red wine, these highly aromatic lamb shanks make a perfect dish for Sunday lunch.

Serves 4–6:

1 large onion (about 14 oz)

10 oz celery with leaves

4 lamb shanks
(about 1 lb each)

6 tbsp olive oil

salt

pepper

1 clove of garlic (cut in half)

4 tbsp tomato paste

1 star anise

1 tsp coriander

8 sprigs thyme

⅝ cup red wine

1 untreated lemon (sliced)

1 ¾ cups lamb stock

1 Coarsely mince the onion and the celery; also roughly mince the green leaves of the celery. Remove the skin and sinews from the shanks. Brown the lamb shanks well all round in 4 tbsp hot olive oil in a large roasting pan, season with salt and pepper. Remove from the roasting pan. Now add the onion, celery, and garlic to the remaining olive oil in the roasting pan and brown. Add the tomato paste, star anise, coriander, and half of the thyme, and fry briefly with the onion, celery, and garlic. Add the red wine and cook briefly to reduce.

2 Return the shanks to the roasting pan and add ⅞ cup lamb stock, and bring briefly to the boil. Cover and put in the oven, preheated to 355 degrees (fan oven 320 degrees), on the second shelf from the bottom, and braise for 2 hours. Halfway through the cooking time turn the shanks, add the rest of the stock and ½ lemon, and continue braising but without a lid.

3 Season the sauce with salt and pepper. Sprinkle the celery leaves on top, garnish with the remaining lemon slices.

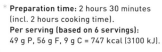

Preparation time: 2 hours 30 minutes (incl. 2 hours cooking time).
Per serving (based on 6 servings):
49 g P, 56 g F, 9 g C = 747 kcal (3100 kJ).

CLEANING
Removing the thick skin and coarse sinews from the shanks prevents the lamb from tasting of mutton.

Culinary heating against the cold

"HAVE NO QUALMS, you can give me snow to eat", wrote the Austrian poet Paul Celan. Instead of taking the poet at his word, try our nourishing Sauerkraut Stew with mouth-watering Curd Fritters. Or try to fend off the winter cold with a spicy Texas Chili and Gypsy-Style Sliced Pork, cooked in sauce. This will make even snow-lovers melt inside!

Sauerkraut Stew

A light version of this winter dish, with less fat and delicate little meatballs.

Serves 4:

14 oz mixed ground meat

1 medium egg

salt

pepper

1 lb potatoes

5 oz carrots

3 onions

3 tbsp oil

2 tbsp sugar

1 can sauerkraut
(1¾ lb drained weight)

1 tbsp paprika powder

4½ cups beef stock

2 tbsp minced chives

1 Knead the ground meat and egg together, and season generously with salt and pepper. Shape into small meatballs (diameter about ¾ in). Peel the potatoes and carrots, and cut into ¾-in pieces.

2 Cut the onions into small cubes and fry in the hot oil until transparent. Add the sugar and allow to caramelize. Add the drained sauerkraut and paprika powder, then fry briefly. Add the stock and the meatballs. Cover and cook over medium heat for 25 minutes. After 15 minutes, add the potatoes and carrots. Sprinkle the minced chives on top.

* **Preparation time:** 50 minutes.
Per serving: 29 g P, 27 g F, 27 g C = 480 kcal (2012 kJ).

MEATBALLS
Small, even meatballs are best for this dish: Wetting your hands with cold water makes the job of shaping the meatballs easier and less messy.

Alfredo Tagliatelle

There are no doubt numerous pasta recipes with the name Alfredo.
But our Alfredo is a particularly good cook!

Serves 2: 1 Wash and prepare 9 oz **soup vegetables** and cut them into
small cubes. Cook them for 2 minutes in boiling salted water, pour away
the water, and run under cold water. Cut 1 **onion** into cubes. **2** Cook
9 oz **tagliatelle** in salted water, following the instructions on the packet.
3 Heat 2 tbsp **butter** in a pan, add the onion, and fry lightly for 2 minutes
over medium heat. Add the vegetables and fry for another minute.
Add 4 ½ oz diced **cooked ham**. **4** Add ⅞ cup **whipping cream** to the pan.
Continue cooking until it becomes creamy and stir in ¼ cup grated
Parmesan. Season with salt and pepper. Drain the tagliatelle and stir
into the sauce. Sprinkle 1 tbsp of **chives** on top.

* **Preparation time:** 25 minutes. **Per serving:** 38 g P, 54 g F, 92 g C = 1008 kcal (4219 kJ).

Texas Chili

*Spicy and nourishing like the American South:
beef, beans and fiery chili peppers with sour cream.*

Serves 4: 1 Cut 1¾ lb **braising beef** into cubes of about ¾ in. Mince
1 **onion**, cut open 2 **red chili peppers**, remove the seeds and mince. In
two batches, briskly brown the cubed meat all over in 2 tbsp of hot **oil**
(add another 2 tbsp of oil for the second batch). Season each portion with
salt and pepper, and 1 tsp of **hot paprika**. Remove from the pan. Now add
2 tbsp **oil** to the pan and fry the chili peppers, onion, and 2 crushed **cloves
of garlic** in it. **2** Stir in 2 tsp ground **cumin**, 2 tbsp **tomato paste**, and
2 tbsp minced **oregano leaves** (or 1 tsp **dried oregano**) and fry briefly with
the other ingredients. Return the meat to the pan and add 1 can **tomatoes**
with the juice (14 oz drained weight) and 1¾ cups **meat stock**, and bring
to the boil. Cover and cook over low heat for 1½ hours. **3** Drain 1 can
kidney beans (14 oz drained weight), add to the pan and bring again to
the boil briefly. Season generously with salt and pepper. Serve with 7 oz
sour cream. Garnish with paprika powder and oregano leaves if you like.

* **Preparation time:** 1 hour 50 minutes. **Per serving:** 49 g P, 36 g F, 15 g C = 581 kcal (2432 kJ).

Winter Salad

This light, refreshing, refined salad makes a perfect appetizer: Belgian endive, corn salad and pomegranate with a cinnamon and lime vinaigrette.

Serves 2: 1 Wash and prepare 5 oz **corn salad** and spin-dry. Separate the leaves of 1 **Belgian endive**. Cut out the bitter cone-shaped centre. Cut 1 **pomegranate** into quarters lengthways and take out the seeds. **2** Mix together 1 tsp grated **lime zest (untreated)**, 3 tbsp **lime juice**, 2 tbsp **honey**, ½ tsp **cayenne pepper**, 2 pinches ground **cinnamon**, ½ tsp **prepared mustard**, salt, pepper and 3 tbsp **oil** in a screw-top jar, close carefully and shake vigorously. **3** Arrange the corn salad and Belgian endive on a dish, sprinkle the pomegranate seeds on top and pour the dressing over it.

Preparation time: 20 minutes.
Per serving: 2 g P, 16 g F, 24 g C = 248 kcal (1042 kJ).

Curd Fritters

You don't have to wait for New Year's Eve:
anyone who loves doughnuts won't be able to resist these.

For about 12 pieces: 1 Mince ⅓ cup dried **apricots**. Mix together 2 medium **eggs**, ¼ cup **sugar**, 1 pinch of salt, and the grated zest of 1 **orange**, using a hand-held mixer for 5 minutes until very creamy. Stir in 12 oz **low-fat yoghourt**. Sift 2 cups **flour** and 1½ tsp of **baking powder**, then stir in ½ cup **milk**. **2** Stir in the cubed apricots. Heat up 12½ cups **oil** in a chip pan or a high, wide saucepan to 320 degrees. Using a tablespoon dipped in the hot oil, take small amounts of the batter to make the fritters. Make 4 fritters at the same time over medium heat, cooking them for 3–4 minutes. **3** Drain the fritters on kitchen paper. Mix together ¼ cup **sugar** and 1 sachet of **vanilla sugar** and dip the hot fritters in it. They are delicious served with ready-made chocolate or orange sauce.

Preparation time: 50 minutes. **Per piece:** 5 g P, 10 g F, 24 g C = 208 kcal (869 kJ).

Apple Rice Dessert

A perfect dish to revive your spirits during the dark days of winter, or any other time: creamy rice with apples, poppy seeds and almonds.

Serves 2: 1 Bring to the boil 2 ¼ cups **milk** with ⅝ cup **short-grain rice**, 2 tbsp **sugar**, ½ **vanilla bean split** open and strips of **lemon zest (untreated)** 2 in long. Cover and simmer gently over low heat for 30 minutes. Stir frequently so to make sure that the rice does not stick. Wash 1 **red apple**, cut it into quarters, remove the seeds and cut into slices. Mix together with 5 oz **apple compote** (from a jar) and 1 tbsp **lemon juice**. **2** Melt 3 tbsp **butter** in a pan and add 2 tbsp **poppy seeds**, 2 tbsp **slivered almonds**, 1 tbsp sugar, and ½ tsp **ground cinnamon**, and brown slowly. Stir the apple mixture into the rice pudding. Gently cook over low heat for 2 minutes, stirring all the time.

* **Preparation time:** 40 minutes. **Per serving:** 17 g P, 38 g F, 115 g C = 870 kcal (3648 kJ).

Sausage with Onion Sauce

Even gourmets will enjoy this curried sausage!
Here is a delicious recipe to make it.

Serves 2: 1 Cut 7 oz **onions** into thin strips. Melt 2 tbsp **butter**, add the strips of onions and fry 5 minutes over medium heat until golden brown. Add 4 tbsp hot **curry paste** and ⅞ cup water. Bring everything to the boil and simmer for 5 minutes uncovered. **2** Fry 3 **sausages** (3½ oz each) in 3 tbsp hot **oil** for 5–6 minutes over medium heat. Season the sauce generously with salt, pepper, and **Cayenne pepper**, and serve with the sausage. Sprinkle minced chives on top. Serve with potato segments or Rösti.

Preparation time: 20 minutes. **Per serving:** 26 g P, 60 g F, 12 g C = 691 kcal (2894 kJ).

Baked Potatoes with Sour Cream

Steaming hot potatoes, served with a sour cream, avocado, and paprika sauce. This contains many good things to boost the body's defense system.

Serves 4: 1 Scrub clean 4 floury **potatoes** (10 oz each). Brush each with 1 tbsp **oil**, sprinkle a little salt on top and place on greased cookie sheet. Bake in the oven, preheated to 355 degrees (fan oven 340 degrees), on the second shelf from the bottom for 60–70 minutes. Cut 1 **avocado** (10 oz) in half and remove the pit. Scoop out the flesh and mince. Stir in 2 tbsp **lime juice**. **2** Wash and prepare 1 **red** and 1 **yellow bell pepper** and mince. Mince ½ bunch of **chives**. Slit open 1 red bell pepper, remove the seeds, and mince. Mix together ¾ cup **sour cream** with ⅜ cup **creamy yoghourt**, 1 crushed **clove of garlic**, pepper, 1 tsp grated **lime zest**, and season with a little **salt**. **3** Add the peppers, avocado, and chives, seasoning again if necessary. Open up the potatoes lengthways with a knife and squeeze slightly to open them further. Stuff with the sour cream sauce. Sprinkle 2 tsp of **red caviar** on top. Garnish with 4 tbsp of **cress**.

* **Preparation time:** 1 hour 15 minutes.
  Per serving: 10 g P, 35 g F, 35 g C = 502 kcal (2100 kJ).

Cream Puffs with Egg Liqueur

The orange may be visually concealed here but its aroma is clearly present: in the pastry and in the vanilla and egg-liqueur cream.

For 6 pieces:

2 tsp grated orange zest (untreated)

salt

3 tbsp butter or margarine

good ¾ cup flour

2 medium eggs

¼ tsp baking powder

1 cup whipping cream

1 ½ tsp vanilla sugar

8 tbsp egg liqueur

1 tbsp confectioners' sugar

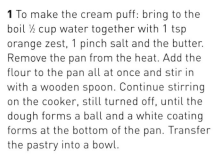

1 To make the cream puff: bring to the boil ½ cup water together with 1 tsp orange zest, 1 pinch salt and the butter. Remove the pan from the heat. Add the flour to the pan all at once and stir in with a wooden spoon. Continue stirring on the cooker, still turned off, until the dough forms a ball and a white coating forms at the bottom of the pan. Transfer the pastry into a bowl.

2 Knead the eggs into the pastry, one by one, using the hook attachment of the hand-held mixer. Quickly knead the baking powder into the pastry. Put the pastry in a pastry bag with a large star-shaped nozzle. Pipe 6 cream puffs (2 in in diameter) onto a cookie sheet, lined with grease-proof paper. Bake in the oven, preheated to 430 degrees (fan oven 390 degrees), on the second shelf from the bottom for 22–25 minutes.

3 Immediately after removing the cream puffs from the oven, cut off the top to make a lid and leave to cool down. Beat the cream with the vanilla sugar until thick. Add 5 tbsp egg liqueur and 1 tsp orange zest and continue whipping briefly. Pipe the cream into the cooled bottom part of the cream puffs, drizzle 3 tbsp egg liqueur over the cream filling and place the lid on top. Sprinkle with confectioners' sugar before serving.

THROWAWAY PASTRY BAG
Choux pastry is difficult to wash out from fabric pastry bags. The practical solution is to use disposable piping-bags.

* **Preparation time:** 45 minutes (plus cooling time).
  Per serving: 7 g P, 20 g F, 20 g C = 300 kcal (1253 kJ).

Breadcrumb-Coated Dumplings

Breadcrumb-coated dumplings sound as good as they taste and they are easy to make: potato dumpling dough from a packet is later coated in breadcrumbs.

Serves 4: 1 Mince ½ bunch of **<u>flat-leaved parsley</u>**. Stir 1 packet of **<u>potato dumpling dough</u>** into cold water, following the instructions on the packet. Add 1 tbsp parsley and allow the dough to swell. Then make 12 dumplings, using wet hands. Put the dumplings into boiling salted water, bring back to the boil, then cook for 15–20 minutes over low heat. **2** Grate the zest of 1 **<u>lemon</u>**, crush 3 tsp **<u>coriander seeds</u>**, melt 6 tbsp **<u>butter</u>**. Add 12 tbsp **<u>breadcrumbs</u>** and coriander to the melted butter and fry until crisp while stirring constantly. Season with salt and pepper. Add 1 tbsp parsley and lemon zest. Drain the potato dumplings. Turn the potato dumplings into the hot breadcrumbs until they are entirely coated in them.

Preparation time: 35 minutes (plus standing time).
Per serving: 7 g P, 20 g F, 54 g C = 425 kcal (1777 kJ).

Gypsy-Style Pork Pieces

A dish whose name conjures up images of Hungary: the paprika adds a fiery note to this quick-fried dish, which is ready in a mere 20 minutes.

Serves 2: 1 Cut 1 **onion** into thin strips. Wash and prepare 1 **red bell pepper**, and cut into ⅜-in cubes. Briskly fry 10 oz **pork pieces** in 2 tbsp hot **oil** over high heat until golden brown. Season with salt, pepper, and 1 tsp **paprika powder**, and remove the meat from the pan. **2** Now add 1 tbsp **oil**, sliced pepper, onion, and 1 crushed **clove of garlic** to the pan juices and fry. Add 1 tsp paprika powder and fry briefly. Add 1 cup **vegetable stock** and ½ cup **spicy ketchup** and cook over medium heat for 5 minutes without a lid. Return the meat to the pan and briefly heat up again. Sprinkle 2 tbsp of **minced chives** on top.

Preparation time: 20 minutes. Per serving: 36 g P, 18 g F, 16 g C = 374 kcal (1565 kJ).

Classic Meatballs

The mother of all meatballs: made with mixed ground meat, onions, garlic, and a pinch of hot mustard.

Serves 4: 1 Mince 2 **onions** and 1 **clove of garlic**. Fry until transparent in 1 ½ tbsp **butter** and leave to cool. Soak 1 stale **bread roll** in hot water for 10 minutes, remove and squeeze out the water. Mix together with the onions, 1 ¾ lb **mixed ground meat**, 1 medium **egg**, salt, pepper, and ½ tsp hot **mustard**. **2** Heat 2–3 tbsp **oil** in a pan, add the meatballs, and fry over medium heat for about 6 minutes on each side. It is delicious served with potato purée with fried onions.

* **Preparation time:** 40 minutes. **Per serving:** 40 g P, 46 g F, 7 g C = 598 kcal (2507 kJ).

Citrus-Pineapple Cake

This yeast cake is so very easy to make that it is also one of the most popular cakes.

For 20 pieces: 1 Peel 1 small **pineapple** (about 2 lb 10 oz), cut into 16 slices about ¼ in thick. Remove the stem with a corer. Grate the zest of 2 **lemons** and squeeze 8 tbsp of juice. Beat together ⅞ cup softened **butter**, 1⅓ cups **confectioners' sugar**, the lemon zest, and 1 pinch of salt with a hand-held mixer for 8 minutes until the mixture becomes creamy. **2** Beat in 4 medium **eggs**, one at a time, whisking each one for ½ minute. Sift together 3 cups **flour**, 6 tbsp **cornstarch**, and 2 tsp **baking powder**. Add 5 tbsp **lemon juice** and 6 tbsp **orange juice**, and stir in. Spread the dough on a greased cookie sheet (16 x 12 in). Arrange the pineapple slices on top. **3** Bake in the oven, preheated to 390 degrees (fan oven 355 degrees), on the second shelf from the bottom for 25 minutes. After 15 minutes, place 1 **candied cherry** (you will need about 5 oz in all) in the hole in the middle of each piece of pineapple and continue baking. Bring bare ½ cup **apricot jelly** and 3 tbsp lemon juice to the boil. Spread this mixture over the cake to glaze it and leave to cool slightly until lukewarm.

* **Preparation time:** 50 minutes (plus cooling time).
  Per serving: 3 g P, 10 g F, 40 g C = 264 kcal (1105 kJ).

Mashed Potato with Roast Onion

A classic dish from our childhood: mashed potatoes with crisp fried onions. It is popular with everyone and it can even be served on its own.

Serves 2: 1 Mince 3 **onions**. Fry in 2 tbsp **butter** and 1 tbsp **olive oil** over medium heat until golden brown, stirring all the while. **2** Meanwhile, wash and peel 10 oz **potatoes**. Cook in salted water and drain. Wait briefly until the potatoes stops steaming, then mash them. **3** Bring ⅝ cup **milk** and 2 tbsp butter to the boil with salt, pepper, and a little **nutmeg**. Add the mashed potatoes and fried onions and mix very well. Sprinkle with **chives** before serving.

Preparation time: 35 minutes.
Per serving: 6 g P, 31 g F, 24 g C = 393 kcal (1645 kJ).

69

Tortellini Gratin

There are only few things that taste better than tortellini. This tortellini gratin is one of them!

Serves 4:

2 tbsp butter

5 oz frozen spinach (defrost-ed)

salt

pepper

nutmeg

1 tbsp olive oil

14 oz tortellini (fresh)

4 ½ oz Mozzarella

1 Make the sauce as explained below.

2 Heat the butter in a pan, squeeze the spinach to remove as much water as possible and fry for 2 minutes. Season with salt, pepper, and a little nutmeg. Grease an oven-proof gratin dish with olive oil and arrange the spinach in it.

3 Cook the tortellini following the instructions on the packet and drain thoroughly. Spread on top of the spinach and pour the hot tomato sauce on top. Slice the Mozzarella and spread over the tortellini, then bake in the oven, preheated to 390 degrees (fan oven 355 degrees) on the second shelf from the bottom for 15–20 minutes.

* **Preparation time:** 1 hour.
Per serving (excluding sauce): 24 g P, 33 g F, 50 g C = 593 kcal (2492 kJ).

PREPARE THE
TOMATO SAUCE:
Mince 2 onions and 2 cloves of garlic. Pour 1 can of tomatoes (14 oz drained weight) into a strainer and crush. Collect the juice. Heat 2 tbsp olive oil, add the onions and cloves of garlic and fry over medium heat for 2 minutes until trans-parent. Crumble 1 dried chili pepper and add to the pan. Now add the tomatoes, salt, and a little oregano, and cook for 25 minutes. Season with salt, pepper, and 1 pinch of sugar.
TIP: Make twice the amount of tomato sauce you need and keep the rest refrigerated in a closed container. It will keep for 2–3 days and can be served with all kinds of pasta.

Onion Soup

This soup is guaranteed to warm you up on the coldest winter's day.

Serves 2:

1 Cut 9 oz **onions** into thin rings. Heat 1 tbsp **butter** and 1 tbsp **oil** in a pan. Add the onions and fry until golden brown over medium to high heat. Season with salt, pepper, and a little **nutmeg**, 1 pinch of sugar, and a little ground **caraway**. Add 5 tbsp **white wine** and continue cooking for a little longer. Now add 2¼ cups **vegetable stock**, cover and cook over medium heat for another 15 minutes. **2** Wash and prepare the **scallions** and cut into thin rings and add to the soup 2 minutes before the end of the cooking. Toast 2 slices of **country bread** and rub with 1 peeled **clove of garlic**. Season the soup again if necessary. Sprinkle with crushed **cranberries** and serve with the bread.

* **Preparation time:** 30 minutes.
Per serving: 5 g P, 12 g F, 30 g C = 254 kcal (1062 kJ).

*Winter vegetables such as leeks, carrots, celery, and parsley
are a delicious addition to any dish, and not only in the depths of winter.*

Serves 2: 1 Mince 3–4 stems/sprigs of **dill**. Sprinkle salt and pepper
on the 2 **fillets of cod or bream**, and roll in the minced dill. **2** Wash and
prepare 1 bunch of **winter vegetables**. Cut the vegetables into thin strips
and arrange in a steamer. Season with salt and pepper. Place the fish
on top of the vegetables. Cut 1 **lemon** into slices and arrange round the
fish. Cover, place in a saucepan of boiling water and steam for 7 minutes.
3 Sprinkle with a little **olive oil** before serving. Boiled potatoes are a
perfect accompaniment.

* **Preparation time:** 35 minutes. **Per serving:** 32 g P, 11 g F, 11 g C = 277 kcal (1157 kJ).

Fried Pineapple

*The dessert that made pineapple famous: hot pineapple,
caramelized with honey and served with ice cream.*

Serves 2: 1 Grate the zest of 1 <u>lime</u> and squeeze 3 tbsp of juice. Stir both
with 2 tbsp <u>honey</u> and ¼ tsp <u>ground ginger</u>. Take 1 quarter of a <u>pineapple</u>
(about 14 oz), peel, remove the hard stem, and cut into slices ⅝ in thick.
Remove 12 <u>cape gooseberries</u> from their husks. Thread the pieces
of fruit on 4 wooden skewers. **2** In a large pan, heat 2 tbsp <u>butter</u> and
fry the fruit on the skewers for 3–4 minutes on each side until golden
brown. Add the honey mixture and briefly bring to the boil. Arrange each
skewer on a dish and pour the sauce on top. This is delicious served
with lemon sorbet.

* **Preparation time:** 25 minutes. **Per serving:** 1 g P, 9 g F, 35 g C = 232 kcal (970 kJ).

American Pancakes

Piled high, these pancakes make a delicious breakfast:
light, airy pancakes served with an orange-maple syrup sauce.

Serves 4: 1 Wash 1 **<u>orange</u>** in hot water and peel, removing only a thin layer of the zest (without any white pith) and cut the zest into thin strips. Heat ⅞ cup **<u>orange juice</u>** and ½ cup **<u>maple syrup</u>** in a small pan and re-duce to half the original volume over high heat. Put to one side **2** Mix together 3 level tsp **<u>baking powder</u>** and 2 cups **<u>flour</u>**. Now beat together 1 cup **<u>milk</u>**, 1 tbsp **<u>lemon juice</u>**, 1 sachet **<u>vanilla sugar</u>**, 1 pinch **<u>salt</u>**, and 4 medium **<u>eggs</u>**, using a hand-held mixer. Gradually stir in the flour mixture and continue stirring until completely smooth. **3** Heat 3 tbsp **<u>clarified butter</u>** in a large pan. Pour 6 small amounts of batter and sprin-kle 1 tsp **<u>strips of orange zest</u>** on each of them. Fry over medium heat for 3–4 minutes on each side until golden brown. Remove from the pan. Add another 1 tbsp clarified butter in the pan and make the rest of the pancakes. Pour some orange-maple syrup on top of the pancakes.

* **Preparation time:** 30 minutes. Per serving: 15 g P, 7 g F, 63 g C = 468 kcal (1965 kJ).

Coconut Soup

Enjoy some oriental warmth in your kitchen: this sophisticated vegetable soup with pieces of chicken is as delicious and nourishing as your grandmother's chicken soup.

Serves 2: 1 Peel 9 oz **carrots** and **potatoes**, and cut into ⅝-in cubes. Mince 1 **onion**. Brown the carrots, potatoes, and onion lightly together with 1 crushed **clove of garlic** in 2 tbsp of **oil**. Season with salt and pepper. Add 1¾ cups **vegetable stock** and ⅞ cup **coconut milk** and bring to the boil. Add 2 **chicken breast fillets** (4½ oz each), cover and cook for over medium heat for 12 minutes. Wash and prepare 3 oz **snow peas** and cut diagonally. **2** Remove the chicken breasts and leave to rest briefly. Add the snow peas to the soup and crumble ½–1 **dried chili peppers** into the soup. Cook for 2–3 minutes. Cut the chicken into slices and heat up in the soup again. Season with salt and pepper, and 1–2 tsp **lemon juice**. Add 4 tbsp coarsely minced **cilantro leaves** (or **parsley**) and serve.

* **Preparation time:** 25 minutes. **Per serving:** 34 g P, 28 g F, 21 g C = 478 kcal (2000 kJ).

Colorful Pasta Casserole

Casseroled pasta? Yes, it is possible if you add enough liquid.
The pasta and the vegetables will then cook together.

Serves 2–4: 1 Wash and prepare 5 oz each of <u>**carrots**</u>, <u>**celeriac**</u>, <u>**celery**</u>, and <u>**onions**</u>, and mince. Finely slice 2 <u>**cloves of garlic**</u>. **2** Heat 2 tbsp <u>**oil**</u> in a shallow saucepan, add the vegetables and fry lightly over medium heat for 5 minutes. Season with salt and pepper and add 10 oz <u>**short spaghetti**</u>. **3** Stir together 2¼ cups <u>**tomato juice**</u> and 2¼ cups <u>**vegetable stock**</u>. Pour half into the pan and bring to the boil. Simmer over medium heat for 20 minutes, adding the rest of the liquid little by little. **4** Add 3 oz <u>**green olives**</u>, heat through and season with salt and pepper.

* **Preparation time:** 45 minutes.
  Per serving (based on 4 servings): 12 g P, 10 g F, 59 g C = 380 kcal (1590 kJ).

Quick Pizzas with Mozzarella

Hot, tasty, quick to make and in the colors of Italy: put some Mozzarella, cherry tomato and pesto on a toasted hamburger bun and you've got your pizza!

For 4 pieces: 1 Fry 1 tbsp of **pine nuts** in a pan without fat. Cut 2 **toasted hamburger buns** in half. Spread 1 tsp of **pesto** (from a jar) on each half. **2** Carefully drain 4 ½ oz **Mozzarella**. Cut into slices and arrange on the rolls. Garnish each pizza with 5 **cherry tomatoes**. Brown lightly under the preheated oven broiler on the second shelf from the top for about 6 minutes. **3** Season the pizzas with salt and pepper, and sprinkle some pine nuts and **strips of basil leaves** on top.

Preparation time: 20 minutes. **Per serving:** 9 g P, 12 g F, 12 g C = 190 kcal (798 kJ).

Quick Pizzas with Salami

*They are as quick to garnish with zucchini, Mozzarella and salami
as they are to cook in the oven.*

For 4 pieces: 1 Cut 2 <u>**toasted hamburger buns**</u> into half and spread
with 1 tsp <u>**paprika paste**</u> from a jar. **2** Carefully drain 4 ½ oz <u>**Mozzarella**</u>,
cut into slices and arrange on the rolls. Grate 1 small <u>**zucchini**</u>, season
lightly with salt and pepper, and sprinkle on the Mozzarella. **3** Cut
3 oz <u>**salami**</u> into strips and arrange on the pizzas. Brown lightly under
the preheated oven broiler on the second shelf from the top for about
6 minutes.

Preparation time: 15 minutes. **Per piece:** 13 g P, 14 g F, 12 g C = 218 kcal (414 kJ).

Caribbean-Style Carpaccio

Quick to make and very effective: cold meats served with an exotic dressing.

Serves 2–4: 1 Scoop out the flesh of 3 **passion fruits**. Mix the passion fruit flesh together with salt, sugar, pepper, and 4 tbsp **olive oil**. Allow to stand for 10 minutes, then pour through a strainer to remove the seeds. **2** Mince a **small cucumber**, cut 2 **scallions** into fine rings, and mince 1 oz salted **peanuts**. Add to the vinaigrette. **3** Arrange the **cold meats** on a dish and sprinkle the vinaigrette on top.

* **Preparation time:** 15 minutes.
  Per serving: 13 g P, 14 g F, 12 g C = 218 kcal (414 kJ).

Papaya and Steak Salad

Who says that salad is a summer dish? Make a delicious winter salad with winter leaves, exotic fruit, and juicy steak!

Serves 2: 1 Mix together 1 tsp **tomato paste**, ½ tsp **ground cinnamon**, and 2 tbsp **white wine vinegar** with 2 tbsp of **oil**. Wash and prepare 1 **Belgian endive** and cut into strips. Wash and prepare 7 oz **romaine lettuce**, then tear or cut it into small pieces. **2** Peel 1 **papaya**, cut in half, and remove the pit. Cut the flesh into strips. Cut 1 **avocado** in half, remove the pit, and scoop out the flesh. Cut into strips. Stir half the vinaigrette into the papaya and avocado. **3** Sprinkle 2 **sirloin steaks** (5 oz each) with 1 tbsp **paprika**, rub in a little salt and pepper, and fry in a pan in 2 tbsp **oil** for 3–4 minutes on each side. **4** Arrange the Belgian endive and lettuce on a dish. Cut the steaks into slices and arrange on the salad. Put the papaya-avocado mixture on top, then sprinkle with the rest of the vinaigrette.

* **Preparation time:** 30 minutes. **Per serving:** 37 g P, 56 g F, 5 g C = 672 kcal (2820 kJ).

Coconut-Couscous Salad

Have you ever made couscous? Honestly, it is so easy that it makes boiling water seem complicated!

Serves 2: 1 Bring to the boil ⅞ cup **vegetable stock** with 2 tsp **curry powder** and 1 tbsp **olive oil**. Add 7 oz **instant couscous**, bring to the boil briefly, remove from the heat, cover, and leave to stand for 5 minutes. **2** Cut 7 oz **pineapple** into slices and fry on both sides in a non-stick pan without fat over high heat, then cut into cubes. **3** Peel 8 oz **salad cucumber**, cut into half lengthways, then cut into cubes. Wash and prepare 1 **red bell pepper**, remove the seeds and cut into dice. Fry 2 oz **coconut flakes** in a pan without fat until slightly brown. Remove the bones and skin from ½ **broiled chicken** and cut into cubes. Mix together 2 tbsp **lemon juice** and 3 tbsp olive oil. Then add all the ingredients mentioned and stir into the couscous. Season with salt and pepper, and serve immediately because otherwise the coconut flakes will become soggy.

Preparation time: 25 minutes. **Per serving:** 52 g P, 39 g F, 81 g C = 888 kcal (3734 kJ).

Sweet-Spicy Medallions

Good honest pork and wild exoticism – what a combination!

Serves 2: 1 Cut 9 oz **pineapple** into cubes. Cut 2 **red bell peppers** into quarters. Remove the seeds and cut into cubes. Cut 2 **onions** into strips. Thinly slice 2 **cloves of garlic**. Remove the seeds of 2 **red chili peppers** and cut into thin strips. **2** Heat 2 tbsp **olive oil** in a pan. Season 6 **pork medallions** (2 oz each) with salt and fry in the hot oil for 3–4 minutes on each side. Remove from the pan and keep warm. **3** Add the garlic and chili peppers to the pan and fry briefly. Add the peppers and onions, and fry over medium heat for 2 minutes. Now add the pineapple, 5 tbsp **soy sauce**, 1–2 tbsp **sugar**, and 3 tbsp water in the pan, and cook for 2 minutes. **4** Briefly heat the pork medallions in the sauce and sprinkle with 1 oz **roast peanuts** before serving.

Preparation time: 40 minutes.
Per serving: 41 g P, 21 g F,
35 g C = 500 kcal (2094 kJ).

Banana-Nut Cake

If you are looking for something special for tea, here is the perfect cake. It is impressively delicious!

For 16 pieces:

3 ½ oz chocolate with nuts

5 bananas

3 tbsp lemon juice

⅞ cup soft butter

1 ⅓ cups confectioners' sugar

grated zest of 1 lemon (untreated)

salt

4 medium eggs

3 cups flour

2 tbsp baking powder

4 ½ oz minced filbert kernels

1 packet lemon cake frosting (3 ½ oz)

1 Mince 3 oz of nut chocolate. Peel 4 bananas, cut into cubes and stir in 2 tbsp lemon juice. Mix together butter, confectioners' sugar, lemon zest, and 1 pinch of salt with a hand-held mixer for 8 minutes until very creamy. Beat in the eggs one by one, whisking each one for ½ minute before adding the next one.

2 Mix together the flour and baking powder, and add the filberts and minced chocolate. Stir well. Now fold in the cubed bananas. Pour this mixture into a rectangular pan (12 in long), lined with waxed paper. Bake in the oven, preheated to 340 degrees (fan oven 300 degrees) on the second shelf from the bottom for 70 to 80 minutes.

3 Leave to cool down. Prepare the lemon cake frosting and spread over the cake. Coarsely mince the remaining chocolate with nuts, peel the remaining banana, slice it, sprinkle with 1 tbsp lemon juice, and use to garnish the cake. Leave the frosting to set.

NUTTY ALTERNATIVES
You can also use pecan nuts or walnuts instead of filberts. In this case you should use milk chocolate instead of nut chocolate.

* **Preparation time:** 1 hour 45 minutes (plus cooling time).
Per piece: 5 g P, 22 g F, 35 g C = 345 kcal (1480 kJ).

More color on the plates

In March we see the first stirrings of Spring, but we shan't go into raptures about the delights of the season or anything like that. Nevertheless we cannot help but feel its poetic effect: as nature outside blossoms and bursts into color in the fields and woods, with flowers and new shoots, so our dishes becomes more colorful. And this triggers feelings of new life and enthusiasm...

Chicken Tikka Massala

Curiously enough, this Indian dish did not travel from India to Europe but from Europe to India.

Serves 2:

14 oz chicken breast fillets

2 oz Tikka-Massala mixture

3 tbsp creamy yoghourt

4 small red onions

1½ oz raw ginger

1 tbsp oil

1 can minced tomatoes (14 oz drained weight)

1 tbsp tomato paste

⅜ cup whipping cream

salt

black pepper

1 Cut the chicken fillet into cubes and stir into a bowl with the spicy Tikka-Massala mixture and the creamy yoghourt. Leave to marinate for 1 hour.

2 Mince 2 onions and slice the other 2. Peel the ginger and mince. Heat the oil in a pan, and fry the onions and the ginger. Add the meat and continue frying for 1 more minute.

3 Add the can of tomatoes, tomato paste, and ½ cup water to the pan, and bring to the boil. Cover and cook for 10 minutes.

4 Add the end of the cooking time, add the cream and season with salt and pepper.

* **Preparation time:** 25 minutes (plus marinating time). **Per portion:** 52 g P, 22 g F, 12 g C = 456 kcal (1910 kJ).

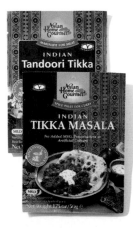

EXOTIC AROMAS
There are many ready-made spicy sauces for meat, called Tikka, available in gourmet shops. Tandoori Tikka develops its hot, spicy aroma best with broiled or roast meat.

Ravioli with Basil and Cream Sauce

This dish is very quick to prepare because the ravioli is fresh from the refrigerator and the cream-based sauce is easy to make.

Serves 2: 1 Mince 1 **clove of garlic** and 1 **onion**. Pull the leaves off 4 sprigs of **basil** and put them and the stems to one side. Heat 1 tbsp oil, add the garlic and onions and fry until transparent. Add ½ cup **vegetable stock** and 7 oz **whipping cream**. Add the basil stems and cook over medium heat for 8–10 minutes. **2** Cook 14 oz fresh **ravioli** in plenty of boiling salted water, following the instructions on the packet. **3** Remove the basil stems from the sauce and add 5 oz **half-fat cream**. Bring briefly to the boil. Coarsely rip up ⅔ of the basil leaves. Drain the ravioli and add them to the sauce together with the minced basil leaves. Season with salt and pepper. Sprinkle with the rest of the basil leaves.

Preparation time: 25 minutes. **Per serving:** 28 g P, 76 g F, 74 g C = 1088 kcal (4554 kJ).

Fish Stick Hot-Dogs

Nobody will miss the little sausage! This Danish specialty with fish sticks is popular with young and old alike.

Serves 2: 1 Beat together vigorously 2 tbsp prepared **mustard**, 1 tsp brown **sugar**, 2 tsp **lemon juice**, and 6 tbsp **oil**. Remove the leaves of ½ bunch of **dill** and stir into the mixture. Season generously with salt and pepper. Wash, dry and prepare 2 **romaine lettuces**. Cut 5 oz **cucumber** into thin slices. **2** Cook 8 **fish sticks** in the preheated oven following the instructions on the packet. **3** Put the **hot-dog rolls** in the oven briefly with the fish sticks. Cut the rolls lengthways, and fill with salad, cucumber, fish sticks, the sauce, and ¾ oz **fried onions**. Garnish to taste with dill and slices of lemon.

Preparation time: 20 minutes.
Per serving: 26 g P, 46 g F, 78 g C = 825 kcal (3458 kJ).

Fish Curry

Tender cod is served in a mouth-watering golden curry sauce, made with coconut milk and ginger. Snow peas and frozen garden peas add a note of color and aroma.

Serves 2: 1 Cut 1 **onion** into thin slices, peel ¾ oz raw **ginger**, and grate finely. Brown both lightly in 2 tbsp **oil**. Add 1 tbsp **curry powder**, stir in, and cook briefly. Add ⅞ cup **vegetable stock** and ½ cup **coconut milk**. Cook and reduce without a lid for 5–7 minutes. Cut the **cod fillets** into pieces 1¼ in wide, season with salt, pepper, and 2 tsp **lemon juice**. **2** Halve 3½ oz **snow peas** diagonally and add to the sauce together with 3½ oz **frozen garden peas**. Arrange the sander on top. Cover and cook over medium heat for 6 minutes. Turn the fish after 3 minutes. Season with salt, pepper, curry powder, and 1 pinch of **sugar**, stirring very carefully.

Preparation time: 30 minutes. Per serving: 34 g P, 20 g F, 15 g C = 379 kcal (2588 kJ).

Welsh Pork tenderloin

Nourishing dish with a fruity aroma: apple, leeks, raisins, and filberts are a perfect accompaniment to this pork-based dish.

Serves 2: 1 Wash and prepare 14 oz **leeks**, then cut the white and pale green parts into ¾-in rings. Cut 1 cored **red apple** into quarters and then into slices. Take 10 oz **pork tenderloin** and season with salt and pepper. Heat 2 tbsp **oil** in a pan and brown the meat well on all sides. Remove the meat from the pan. Heat 1 tbsp **butter**, add the leeks and apple, and cook for 1 minute while stirring. Add 2 tbsp coarsely minced **filberts** and 2 tbsp **raisins** and cook briefly. **2** Now add ⅞ cup **vegetable stock**, 2 tsp Dijon **mustard with seeds**, and stir well. Add the pork tenderloin, cover, and cook over medium heat for 15 minutes, turning the meat half-way through the cooking time. Leave to rest briefly wrapped in aluminum foil. If you like, thicken the sauce with 1–2 tbsp **light-colored gravy thickener** and if necessary season again. Cut the meat into slices, and serve with the sauce.

* **Preparation time:** 35 minutes.
  Per serving: 37 g P, 26 g F, 20 g C = 468 kcal (1960 kJ).

Salad with Sweet Dill Dressing

This dish pays homage to our grandmothers who when we were children prepared this salad with sweet creamy sauce! A very sweet memory!

Serves 2: 1 Wash and prepare 1 head of **chicory**, spin-dry and tear into bite-sized pieces. Wash 1 **lemon** under hot water and finely grate half the zest. Squeeze 2–3 tbsp **lemon juice**. **2** Mix together 7 oz **sour cream**, lemon zest and juice, and 1–2 tbsp **sugar**, salt and pepper. Finely cut ½ bunch of **dill** and stir into the sauce. Pour the sauce onto the salad and mix well. Sprinkle plenty of freshly-ground pepper and serve immediately.

Preparation time: 20 minutes. **Per serving:** 4 g P, 10 g F, 16 g C = 176 kcal (734 kJ).

Mint Chocolate Ice Cream

Deliciously refreshing and very quick to make. For the best consistency, take out of the freezer 15 minutes before serving.

Serves 4:

5 oz bar mint chocolate

1 leaf clear gelatin

1 cup whipping cream

1½ tsp vanilla sugar

2 tbsp peppermint liqueur (or peppermint syrup)

2–3 tbsp cocoa powder

mint leaves for decoration

1 Coarsely mince the bar of chocolate. Soak the gelatin in cold water.

2 Beat the whipping cream and vanilla sugar until stiff. Heat the peppermint liqueur. Squeeze the gelatin to remove the water and dissolve in the warm liqueur. First fold the gelatin and liqueur into the whipped cream, then the chocolate.

3 Spoon the chocolate mint cream mixture into four heart-shaped (or round) soufflé ramekins, smooth the surface flat, and cover with Saran wrap. Put in the freezer for 3–4 hours. Move to the refrigerator for 15–20 minutes before serving. Sprinkle cocoa powder on top, and garnish with mint leaves before serving.

* **Preparation time:** 10 minutes (plus freezing and cooling time).
Per serving: 3 g P, 24 g F, 33 g C = 369 kcal (1550 kJ).

MINT CHOCS: RANGING FROM MILD TO SHARP
The menthol contained in the serrated leaves of the peppermint plant is responsible for the refreshingly cool filling in mint chocolates.

Aromatic Chicken

Do you fancy some delicious chicken in a bag? Cooked in waxed paper, with oranges, carrots, and rosemary, it will seduce you with its mouth-watering aroma when you open the parcel.

Serves 2: 1 Peel 10 oz **carrots**, grate or cut into very thin slices. Cut 4 thin slices from an unpeeled **orange**, and squeeze the remaining juice. Cut 2 pieces of waxed paper (16 x 16 in). Season 2 **chicken breast fillets** with salt and pepper and fry on all sides in 2 tbsp **oil** in a pan over high heat. Add 2 small **sprigs of rosemary** and cook briefly with the chicken. Remove everything from the pan and put to one side. **2** Briefly brown the sliced carrots and slices of oranges, add 6 tbsp **orange juice** and season with salt, pepper and 1 tsp **honey**. Pour this sauce onto the middle of the piece of waxed paper and place the chicken fillet with the rosemary sprig on top. Fold the waxed paper to seal the parcel, twisting the ends and tying them if necessary. Place on a cookie sheet and cook in the oven, preheated to 390 degrees (fan oven 355 degrees) on the second shelf from the bottom for 20 minutes.

Preparation time: 40 minutes. **Per serving:** 30 g P, 11 g F, 10 g C = 260 kcal (1090 kJ).

Carrot and Potato Rösti

Crisply fried Rösti made from grated potatoes are delicious.
But with the addition of carrots, they are simply irresistible!

Serves 2: 1 Mince 1 **onion**. Peel and coarsely grate 7 oz **carrots**. Peel and coarsely grate 7 oz **potatoes**. Pat dry the grated carrots and potatoes, and mix with the onion, 1 tbsp **flour**, and 3 **egg yolks**. Season generously with salt, pepper, and **nutmeg 2** Heat 2 tbsp **oil** in a non-stick pan. Take half of the Rösti mixture, divided in 4–5 portions and fry for 3–4 minutes on each side until crispy brown. Cook the remaining mixture in 2 tbsp oil in the same way.

* **Preparation time:** 30 minutes. **Per serving:** 6 g P, 26 g F, 22 g C = 353 kcal (1497 kJ).

Veal Cream Goulash

Braised dishes are unique: their long cooking time brings out all the flavor of the ingredients – enough to make this goulash addictive!

Serves 4:

¾ oz dried ceps

2–3 onions

4 cloves garlic

2 lb 3 oz shoulder of vealsalt

pepper

3 tbsp oil

4 tbsp flour

1¾ cups chicken stock

1 cup whipping cream

9 oz mushrooms

1½ tbsp butter

1–2 tbsp lemon juice

1 Soak the ceps in ⅞ cup water. Mince the onions and garlic. Cut the veal into cubes, season with salt and pepper.

2 Heat the oil in a pan, add the meat in small amounts and brown over high heat. Remove from the pan. Add the onions and garlic to the pan and fry over medium heat until transparent. Squeeze the ceps and collect the water. Add the ceps to the pan. Sprinkle with flour and stir in. Now add the meat, stock, and ceps water to the pan.

3 Cover lightly and braise the goulash over medium heat for 45 minutes. Stir in the cream and cook for another 15–20 minutes without the lid on.

4 10 minutes before the end of cooking time, wash and prepare the mushrooms, braise lightly in the butter, and add to the goulash. Season with salt, pepper, and lemon juice.

* **Preparation time:** 1 hour 10 minutes.
Per serving: 55 g P, 38 g F, 10 g C = 604 kcal (2527 kJ).

CUTTING THE MEAT INTO CUBES
First cut the shoulder of veal in slices, then into cubes, using a sharp knife.

Spaghetti with Tuna Fish

Extremely quick to prepare: you can make the lemon-butter sauce with tuna fish while the pasta is cooking.

Serves 2: 1 Thoroughly drain 1 can of **tuna fish** (natural, 4½ oz drained weight) and separate the chunks into flakes. Cook the **spaghetti** in plenty of salted water, following the instructions on the packet. Cut 1 **red bell pepper** in half lengthways, remove the seeds, and cut diagonally into strips. **2** Heat 4 tbsp **butter** in a pan, then add the strips of pepper together with 4 tbsp **lemon juice**. Cook for 1 minute over medium heat. **3** Drain the spaghetti and stir quickly into the sauce. Add the tuna fish and 2 tbsp **chervil leaves**, and fold in carefully.

* **Preparation time:** 20 minutes.
  Per serving: 23 g P, 30 g F, 73 g C = 660 kcal (2765 kJ).

Spinach Pizza

Spinach and Gorgonzola go together like spaghetti and Parmesan, or pizza and tomatoes.

Serves 2: 1 Thaw 1 lb **frozen spinach** following the instructions on the pack, then squeeze to remove as much water as possible. Mince 1 **onion** and fry with 1 clove of crushed **garlic** in 3 tbsp **olive oil** until transparent. Add the spinach and season generously with salt, pepper, and **nutmeg**. **2** Knead 1 pack **pizza dough** (8 oz) with ½ cup lukewarm water. Divide into 2 halves. Roll out the dough on a floured surface until each half measures 9 in in diameter. Put on a cookie sheet lined with waxed paper. Garnish with the spinach, 5 oz **cherry tomatoes**, and 5 oz coarsely crumbled **Gorgonzola**. **3** Bake in the oven, preheated to 480 degrees (fan oven not recommended) on a base, placed directly on the bottom of the oven, for 15 minutes. Roast 1 oz **pine nuts** in a pan without fat and sprinkle over the pizza.

Preparation time: 40 minutes.
Per serving: 34 g P, 66 g F, 79 g C = 1059 kcal (4430 kJ).

Fish in a Peanut Crust

Fast food can also be tempting: juicy morsels of cod,
coated in a crispy peanut crust, and served with a hot, spicy chili dip.

Serves 2: 1 Mince 3 ½ oz **peanuts** and mix with 3 tbsp **breadcrumbs**.
Defrost 2 **frozen fillets of cod or bream** (4 ¾ oz each), and cut into sticks
2 ¾ x 1 ¼ in). **2** Beat 2 **eggs**. Roll the fish pieces in the **flour**, dip them
in the eggs, and roll in the crumbed peanuts. **3** Mix together 5 oz **full
fat yoghourt** with 1 tbsp **lime juice**, 3 oz diced **cucumber**,
1 tbsp minced **cilantro**, and 5 tbsp **sweet chili sauce**.
Season with salt and pepper. **4** Fry the fingers in ⅜ cup
oil for 3–4 minutes on each side over medium heat.

Preparation time: 30 minutes.
Per serving: 47 g P, 56 g F, 36 g C = 830 kcal (3483 kJ).

Apple Puree Cake

Don't you love licking the whisk and dipping your finger in the pastry bowl? If so this mouth-watering, moist cake is right up your street.

For 14 pieces: 1 Melt ¾ cup **butter** in a warm bain-marie. Mince 3 oz **white chocolate**, add to the butter, melt, and leave the mixture to cool down until lukewarm. **2** Beat together 3 medium **eggs**, ⅞ cup **sugar**, the pulp of 1 **vanilla bean**, and 1 pinch of salt with a hand-held mixer for 5 minutes until creamy. Add 10 oz **apple puree** (from a jar) and beat for another 2 minutes. Stir in the butter mixture. Sift 3 tsp **baking powder** and 1½ cups **flour** into the above mixture and stir in briefly. Spoon the cake batter into a greased rectangular pan (10 in long). **3** Bake in the oven, preheated to 340 degrees (fan oven 300 degrees) on the second shelf from the bottom for 55 minutes. Leave for 10 minutes in the pan, then turn out and leave to cool. Cut 1 **red apple** into quarters, core and cut into thin slices. Cook these slices in ½ cup **apple juice** for 2 minutes and drain. Mince 3 oz **white chocolate**, melt in a hot bain-marie, and pour over the cake. Garnish with the slices of apple and **mint** leaves.

Preparation time: 1 hour 30 minutes (plus cooling time).
Per piece: 4 g P, 16 g F, 30 g C = 279 kcal (1172 kJ).

Avocado Salad

Avocados are rich in vitamin E, which helps to protect the skin against the sun.

Serves 2: 1 Wash 5 oz **cherry tomatoes** and cut in half. Cut 1 red **onion** into thin slices. Wash the heart of 1 **romaine lettuce** and cut into bite-sized pieces. Cut 1 **avocado** in half, remove the pit, and carefully remove the flesh with a tablespoon, then cut into bite-sized pieces. **2** Mix together 1–2 tbsp **lemon juice**, 5 tbsp **olive oil**, salt, pepper, and 1 pinch of **sugar**, and add to the vegetables. **3** Season 7 oz **fillet of cod or bream** with salt, add ⅜ cup **white wine**, cover, and cook over medium heat for 5 minutes. Remove from the pan and crumble lukewarm into the salad.

Preparation time: 30 minutes. **Per serving**: 22 g P, 49 g F, 5 g C = 540 kcal (2264 kJ).

Curd Cheese Terrine

The ham conceals a delicious curd cheese mixture, flavored with herbs and pepper, served on a bed of green salad.

Serves 4: 1 Mix together 14 oz **full cream curd cheese** with 1 tbsp **minced chives**, 1 tbsp minced **dill**, 1 tbsp **lemon juice**, 1 tsp drained green **peppercorns** in brine, salt, and a few dashes of **Tabasco**. **2** Line 4 small ramekins (each ½ cup) with Saran wrap. Line each ramekin with 1 slice of **prosciutto** and spoon the curd cheese mixture inside it. Place in the refrigerator for 2 hours. **3** Turn out the terrine, remove the foil and cut into slices. Serve with **green salad**.

* **Preparation time:** 30 minutes (plus cooling time).
  Per serving: 14 g P, 33 g F, 3 g C = 362 kcal (1515 kJ).

Sauerkraut Gratin

A delicious, filling dish: half an hour preparation is all you need; the oven does the rest.

Serves 2: 1 Peel 18 oz **potatoes** and cut into slices ⅙-in thick. Cook in 1¼ cups **milk**, ⅔ cup **whipping cream** with 1 **bay leaf**, and ½ tsp salt for 10 minutes over medium heat, stirring constantly. Then put to one side. Drain 1 can of **sauerkraut** (1¼ lb drained weight) in a strainer. Coarsely mince 1 medium **onion**. **2** Heat 1 tbsp **oil** in a pan, add the onion, and fry until golden brown. Add 7 oz **mixed ground meat** and fry for 4–5 minutes until crumbly. Season with salt, pepper, and ½–1 tsp **paprika powder**. Add the sauerkraut and 1 tsp caraway, then fry for 3–5 minutes over medium heat, stirring occasionally. **3** Grease a gratin dish (6 x 6 in). Arrange alternate layers of potatoes and sauerkraut-ground meat in the gratin dish until there are 4 layers on top of each other. Pour the rest of the cream-milk mixture (in which you cooked the potatoes) on top and sprinkle with 3–4 tbsp **grated cheese**. **4** Bake in the oven, preheated to 390 degrees (fan oven 355 degrees) on the middle shelf for 20–25 minutes. Then switch off the oven and leave for 5 minutes before serving.

* Preparation time: 50 minutes. Per serving: 37 g P, 63 g F, 37 g C = 879 kcal (3680 kJ).

Cinnamon Couscous

Couscous is to the people of Arab countries what potatoes are to Europeans. It can be prepared as a sweet dish with dates and almonds, or as a savory dish.

Serves 2: 1 Cut up 2 oz **dates** into strips. Coarsely mince 3 tbsp **almonds**. Bring ⅝ cup water and ¼ tsp **cinnamon powder** to the boil. Add 5 oz **couscous** and 2 tsp **oil**. Turn off the heat, cover, and leave to swell for 4 minutes. Lightly fry the almonds and dates in 1 tbsp **butter**. **2** Add 6 tbsp **orange juice**, season with salt, pepper, and ground **cumin**. Stir in 1 tbsp **butter**, cut into pieces, into the couscous. Fluff it up with two forks.

Preparation time: 15 minutes. **Per serving:** 11 g P, 28 g F, 72 g C = 589 kcal (2465 kJ).

Orange Soup

This refreshing fruit soup becomes visually even more striking when prepared with blood oranges.

Serves 2: 1 Take 5 tbsp from 2¼ cups **orange juice** and add 2 level tsp **cornstarch**. Bring the rest of the juice, 1½ tsp **vanilla sugar**, 1 small **cinnamon stick**, and 4 **pods of cardamom** to the boil. Add the cornstarch mixture, bring to the boil while stirring, cover, and put to one side.
2 Beat 1 medium **egg white** and 1 pinch of salt until stiff. Very carefully drizzle 2 slightly heaping tbsp **sugar** into the stiffly beaten egg and continue whisking for another 2 minutes. Using 2 teaspoons, take small amounts and place on the hot soup. Leave to draw in the covered pan over a very low heat for 10 minutes but do not boil any more. Make sure you keep the lid on all the time! Remove the cinnamon and cardamom before serving.

* **Preparation time:** 20 minutes. **Per serving:** 4 g P, 0 g F, 48 g C = 228 kcal (952 kJ).

Spinach with Butterfly Pasta

Butterflies in your stomach: with crispy bacon and a hint of lemon, everyone will love this dish.

Serves 2: 1 Take 2 oz **bacon** and cut into wide strips. Wash and prepare 10 oz raw **leaf spinach** (or defrost 7 oz **frozen leaf spinach** and drain thoroughly). Fry the fat out of the bacon in 2 tbsp **oil**, remove the bacon from the pan, and put to one side. Add the spinach to the pan in the bacon fat, cover, and cook until done. Drain well. **2** Boil 7 oz **butterfly pasta** in salted water, following the instructions on the packet. Melt 3 tbsp **butter** and slowly brown over medium heat. Add 1 tsp **lemon rind**, cut into **strips** (or **grated**), and fry briefly. Drain the pasta and add the spinach and bacon together with the melted butter. Season with salt, pepper, and 1–2 tbsp **lemon juice**.

Preparation time: 25 minutes. **Per serving:** 20 g P, 38 g F, 70 g C = 708 kcal (2966 kJ).

Apple-Bacon Crêpes

A delight to the palate! The taste of these light, spicy crêpes is enhanced by the addition of tasty bacon and a juicy apple.

Serves 2:

2 oz bacon

1 red apple (5 oz)

1 tbsp lemon juice

3 tbsp butter

2 medium eggs (separated)

salt

pepper

nutmeg

6 tbsp milk

good ½ cup flour

½ tsp baking powder

2 tbsp oil

1 Cut the bacon into 1¼-in strips. Cut the apple into quarters, core, and cut into slices diagonally. Stir in the lemon juice. Melt 2 tbsp butter and stir in the egg yolks, a little salt, pepper, nutmeg, milk, flour, and baking powder.

2 Beat the egg whites stiff and fold into the flour mixture. Heat the oil in a non-stick pan (8 in diameter). Add the bacon and apple, fry and remove. Melt the rest of the butter and add the batter to the pan. Fry over medium heat for 5–7 minutes. Cut the crêpe into four, turn over, and fry for another 5 minutes.

3 Crumble the crêpe, add the bacon and apple and fry briefly again. Delicious served with herb curd.

Preparation time: 30 minutes.
Per serving: 16 g P, 50 g F, 32 g C = 644 kcal (2696 kJ).

CRUMBLING CRÊPES
The best way to crumble a fried egg-based crêpe is to do it in the pan with a fork and spatula.

Minute Steak

With aromas of the Mediterranean: marinated mini-size beef tenderloin slices are served with sauce made with sun-dried tomatoes and pine nuts.

Serves 2: 1 Stir together 1 crushed <u>**clove of garlic**</u>, ½ tsp dried <u>**thyme**</u>, 1 tsp <u>**lemon zest (untreated)**</u>, a little pepper, and 1 tbsp <u>**olive oil**</u>, and spread on 8 slices of <u>**beef tenderloin**</u> (1½ oz each). Leave to marinate for ½ hour. Mince 1 <u>**onion**</u> and fry lightly with 1 crushed <u>**clove of garlic**</u> in tbsp <u>**oil**</u>. Roast 1 oz <u>**pine nuts**</u> in a non-stick pan without fat. **2** Mince 2 oz <u>**dried tomatoes**</u> and puree with the onion mixture, 1 tbsp olive oil and 4 tbsp <u>**vegetable stock**</u>. Add the pine nuts and 3 tbsp flat-leaved <u>**parsley**</u>. Season with salt and pepper. Fry the meat briskly in 2 portions in 1 tbsp hot oil each time for 1–2 minutes on each side. Serve with the sauce.

Preparation time: 25 minutes (plus marinating time).
Per serving: 38 g P, 36 g F, 5 g C = 498 kcal (2085 kJ).

Duck in Red Wine

Choose Barbary duck breasts: they are very tasty and meaty, and, compared to other kinds of duck, have very little fat.

Serves 2–4: 1 Cut 5 oz **bacon** into strips. Wash and prepare 7 oz **mushrooms**. Cut 2 **cloves of garlic** into slices. **2** Score the skin of 2 **duck breasts** (12 oz) to form a diamond-shaped pattern. Put in a cold pan with the skin facing downward and fry over medium heat for 10 minutes. Then season with salt and pepper, turn, and fry for another 2 minutes. Now wrap the meat in aluminum foil and leave to rest. Pour away the fat. **3** Add the bacon, mushrooms, and garlic to the pan. Fry for 2–3 minutes while stirring and add 1 cup **red wine** and ½ cup **chicken stock**, bring to the boil, and thicken with **dark gravy thickener**. **4** Drain 1 jar of **cocktail onions** (6 oz drained weight), add to the sauce, and season with salt and pepper. Cut the duck breasts into slices and serve with the sauce.

* **Preparation time:** 40 minutes.
  Per serving: 39 g P, 36 g F, 2 g C = 490 kcal (2048 kJ).

Mushroom Polenta

*This very nourishing country dish is greatly enhanced
by the addition of ceps and mushrooms.*

Serves 2: 1 Soak ¼ oz **dried ceps** in hot water. Wash and prepare 7 oz
mushrooms, and cut into quarters. Mince 2 **onions**. **2** Fry the onions in
2 tbsp **olive oil** until transparent. Squeeze the ceps to remove as much
water as possible, add to the pan, and pour in 1 ¼ cups **vegetable stock**.
3 Bring this mixture to the boil and carefully add 3 oz **polenta** (maize
semolina). **4** Bring to the boil again and simmer for 20 minutes over
medium heat, stirring occasionally. Shortly before the end of the cooking
time, fry the mushrooms in 1 tbsp olive oil, and add to the polenta.
5 Add 2 oz grated **Parmesan** and 2 tbsp **butter**. Season with salt and
pepper. Sprinkle with **minced chives** before serving.

Preparation time: 25 minutes. **Per serving:** 16 g P, 35 g F, 31 g C = 498 kcal (2088 kJ).

Marinated Zucchinis

Zucchinis can be rather bland vegetables. But marinated in some herbs and spices, they are quite delicious.

Serves 2: 1 Wash and prepare 14 oz **zucchinis**, cut into three and then into sticks. Cut 1 **clove of garlic** into thin slices. Cut 1 red **chili** pepper open, remove the seeds, and cut into thin strips. Mince 1 **onion**. Divide the zucchinis into 2 portions and fry each in 1 tbsp hot **olive oil** on a griddle or in a pan. Season with salt and pepper and place in a bowl.
2 Lightly fry the onions, garlic, 4 sprigs of **thyme**, and chili pepper in 1 tbsp olive oil. Add 2 tbsp **lemon juice** and ½ cup **vegetable stock**. Pour into a bowl and beat in 2 tbsp olive oil. Season with salt, pepper, and 1 pinch of **sugar**. Pour over the zucchinis and leave to marinate for 2 hours.

Preparation time: 25 minutes (plus marinating time).
Per serving: 3 g P, 26 g F, 9 g C = 279 kcal (1171 kJ).

Caramel Cream

Whoever would think of melting caramel toffees to make a dessert instead of eating them? Our test kitchen! The result was fantastic!

Serves 6: 1 Mince 3 oz hard **caramel toffees**. Add to 1 ¾ cups **milk**, bring to the boil melting the toffee in the process, stirring frequently. Stir together 1 oz **starch** and 4 tbsp **caramel liqueur** (or caramel syrup) until smooth and add to the milk. Bring back to the boil while stirring. Pour into a bowl and allow to stand until lukewarm. **2** Remove 6 oz cape **gooseberries** (up to 6 pieces) from their husks and cut in half. Stir 5 oz **mascarpone** into the crème caramel. Arrange 2 **wafers** next to each other on 6 plates. Put half the crème and half the halved cape gooseberries on top. Cover with the rest of the wafers, cream, and gooseberries. Garnish with the remaining gooseberries.

* **Preparation time:** 30 minutes (plus cooling time).
  Per serving: 5 g P, 22 g F, 33 g C = 368 kcal (1539 kJ).

Red Wine and Raspberry Dessert

A heavenly dream made of frothy cream and the most delicious fruit: red wine dessert with raspberries.

Serves 4–6: 1 Bring to the boil 7 oz **frozen raspberries**, ¼ cup **sugar**, and the pulp of 1 **vanilla bean**. Stir together 1 tbsp **cornstarch** and 2 tbsp **orange juice** until smooth, then add to the boiling raspberry mixture. Bring to the boil again and pour into a bowl, add 3½ oz frozen raspberries and leave to cool down. **2** Mix together ⅝ cup **red wine**, ⅝ cup water, ¼ cup **sugar**, 1 tbsp **lemon juice**, 1 **egg yolk**, and 2 tbsp cornstarch. Heat gently, stirring all the time, and cook for 5 minutes until the mixture thickens. Leave to cool. **3** Beat 4½ oz **whipping cream** until stiff. Fold the cooled red wine mixture into the cream. **4** Arrange the cooled raspberry compote and red wine cream in alternate layers in glasses. Place in the refrigerator for 2 hours.

Preparation time: 25 minutes (plus cooling time).
Per serving (based on 6 servings): 2 g P, 6 g F, 27 g C = 195 kcal (822 kJ).

117

Waffles with Avocado Sauce

Spicy and light: an exotic waffle with avocado, tomatoes, cilantro, and dash of Tabasco.

Serves 4:

1 ¼ cups whole-wheat flour

2 medium eggs (separated)

1 cup skimmed milk

2 tbsp butter

10 oz tomatoes

3 scallions

½ avocado (5 oz)

1 tbsp lemon juice

2 tbsp minced cilantro (or flat-leaved parsley)

salt

pepper

Tabasco sauce

3 ½ oz full fat yoghourt

1 To make the waffle batter, stir together the flour, egg yolks, and milk. Allow to stand for 10 minutes. Melt the butter and leave to cool. Cut the tomatoes in four, remove the seeds and mince. Cut scallions into thin rings.

2 Scoop out the avocado flesh with a large spoon. Mince very finely and immediately pour lemon juice on top. Add the cilantro, scallions, and tomatoes to the diced avocado. Season with salt and pepper, and a dash of Tabasco. Beat the egg white until stiff with 1 pinch of salt. Fold the beaten egg white and butter into the waffle batter. Season with salt and pepper.

3 Heat the waffle iron, grease if necessary. Bake 6 waffles one after the other. Garnish with the avocado sauce and yoghourt.

Preparation time: 40 minutes.
Per serving: 12 g P, 17 g F, 35 g C = 344 kcal (1440 kJ).

NO IRONS IN THE FIRE? NO PROBLEM!

Congratulations if you are the proud owner of a waffle iron. If not, you can still make waffles without one. Heat 1 tbsp oil in a non-stick saucepan (11 in diameter), add the batter, and bake in the oven, preheated to 390 degrees (fan oven 355 degrees) on the second shelf from the bottom for 10–12 minutes. Turn out the waffle onto a plate, cut into slices, and that's it!
Tip: Wrap the handle of the pan in aluminum foil!

Borscht

*Don't worry: you don't need to be able to pronounce the name
of this East European dish to love it.*

Serves 4: 1 Cut 700 g **white cabbage** into thin strips. Cut 5 oz **onions**
into thin strips and fry lightly with the cabbage in 2 tbsp **oil** over medium
heat. **2** Peel 14 oz **potatoes** and cut into ¾-in cubes. Add to the cabbage
and onion. Add 1 tsp **caraway seeds** and 4½ cups **vegetable stock** to
the pan, bring to the boil, and cook for 20 minutes. **3** Five minutes before
the end of the cooking time, add 1 jar of **beet** (cut into slices, 11 oz
drained weight) to the soup. Cut 7 oz **cold roast pork** into strips
and add to the soup. Season with salt and pepper, and 1 tbsp
minced **dill**. **4** Season 4½ oz **sour cream** with salt and pepper,
stir until smooth and serve with the soup.

* **Preparation time:** 45 minutes.
  Per serving: 20 g P, 15 g F, 21 g C = 298 kcal (1248 kJ).

Poppy Seed Curd Cake

There are combinations of taste that are simply made in heaven – such as tomatoes and basil. Pears, curd, and poppy seeds are another such example.

For 14 slices: 1 Melt 7 tbsp **butter**. Crumble 7 oz **Graham crackers** and stir into the butter. Then press this mixture onto the base of a greased springform mold while also shaping a border ¾ in high all round. Drain 1 can **pears** (15 oz drained weight) and cut into slices. **2** Mix together ⅝ cup softened butter and ¼ cup **sugar** with a hand-held mixer for 5 minutes until very creamy. Stir in 3 medium **egg yolks**. Now stir in 9 oz **low-fat curd**, ¾ oz cornstarch, and a drop of **vanilla extract**. Beat 3 **egg whites** until stiff with 1 pinch of salt, carefully add ¼ cup sugar and continue whisking for another 3 minutes. Fold into the curd mixture. Spoon into the springform mold. **3** Mix 2 tbsp **poppy seeds** with 9 oz **sponge cake mix**. Spoon the mixture on top of the curd mixture and garnish with the pears. Bake in the oven, preheated to 355 degrees (fan oven 320 degrees) on the second shelf from the bottom for 55–60 minutes. Spread 2 oz **apricot jelly** over the hot cake and allow to cool in the pan. Sprinkle with 2 tsp **confectioners' sugar**.

* **Preparation time:** 1 hour 30 minutes (plus cooling time).
Per piece: 7 g P, 20 g F, 33 g C = 339 kcal (1419 kJ).

Königsberger Meatballs

The pleasantly sharp caper sauce combines beautifully with the dried tomatoes in this meatball recipe from Prussia.

Serves 4:

1 onion

2 slices white bread

9 oz ground beef

9 oz ground pork

1 tbsp prepared mustard

2 medium eggs

salt

pepper

1 oz dried tomatoes

3 ½ cups vegetable stock

2 tbsp butter

3 tbsp flour

½ cup white wine

⅝ cup whipping cream

2 tbsp bottled capers with 1 tbsp juice from the jar

4 tbsp minced parsley

1 Mince the onion very finely. Soak the slices of white bread in cold water and squeeze to remove as much water as possible. Add the onions, ground beef, ground pork, mustard, eggs, 1 pinch of salt and pepper, and knead into a smooth dough. Season again if necessary. With wet hands, shape 14–16 meatballs. Mince the dried tomatoes.

2 Bring the vegetable stock to the boil, add the meatballs, cover, and cook over medium heat for 15 minutes. Carefully transfer the meatballs into a colander while catching the stock. Melt the butter, add the flour, and brown lightly while you continue stirring. Now stir in the wine, 2 ½ cups stock, and the whipping cream. Add the minced tomatoes, bring to the boil and simmer for 10 minutes, while stirring frequently. Heat the meatballs briefly in the sauce.

3 Add the capers, caper juice, and parsley. If necessary season with salt and pepper. Delicious served with boiled potatoes and roast pine nuts.

* **Preparation time:** 40 minutes.
Per serving: 31 g P, 44 g F, 14 g C = 577 kcal (2417 kJ).

MAKE ME ROUND!
Want to make beautifully round meatballs, all the same size? No problem with an ice cream scoop! Just scoop out small amounts of the meatball mixture, using the ice cream scoop use your hands, previously moistened, for the last few meatballs.

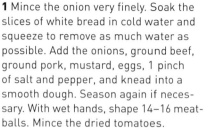

No time for boredom

THE WEATHER in April is changeable, inconsistent, capricious – but never boring or predictable. The same goes for our April recipes. No one will ever say: 'not that again ...!' Let yourself to be pleasantly surprised every day.

Saddle of Lamb

Saddle of lamb fillet is best served pink – that way it remains tender and juicy.

Serves 4:

5 oz onions

4 tbsp butter

4 tbsp olive oil

2 sprigs thyme

2 oz breadcrumbs

1 ¼ oz minced filberts

2 tbsp flat-leaved parsley

salt

pepper

4 lamb fillets (7 oz each)

2 tbsp balsamic vinegar

½ cup Marsala or medium sherry

⅞ cup chicken stock

dark gravy thickener

1 Mince the onions. Fry in 1½ tbsp butter and 2 tbsp olive oil over medium heat until golden brown. Remove the thyme leaves from the stems, mince coarsely, add to the pan, and fry briefly.

2 Allow the onions to cool on a plate. Mix in 2 tbsp butter, the breadcrumbs, filberts, and parsley. Season with salt and pepper.

3 Season the lamb fillets with salt and pepper. Heat 2 tbsp olive oil in a pan and briskly fry the meat on both sides over high heat. Arrange the meat in an oven-proof dish and spread the bread-crumb mixture on top.

4 Bake in the oven, preheated to 410 degrees (fan oven 375 degrees) on the second shelf from the bottom for 10–12 minutes until golden brown.

5 Return the pan to the heat and add the Marsala and balsamic vinegar. Cook until the liquid has reduced to half the amount. Add the stock, bring to the boil, and thicken with the gravy thickener. Season with salt and pepper. Allow the meat to rest briefly and serve with the sauce.

* **Preparation time:** 35 minutes.
Per serving: 44 g P, 33 g F, 18 g C = 546 kcal (2286 kJ).

COMPLETE CRUST
Scatter the breadcrumbs generously over the meat to ensure a very crisp coating.

Quick Mashed Potatoes with Herbs

Looks and tastes sensational – in just 15 minutes.

Serves 2: 1 Mix together 2 tbsp minced mixed **herbs** (chervil, parsley, dill, and chives) with 3 tbsp **olive oil**, and puree finely in a blender. **2** Prepare the mashed potato, following the instructions on the packet. Mix half the mashed potato with the herb-oil mixture (up to 2 tbsp) and fold into the rest of the mashed potatoes. Sprinkle with the rest of the herb-oil mixture.

* **Preparation time:** 15 minutes. Per serving: 4 g P, 15 g F, 36 g C = 298 kcal (1251 kJ).

Rolled Plaice

Rolled herb-flavored plaice fillets, served with a white wine sauce and thin strips of vegetables: Refined and sophisticated, it only takes 45 minutes to prepare.

Serves 4: 1 Defrost 4 **frozen plaice fillets** (5½ oz each). Strip the leaves of ½ bunch of **parsley** and **chervil** and mince. Cut each piece of plaice lengthways to make 2 fillets, season lightly with salt and pepper. Sprinkle ½ tsp **herb mustard** on top of each fillet. Sprinkle the herbs on top, roll up and secure with wooden skewers. **2** Wash and prepare 5 oz each **carrots**, **scallions**, and **snow peas**, and cut into thin sticks, about 2 in long. Fry lightly in 2 tbsp melted **butter**. Add 3 tsp flour and 1 pinch **saffron strands** and fry briefly. **3** Stir in ½ cup **white wine**. Add ⅝ cup **vegetable stock** and 3½ oz **crème fraîche** and bring briefly to the boil. Season with salt and pepper and 1 pinch of **sugar**. Arrange the rolled plaice fillets on the vegetables. Cover and cook over medium heat for 8 minutes. Turn the rolled plaice after 4 minutes. Delicious served with mixed wild rice.

* **Preparation time:** 45 minutes. **Per serving:** 31 g P, 17 g F, 8 g C = 319 kcal (1333 kJ).

Radish and Parsley Soup

This creamy soup is a delicious spring-like appetizer to a meal. The addition of raw radish leaves gives it a slightly sharp taste.

Serves 4: 1 Wash and prepare 1 bunch of __radishes__ and cut into thin slices. Mince the inner leaves. Pull off the leaves of 1 bunch of __parsley__ and mince. Mince 1 __onion__ and fry lightly with ⅔ of the radishes in 1 tbsp melted __butter__. Add 2½ cups __vegetable stock__, bring to the boil, cover, and cook for 5 minutes over low heat. **2** Add the parsley (up to 2 tbsp) and __radish leaves__ and puree very fine in a blender. Add ⅝ cup __whipping cream__ and bring to the boil again. Add 3 tbsp __mashed potato flakes__ and simmer for 1 minute. Season the soup generously with salt and pepper, and __nutmeg__. Garnish with the rest of the sliced radishes and parsley.

* **Preparation time:** 25 minutes. **Per serving:** 3 g P, 15 g F, 8 g C = 175 kcal (733 kJ).

Chocolate Soufflé

The really special thing about this soufflé is hidden in the centre: in the middle is a chocolate filled with egg liqueur which melts during the baking.

Serves 6:

3 ½ oz cooking chocolate

7 tbsp butter

4 medium eggs (separated)

good ½ cup flour

2 oz slivered almonds

salt

¼ cup sugar

fat and sugar for the molds

4 chocolates filled with egg liqueur

⅝ cup whipping cream

12 tbsp egg liqueur

1 Mince the cooking chocolate and melt together with the butter in a bain-marie over low heat. Add the egg yolks one at a time, stirring thoroughly before you add the next one. Stir in the flour and the almonds. Beat the egg whites stiff with 1 pinch of salt, carefully add the sugar, beat for another 3 minutes, then fold into the chocolate mixture.

2 Grease 6 cups (⅝ cup each) and sprinkle sugar inside. Spoon ⅔ of the mixture into the containers. Place 1 egg liqueur-filled chocolate on the chocolate mixture, then cover with the rest of the mixture. Bake in the oven, preheated to 355 degrees (fan oven 320 degrees), for 25 minutes second shelf from the bottom.

3 Beat the cream semi-stiff. Turn out the soufflés and serve with the egg liqueur and softly whipped cream.

* **Preparation time:** 50 minutes.
Per serving: 9 g P, 31 g F, 40 g C = 495 kcal (2073 kJ).

HOT KISSES
Warm up 1 chocolate marshmallow in the microwave at half power for 15 seconds. Then sprinkle with 1–2 tbsp egg liqueur and serve immediately.

Tagliatelle with Asparagus

Any left-over pepper butter from this recipe will certainly not go to waste: it is delicious with broiled steak.

Serves 2: 1 Drain 2 tsp **green peppercorns** (from a jar) and mince finely. Mince 1 **clove of garlic**. Beat ½ cup **butter** at room temperature with a hand-held mixer until creamy, add 1 tbsp **lemon juice**, add the green pepper and garlic, and season with salt. Divide the butter into strips on Saran wrap, wrap up tightly, and leave in the refrigerator for about 1 hour. **2** Wash 18 oz **green asparagus**, peel the bottom third and cut off the woody ends. Cut the stems diagonally into pieces 1 ½–2 in long. Strip the leaves of ½ bunch **chervil** and mince coarsely. **3** Cook the **tagliatelle** in plenty of salted water, following the instructions on the packet. Put 3 tbsp of the pepper-butter in a pan and melt. Add the asparagus and fry for 4–6 minutes over high heat. **4** Drain the tagliatelle. Add the asparagus and chervil to the tagliatelle and mix well. Season with salt and a little lemon juice according to taste.

Preparation time: 25 minutes (plus cooling time).
Per serving: 18 g P, 22 g F, 90 g C = 637 kcal (2670 kJ).

Waldorf Pappardelle

Clever! The ingredients of the famous Waldorf salad in a pasta dish!

Serves 2: 1 Wash and prepare 7 oz **celery** and cut into long strips with a potato peeler. Mince 2 oz **walnut kernels**. Wash 1 **red apple** (about 9 oz), cut into 8 segments, remove the pips and cut into pieces 1/16 in thick, and immediately sprinkle 1 tbsp **lemon juice** on top. Coarsely mince 1 small **onion**. **2** Cook the **Pappardelle** in plenty of salted water following the instructions on the packet. 30 seconds before the end of the cooking time, add the strips of celery, then drain the pasta with the celery. Meanwhile heat 1 tbsp **oil** in a pan and briskly fry the onions and pieces of apple for 2 minutes over high heat. Season with salt and pepper. Remove from the pan. **3** Add ½ cup **vegetable stock** and ½ cup **whipping cream** to the cooking juices and sediment in the pan. Reduce for 2–3 minutes over high heat. Season generously with 1–2 tbsp lemon juice, salt, and pepper. Briefly reheat the pasta mixture, apple, and onion in the sauce. Sprinkle the minced walnuts on top.

Preparation time: 20 minutes.
Per serving: 21 g P, 40 g F,
105 g C = 868 kcal (3676 kJ).

133

Layered Rhubarb and Curd Dessert

Rhubarb can be very sour depending on the variety and how much sunshine it got when growing. Because of this, you must try the rhubarb compote while preparing it and sweeten according to taste.

Serves 4: 1 Wash and prepare 1¾ lb **rhubarb** and peel off any strings if necessary. Cut into ⅝-in cubes. Mix together 3½ oz **strawberry jelly** and ½ cup **rhubarb juice** (or **grape juice**), bring to the boil and simmer for 2 minutes. Stir together 1 heaping tbsp **cornstarch** and 4 tbsp rhubarb juice until smooth. Carefully stir into the rhubarb, bring back to the boil, pour into a bowl and leave to cool down.
2 Beat together 14 oz **creamy curd**, 4 tbsp **confectioners' sugar** and 1½ tsp **vanilla sugar** with a hand-held mixer for 3 minutes until creamy. Arrange the curd and cooled rhubarb in layers in the glasses.

* **Preparation time:** 25 minutes (plus cooling time).
  Per serving: 10 g P, 10 g F, 38 g C = 300 kcal (1253 kJ).

Egg Liqueur Slices

Many people – both men and women – have a soft spot for egg liqueur. This cake will allow everyone to indulge their secret weakness!

For 20 pieces: 1 Beat 6 medium **egg whites** and 1 pinch of salt until stiff. When the egg whites are nearly stiff, carefully stir in ¾ cup **sugar**, little by little, and continue whisking for another 3 minutes. Briefly stir in the 6 egg yolks. Sift good ¾ cup **flour**, 1½ tbsp **cocoa**, 2 tbsp **cornstarch**, and 3 tsp **baking powder**, and fold into the egg mixture together with 9 oz ground **filberts**. **2** Spread the resulting mixture on a cookie sheet (16 x 12 in), lined with waxed paper. Bake in the oven, preheated to 355 degrees (fan oven 320 degrees) on the second shelf from the bottom for 18–20 minutes. Leave to cool down. Spread 9 oz **cranberry compote** on top. **3** Beat 2½ cups **whipping cream** with 1½ tsp **vanilla sugar** until stiff. Spread over the pastry and press with the back of a spoon to make waves. Sprinkle ⅝ cup **egg liqueur** (e.g. Advocaat) on top. Garnish with **chocolate flakes**.

* **Preparation time:** 50 minutes (plus cooling time).
  Per piece: 6 g P, 20 g F, 26 g C = 312 kcal (1307 kJ).

Vegetable Carpaccio

Like in a restaurant but so easy to make: thinly sliced carrots, kohlrabi, and zucchinis with tomato vinaigrette and pine nuts.

Serves 4: 1 Peel 1 small **kohlrabi** (about 7 oz) and 1 large **carrot** (about 3½ oz) and cut into very thin slices. Also cut 5 oz **zucchinis** into thin slices. Arrange the sliced vegetables on 4 plates. Toast 1–2 tbsp **pine nuts** in a non-stick pan without fat and leave to cool. Strip off the leaves of one pot of **basil** and cut into thin strips. **2** Cut 7 oz **tomatoes** into quarters, remove the seeds and mince. Stir together 3 tbsp **white balsamic vinegar**, a little salt, pepper, 1 pinch of sugar, 1 crushed clove of garlic and 6 tbsp **olive oil**. Add the tomatoes and basil and pour over the vegetables. Sprinkle the pine nuts on top.

Preparation time: 30 minutes. Per serving: 3 g P, 18 g F, 8 g C = 205 kcal (860 kJ).

Casseroled Chicken Leg

A breath of the south: chicken with a medley of vegetables, olive oil, and oregano – uncomplicated, straight from the casserole and served with a creamy basil sauce.

Serves 4: 1 Peel 14 oz **carrots** and cut into pieces. Wash and prepare 9 oz **celery** and cut into pieces. Season 4 **chicken legs** with salt and pepper. Add 3 tbsp **olive oil** in a pan and fry the chicken legs all round until crisp, then place them in deep roasting pan. Then fry the carrots and celery lightly in 1 tbsp olive oil. **2** Season with salt and pepper, 2 tbsp **oregano**, and 1 crushed **clove of garlic**. Add ⅞ cup **chicken stock**, bring to the boil, and pour into the roasting pan. Bake in the oven, pre-heated to 390 degrees (fan oven 355 degrees) on the second shelf from the bottom for 40 minutes. After 30 minutes add 5 oz **cherry tomatoes** and 3 ½ oz **ripe olives**. **3** Strip the leaves of a pot of **basil**, cut into thin strips, add 7 oz **crème fraîche**, a little salt, pepper, and 1 crushed clove of garlic. Serve with the chicken and vegetables.

* **Preparation time:** 55 minutes. **Per serving:** 37 g P, 41 g F, 8 g C = 552 kcal (2308 kJ).

Coq-au-Vin

A classic French dish with red wine and bacon, best prepared in advance.

Serves 2:

3 ½ oz bacon

several chicken breasts
(1 ½ lb)

5 oz small onions

2 onions

2 cloves garlic

1 tbsp oil

salt

1 ¼ cups fruity red wine

½ cup chicken stock
(from a bouillon cube)

3 oz cocktail onions (bottled)

½ bunch parsley

dark gravy thickener

1 Cut the bacon into small cubes. Cut the chicken breasts in half lengthways, then cut each half into 3 pieces. Wash and prepare the mushrooms. Mince the onions and cloves of garlic.

2 Heat the oil in a casserole, add the diced bacon, fry until crisp and remove from the pan. Now add the mushrooms to the fat in the pan and fry briskly, salt and remove from the pan. Season the chicken with salt and fry briskly on all sides in the hot oil. Add the onions and garlic and fry lightly over medium heat for 1 minute while stirring.

3 Now pour the wine and stock into the casserole and bring to the boil. Cover and cook the meat over medium heat for 30 minutes, turning the meat a few times during this time. Drain the cocktail onions and mince. Strip the parsley leaves off the stems and mince them. Add the bacon, mushrooms, and cocktail onions to the casserole 10 minutes before the end of the cooking time.

4 Thicken the sauce with gravy thickener, following the instructions on the packet. Season with salt and pepper. Sprinkle parsley on top before serving.

* **Preparation time:** 1 hour.
  Per serving: 66 g P, 46 g F, 13 g C = 750 kcal (3142 kJ).

COOKING WITH RED WINE
Do not use heavy wines matured in wood, because the "woody notes" become even stronger. Fruity red wines are better for this dish.

Chervil and Mustard Eggs

This is without doubt our editorial team's favorite dish: mustard eggs, served with a delicate, spring-like chervil sauce.

Serves 2: 1 Mince 2 **onions** and fry in 1½ tbsp **butter** until transparent. Sprinkle 3 tbsp **flour** over the onions and brown lightly. **2** Add 1½ cups **milk**, stirring all the while, bring to the boil and cook for 15 minutes over medium heat while stirring. Add 3–4 tbsp hot **mustard** and 1 tbsp minced **chervil**. Season with salt and pepper and keep warm. **3** Boil 4 **eggs** for 7 minutes, put them under cold water and remove the shells. Serve the eggs with the sauce.

Preparation time: 35 minutes.
Per serving: 25 g P, 30 g F, 20 g C = 446 kcal (1870 kJ).

Snow Peas with Sesame Seeds

*A little soy sauce, chili pepper, and roasted sesame seeds
and the snow peas suddenly acquire an oriental touch.*

Serves 2: 1 Wash and prepare 9 oz **snow peas**, cook for 1 minute in
boiling water, drain and put in cold water. Roast 2 tbsp **sesame seeds**
in a non-stick pan without any fat and remove. Wash and prepare
1 **scallion** and cut into thin rings. Cut half of a de-seeded **chili pepper**
into thin strips. **2** Heat 1–2 tbsp **oil** in a pan. Add the snow peas,
scallion and chili pepper to the pan and fry briefly over high heat. Add
the sesame seeds, sprinkle with a little **sugar**, season with salt and
pepper. Remove from the heat and add 1 tbsp **soy sauce**.

Preparation time: 10 minutes. Per serving: 3 g P, 16 g F, 7 g C = 186 kcal (780 kJ).

Oyster Mushrooms in Cream

These creamy, aromatic mushrooms can also be served with a baguette as a sophisticated appetizer.

Serves 2: 1 Wash and prepare 10 oz **oyster mushrooms**. Drain 2 oz **sun-dried tomatoes in oil**, cut into thin strips. Wash and prepare 2 **scallions** and cut into pieces ¾ in long. **2** Heat 2 tbsp **oil** in a pan. Add the mushrooms and fry briskly over high heat for 2 minutes. Add the tomatoes, onions, and ½ cup **whipping cream**. Bring to the boil, then add ½ tsp **thyme** and season with salt and pepper.

Preparation time: 15 minutes. Per serving: 5 g P, 28 g F, 7 g C = 290 kcal (1214 kJ).

Pasta Frittata

The crisp nest of pasta is baked in the oven with cherry tomatoes, paprika, and sheep's cheese.

Serves 2: 1 Cut 1 __red bell pepper__ into four, remove the seeds and mince coarsely. Cut 1 __onion__ into strips. Beat 3 __eggs__ with minced __parsley__. **2** Heat 2 tbsp __oil__ in a non-stick pan. Add the pepper and onion and fry over medium heat for 2 minutes. Crush 1 __clove of garlic__ and add to the pan. Now add 10 oz cooked __fusilli__ and season with salt and pepper. Stir in the eggs and remove from the heat. **3** Arrange 6 __cherry tomatoes__ on the frittata and sprinkle 3 oz crumbled __sheep's cheese__ on top. Bake in the oven, preheated to 375 degrees (fan oven 170 degrees) on the second shelf from the bottom for 20 minutes.

Preparation time: 50 minutes. **Per serving:** 26 g P, 29 g F, 42 g C = 533 kcal (2233 kJ).

Rhubarb and Raspberry Crumble

A mixed double: hot raspberries and rhubarb with cinnamon crumble and vanilla ice cream

Serves 4: 1 Wash and prepare 14 oz **rhubarb** and cut into chunks ¾ in long. Mix together 5 oz **frozen raspberries**, bare ¼ cup **sugar**, and 1½ tsp **vanilla sugar**. Put the mixed fruit in 4 oven-proof ramekins (4¾ in in diameter) or in 1 large oven-proof bowl. Stir together 1 tbsp cornstarch, a drop of **vanilla extract**, and 6 tbsp **orange juice** and pour over the fruit. **2** Melt 4 tbsp **butter**, add 1 cup **flour**, bare ¼ cup sugar, and ½ tsp **cinnamon**, and knead to a crumble consistency. Cover the fruit with this crumble mixture. Bake in the oven, preheated to 390 degrees (fan oven 355 degrees) on the bottom shelf for 25 minutes. Sprinkle confectioners' sugar on top and serve with **vanilla ice cream**.

* **Preparation time:** 50 minutes. **Per serving:** 4 g P, 13 g F, 48 g C = 333 kcal (1396 kJ).

Caramel-Yoghurt Dessert

Crème caramel as made by a pro, but using vanilla-flavored yoghourt and ready-made caramel sauce.

Serves 6: 1 Soak 4 leaves of **gelatin** in cold water. Mix together 10 oz **full fat yoghurt**, 10 oz **vanilla-flavored yoghourt** and 1½ oz **confectioners' sugar**. Heat up 3 tbsp **orange juice**, add the squeezed gelatin and dissolve in the orange juice. Stir this into the yoghurt. Divide the mixture into 4 cups (each ⅝ cup). Refrigerate for at least 4 hours. **2** Loosen round the edges, using a small knife. Dip the cups briefly in hot water and turn out onto a plate. Pour 2 tbsp **caramel sauce** over each one.

* **Preparation time:** 25 minutes (plus cooling time).
 Per serving: 8 g P, 5 g F, 31 g C = 222 kcal (928 kJ).

Romanesco Broccoli and Curd Gratin

This curd gratin can also be made with cauliflower, but it has more visual impact with the green broccoli florets

Serves 2: 1 Wash and prepare 1¾ lb **Romanesco broccoli**, cut into florets and cook in boiling salted water for 4 minutes. Drain and rinse under cold water. **2** Stir together 2 **egg yolks**, 3 oz **curd**, 1 tbsp **olive oil**, 5 tbsp **milk** and 1 tbsp minced **parsley**. Season with salt and pepper. Stir in 2 tbsp **flour**. Beat 2 **egg whites** until stiff with 1 pinch of salt and carefully fold into the mixture. **3** Transfer the batter to an oven-proof dish (12 in in diameter). Arrange the broccoli on top. Season with salt and pepper. Bake in the oven, preheated to 410 degrees (fan oven not recommended) on the second shelf from the bottom for 15 minutes.

Preparation time: 35 minutes. Per serving: 21 g P, 13 g F, 20 g C = 288 kcal (1210 kJ).

Pork Medallions with Rhubarb

Those who have only ever eaten rhubarb as a dessert has missed out!
Rhubarb is simply delicious with meat!

Serves 2: 1 Bring to the boil ¼ cup **sugar**, 2 tbsp **butter**, 3 tbsp **cider vinegar** and ⅓ oz **green peppercorns** in a pan and cook for 5 minutes.
2 Wash and prepare 9 oz **rhubarb** and cut into cubes. Add to the pan and simmer for 5–6 minutes. Season with salt and pepper and keep in a warm place. **3** In a second pan heat 2 tbsp **oil**. Season 2 **pork tenderloin medallions** with salt and fry briskly in the hot oil for 5 minutes on each side over medium to high heat. Serve with the rhubarb.

Preparation time: 30 minutes.
Per serving: 17 g P, 22 g F, 26 g C = 375 kcal (1570 kJ).

Pasta and Beans

There are numerous variations on this traditional Italian pasta and beans dish. This is our favorite version.

Serves 2: 1 Cut 2 oz **bacon** and 2 oz **onions** in small cubes and fry in 2 tbsp **olive oil** until transparent. Crush 2 **cloves of garlic**. Add 3½ cups **vegetable stock** or **chicken stock**, and 1 can minced tomatoes (1 lb drained weight), and bring to the boil. **2** Add 10 oz **frozen vegetables** and cook over low heat for 20 minutes. Add 1 can **white beans** (1 lb drained weight) 3 minutes before the end. Season with salt and pepper. **3** Cook 5 oz **soup noodles** in salted water, following the instructions on the packet. Drain and add to the soup. Add some minced **parsley** and serve with grated **Parmesan**.

Preparation time: 40 minutes.
Per serving: 32 g P, 24 g F, 78 g C = 662 kcal (2780 kJ).

148

Curried Carrots

A completely different side to the personality of this traditional root vegetable: quite frivolous with curry and mango

Serves 2: 1 Peel 18 oz **<u>carrots</u>** and cut diagonally into slices ⅛ in thick. **2** Heat 2 tbsp **<u>butter</u>** in a non-stick pan. Add the carrots, sprinkle 1 tsp **<u>curry powder</u>** on top and fry lightly for 3 minutes. Add 3 tbsp water. Cover and simmer for another 5 minutes. **3** Add ⅝ cup **<u>whipping cream</u>** and cook for another 3 minutes. Cut 7 oz **<u>mangos</u>** into cubes. **4** At the end of the cooking time, add the mango cubes to the carrots. Season with salt, pepper and 1 tbsp **<u>lemon juice</u>**. Garnish with **<u>cilantro</u>**.

Preparation time: 20 minutes. Per serving: 4 g P, 34 g F, 24 g C = 418 kcal (1752 kJ).

Pollock

The best dishes are always the easiest: like this fried pollock on a bed of warm asparagus salad with a chervil-honey vinaigrette.

Serves 2: 1 Wash 10 oz **green asparagus** and cut off the bottom third. Cut the asparagus into thin slices. Cook in salted water for 3 minutes, drain, run under cold water and drain again. **2** Mince 1 **red onion**, put in a strainer and plunge in hot water for 1 minute. Stir together with 5 tbsp oil, 2–3 tbsp **lemon juice**, salt, pepper, and 1 tsp **honey**. Add the asparagus and leave to marinate briefly. Season with salt and pepper. Add 1 tsp minced **chervil**. **3** Salt the **pollock fillets** (6 oz each), coat in **flour** and fry in 1 tbsp **oil** over medium heat for 3–4 minutes on each side. Serve on the asparagus salad.

Preparation time: 30 minutes. Per serving: 36 g P, 31 g F, 13 g C = 478 kcal (2002 kJ).

Caribbean Rice

The sophisticated taste of coconut can be further enhanced if you sprinkle fresh, grated coconut over the rice.

Serves 2: 1 Cut 1 red **chili pepper** in half lengthways, remove the seeds, and cut into strips. Mince 1 **onion**. Lightly fry both in 2 tbsp **olive oil** with 1 tsp **cumin** for 1 minute over medium heat. Add ⅝ cup **long-grain rice** and fry for 30 seconds. **2** Add ⅞ cup **coconut milk** and ⅞ cup **vegetable stock**, stir well and bring to the boil. Cover and simmer over low heat for 20 minutes. **3** Sprinkle some **cilantro** on top.

* **Preparation time:** 35 minutes. **Per serving:** 6 g P, 11 g F, 66 g C = 386 kcal (1618 kJ).

Potato Gratin with Green Peppercorns

Even beginners will find this dish easy to make:
all the uncooked ingredients arranged in layers, the oven does the rest!

Serves 2: 1 Peel 18 oz **potatoes** and cut into thin slices. Cut 2 **red onions** into thin strips. Stir together the potatoes and onions in a bowl and season with salt. **2** Bring to the boil ⅞ cup **whipping cream** together with ½ tsp minced **thyme** and 2 tsp coarsely minced **green peppercorns** (from a jar). Pour over the potatoes, mix well and pour the whole mixture into a greased, oven-proof dish. Bake in the oven, preheated to 390 degrees (fan oven 355 degrees) for 35–40 minutes.

Preparation time: 1 hour. **Per serving:** 7 g P, 30 g F, 34 g C = 438 kcal (1837 kJ).

Burgundian Spinach

*Amazingly effective: the leaf spinach is prepared as usual
but cooked in red wine which adds a very sophisticated touch.*

Serves 2: 1 Wash and prepare 13 oz **spinach** and mince coarsely. Mince
2 **shallots**. Crush 1 **clove of garlic** in a garlic press. **2** Sweat the onions
and garlic in 2 tbsp **butter** over low heat for 3–4 minutes until transparent.
Add ⅞ cup full-bodied **red wine** and reduce until the mixture becomes
syrupy. **3** Add the spinach, cover, and cook for 2–3 minutes, stirring
occasionally. Season with salt and pepper.

Preparation time: 20 minutes.
Per serving: 4 g P, 11 g F, 2 g C = 143 kcal (597 kJ).

Roast Beef with an Oriental Touch

A great combination: the roast is prepared the usual way but it is the sauce which turns it into eastern delight.

Serves 4:

2 tbsp liquid honey

3 tbsp soy sauce

1 tbsp lemon juice

salt

pepper

2 dried red chili peppers

2 star anise

2¼ lb beef top round in the piece

3 tbsp oil

⅝ cup white wine

1 cup beef stock

2 bunches scallions

dark gravy thickener

1 Mix together the honey, soy sauce, lemon juice, and a little salt and pepper. Crumble the chili peppers, mince the star anise and add to the mixture. Put the meat together with the marinade in a freezer bag. Seal well and make sure the marinade is well distributed all over the roast. Leave to marinate for at least 2 hours in the refrigerator.

2 Take the meat out of the marinade and fry briskly on all sides in the hot oil. Now add the marinade, white wine, and stock, and bring to the boil. Put to one side. Put the meat on a cookie sheet and bake in the oven, preheated to 390 degrees (fan oven 355 degrees) on the second shelf from the bottom for 25 minutes.

3 Wash and prepare the scallions and cut into pieces 2⅓ in long. Make several notches at both ends of the pieces, using a sharp knife, then place the pieces in cold water.

4 Wrap the roast in aluminum foil and leave to rest for about 7 minutes. Bring the sauce back to the boil. Thicken with gravy thickener, season with salt and pepper, and pour through a fine strainer. Slice the meat and serve with the drained scallions.

A TENDER REST
The meat fibers relax while the roast is resting and the juices are distributed evenly throughout which makes the meat tender and juicy.

* **Preparation time:** 40 minutes (plus marinating time).
Per serving: 53 g P, 19 g F, 14 g C = 446 kcal (1869 kJ).

Baked Chocolate Eggs

An ideal present or perfect for spoiling yourself!

For 18 pieces:

1 Mix together 1 packet **chocolate cake mix** (about 1 lb) with 3 medium **eggs**, ½ cup **milk**, and ⅝ cup softened **butter**, following the instructions on the packet. Put half the pastry batter in a greased in a pan with 9 egg-shaped holes (if not available, use a muffin pan; the results will not be egg-shaped but still delicious). Bake in the oven, preheated to 355 degrees (fan oven 320 degrees) on the second shelf from the bottom for 15 minutes. **2** Remove from the pan and bake the rest of the pastry batter in the same way. Mince 3½ oz **plain cooking chocolate** and melt in a hot bain-marie or bowl over a saucepan of boiling water. Mince 5 oz **white cooking chocolate** and melt in the same way. Coat 9 eggs with white chocolate and 9 eggs with dark chocolate, then leave to set. **3** Put the rest of the melted chocolate in throw-away pastry bags. Cut a small hole at the end of each one and decorate the eggs according to taste.

Preparation time: 1 hour (plus cooling time).
Per serving: 4 g P, 15 g F, 27 g C = 259 kcal (1090 kJ).

Chocolate Marshmallow Ice Cream

This recipe will enable adults to indulge their secret passion for chocolate marshmallows. Quite irresistible!

Serves 2: 1 If the **chocolate marshmallows** have wafers at the bottom, remove them. Crush the sweets with a fork and stir in ¼ tsp grated **orange zest**. Beat ⅝ cup **whipping cream** and fold into the marshmallow mixture. **2** Put the mixture in a shallow mold, cover with cling film and put in the freezer compartment for about 2 hours. During this time stir the freezing mixture with a spoon 2 or 3 times. **3** Scoop four ice cream balls from the iced mass and put 2 balls in each bowl. Pour 2 tbsp **egg liqueur** over the ice cream and garnish with a chocolate wafer.

Preparation time: 10 minutes (plus freezing time).
Per serving: 6 g P, 29 g F, 40 g C = 463 kcal (1940 kJ).

Veal Roulades

It is not surprising that beef, veal, and pork roulades are so popular: just try these divine veal roulades and you will understand why.

Serves 2:

3 thin veal chops
(about 3½ oz each)

salt

pepper

1 bunch parsley

3½ oz ground pork

3 tbsp herb curd

1 egg yolk
(from a medium egg)

1 onion

2 tbsp oil

⅞ cup veal stock

8 tbsp whipping cream

½ tbsp light gravy thickener

1 Cut the veal chops in half diagonally. Put the pieces, one after the other, in a freezer bag and hit them with a heavy pan to flatten them. Season with salt and pepper. Pull the parsley leaves off the stems and mince. Knead ⅔ of the minced parsley into the ground pork, curd, and egg yolk mixture.

2 Spread the ground pork mixture on the veal escalope, fold the edges over the filling, roll up tightly and secure with cocktail sticks. Mince the onion. Fry the veal roulades briskly in hot oil in a pan. Remove from the pan. Add the minced onion and fry lightly.

3 Add the veal stock and the cream, bring to the boil, add the veal roulades, cover, and cook for 10 minutes over medium heat. Turn the veal roulades after 5 minutes. Thicken the sauce with the gravy thickener. Season with salt and pepper. Add the rest of the parsley to the sauce.

* **Preparation time:** 35 minutes.
Per serving: 49 g P, 42 g F, 6 g C = 594 kcal (2486 kJ).

WELL ROLLED
To make sure the delicious filling does not escape: spread the filling on the escalope, fold up the sides, roll up tight and secure with cocktail sticks.

Asparagus makes an appearance

IT IS THE STAR of the month. Connoisseurs go into raptures over it and grab their asparagus peeler with excitement: whether as soup or salad, whether traditional or exotic, we have some mouth-watering asparagus recipes for you. In addition, we have many more delicious recipes, such as Flounder with Diced Bacon, Spring Soljanka and Pasta Primavera. And last but not least, there are the first strawberries...

Flounder with Diced Bacon

Until the larger flat fish arrive on our table in June, we shall enjoy this delicate-tasting fish, served with diced bacon: quite unbeatable.

Serves 4:

3½ oz bacon

2 onions

1 tbsp oil

3 tbsp butter

8 flounder fillets (ready for cooking, 7 oz each)

salt

flour

3–4 tbsp clarified butter

1 tbsp minced parsley

1 Dice the bacon and mince the onions finely. Sweat the bacon in the oil and butter for 2 minutes. Add the onions and fry for another 5–6 minutes over medium heat while stirring. Keep the bacon mixture warm.

2 Wash the flounder fillets and dab dry. Season with salt and coat in flour.

3 Heat the clarified butter in a large pan. Add the flounders, fry for 1 minute on each side and transfer to a cookie sheet.

4 Bake the flounders in the oven, preheated to 410 degrees (fan oven 375 degrees) on the second shelf from the bottom for 7–8 minutes. Arrange on a plate, sprinkle parsley on top and pour the warm bacon sauce on top.

Preparation time: 40 minutes.
Per serving: 64 g P, 36 g F, 10 g C = 614 kcal (2566 kJ).

A CLASSY ADDITION
To add a festive note to this classic flounder dish, add a couple of spoonfuls of shrimp to the bacon sauce.

Shrimp with a Refreshing Orange Garnish

Contrasts are always exciting. Here the mild taste of the shrimp is juxtaposed with the spicy chili, sharp garlic, and refreshing orange.

Serves 4: 1 Defrost 20 **shrimp**. Cut open 1 **mild red chili pepper**, remove the seeds, and cut into thin strips. Cut 1 **clove of garlic** into thin slices. Remove the zest of 1 **orange (untreated)**, cut it into thin strips, then squeeze out 8 tbsp juice. Remove the shrimp from their shells. Make a slit along the back and remove the black part. **2** Heat 3 tbsp **olive oil** in a large pan and fry the shrimp for 4 minutes, stirring all the time. After 2 minutes add the garlic and chili pepper. Pour in the orange juice and season with salt. Sprinkle 2 tbsp coarsely minced **parsley** and the orange zest on top. This is delicious served with **aioli** (garlic mayonnaise, from a jar) and topped with roast, minced almonds.

Preparation time: 20 minutes. **Per serving:** 31 g P, 10 g F, 4 g C = 230 kcal (962 kJ).

Pasta Primavera

Fresh asparagus, tender snow peas, carrots, garden peas, and aromatic chervil turn this pasta dish into a true celebration of spring.

Serves 2: 1 Peel 7 oz each of **white** and **green asparagus**. Cut 5 oz **snow peas** in half lengthways. Peel 1 **carrot** and cut into slices. Wash and prepare 2 **scallions** and cut into thin slices. **2** Heat 1 tbsp **olive oil** in a pan, add the asparagus and fry for 2–3 minutes over medium heat. Add ⅛ cup **whipping cream**. Now add the snow peas, 3 ½ oz **frozen peas**, and the scallions. Cook for 2 minutes. Season with salt and pepper. **3** Meanwhile, cook 7 oz **penne pasta** in salted water, following the instructions on the packet. 4 minutes before the end of the cooking time, add the carrots. Pour away the water, drain, and mix together with the sauce. Add 2 tbsp minced **chervil**.

*Preparation time: 25 minutes. Per serving: 23 g P, 38 g F, 88 g C = 790 kcal (3315 kJ).

164

Bacon and Cabbage Pizza

A filling meal for 2 hungry people or a substantial snack for 4 to 6 wine or beer drinkers.

Serves 2: 1 Prepare 1 packet of **ready-made pizza dough** (8 oz), following the instructions on the packet. Dice 3 ½ oz **bacon**. Cut 2 **onions** and 7 oz **cabbage** into strips. **2** Fry the onion and bacon in 1 tbsp **oil** until crisp. Add the cabbage and fry for 3 minutes while stirring. Season with salt and pepper. **3** Roll out the pizza dough on a cookie sheet 12 x 10 in. Spread the cabbage mixture on top. Mix together 1 **egg yolk**, 5 oz **crème fraîche**, 1 tbsp **minced chives**, and 1 tbsp **parsley**, and spread this mixture over the cabbage. **4** Bake in the oven, preheated to 410 degrees (fan oven 375 degrees) on the bottom shelf for 20 minutes.

Preparation time: 50 minutes.
Per serving: 23 g P, 65 g F, 79 g C = 1000 kcal (4176 kJ).

Rhubarb Clafoutis

Delicious in a mold: wake up the budding pastry cook within you!

Serves 4: 1 Grease 4 small oven-proof ramekins (2⅓ in diameter or 1 large mold 9½ in diameter) with 2 tbsp **oil**. Wash and prepare 1¼ lb **rhubarb**, cut into pieces ¾ in long, and arrange in the ramekins. Using a whisk, stir together ⅓ cup **sugar**, 1 tbsp **vanilla sugar**, 4 tbsp oil, 2 medium **eggs**, and 1 cup **flour** to shape a smooth dough. Stir ¾ cup **milk**, little by little, into the pastry mixture. Now pour this mixture over the rhubarb. **2** Bake in the oven, preheated to 390 degrees (fan oven 355 degrees) on the second shelf from the bottom for 35–40 minutes. Remove from the oven, sprinkle sugar on top and serve hot. Delicious with ice cream.

Preparation time: 55 minutes.
Per serving: 8 g P, 20 g F,
56 g C = 441 kcal (1850 kJ).

Strawberry Hearts

Chocolate pastry is particularly good with strawberries. The mere sight of these strawberry hearts is enough to make your mouth water.

For 12 pieces: 1 Mince 5 oz **white chocolate** and melt with ⅝ cup **butter** in a hot bain-marie. Mince 2 oz **pistachio nuts**. Beat together 6 medium **eggs**, ⅓ cup **sugar**, and 1 tbsp **orange zest** using a hand-held mixer for 8 minutes until creamy. Now mix together 1½ cups **flour** and 1½ tsp **baking powder**. Stir into the chocolate-butter mixture and add the minced pistachios. **2** Spread the pastry mixture on a cookie sheet (16 x 12 in), lined with grease-proof paper. Bake in the oven, preheated to 390 degrees (fan oven 355 degrees) on the second shelf from the bottom for 15 minutes. Leave to cool. Bring to the boil 7 oz **strawberry jelly** and 2 tbsp **orange juice**, then pass it through a strainer. Wash and prepare 14 oz **strawberries** and cut into slices. **3** Cut out 12 hearts (about 3¼ in long) from the pastry, close to each other. Grate 1 oz white cooking chocolate. Spread the jelly on the hearts and arrange the strawberries on top so that they overlap. Sprinkle the grated chocolate along the edges.

Preparation time: 50 minutes.
Per piece: 6 g P, 16 g F, 31 g C = 297 kcal (1244 kJ).

Spring Soljanka

This Russian dish used to be on the menu of every restaurant in the former East Germany. Here we present a more sophisticated, lighter version.

Serves 4:

1¼ lb braising beef

1 each red and yellow bell peppers

1¼ lb cabbage

7 oz onions

4 tbsp oil

salt

pepper

2 crushed cloves of garlic

4 tbsp red bell pepper paste

4½ cups vegetable stock

3½ oz gherkins with ½ cup juice

sugar

2 tbsp minced parsley

1 Remove all fat and cut the meat into 1¼-in cubes. Wash and prepare the peppers and cut into ¾-in cubes. Wash and prepare the cabbage and cut into ⅜ in strips. Mince the onions. Fry the meat briskly in 2 tbsp hot oil until brown all over. Season generously with salt and pepper and remove the meat from the pan.

2 Heat 2 tbsp oil in the pan, add the onions, peppers, cabbage, and garlic, and fry. Add the pepper paste and fry briefly. Season with salt and pepper. Add the stock, bring to the boil, cover, and cook over medium heat for 20 minutes. Cut the gherkins into cubes and add to the pan with the juice after 15 minutes.

3 Add the meat and cook for another 2 minutes. Season with salt, pepper, and optionally 1 pinch of sugar. Sprinkle parsley on top.

Preparation time: 40 minutes.
Per serving: 40 g P, 18 g F, 11 g C = 370 kcal (1552 kJ).

SPREEWÄLDER GHERKINS
The most famous pickled gherkins come from the Spreewald where gherkins have been grow specially for pickling since the 15th century.

Cream of Asparagus Soup

The most refined soup spring can offer with the irresistible aroma of fresh asparagus, crispy ham, and basil.

Serves 4: 1 Peel 2¼ lb **white asparagus**. Wash the peelings, add to 4½ cups salted water together with 2 tbsp **butter** and 1 tsp **sugar**, bring slowly to the boil, and simmer uncovered over low heat for 15 minutes. Cut the asparagus stems into slices, cut the heads in half, and put to one side. Peel 9 oz **potatoes** and cut into cubes. **2** Pour the asparagus stock through a strainer and bring back to the boil. Add the potatoes and sliced asparagus (but not the asparagus heads yet!), cover, and cook over medium heat for 15–20 minutes. Then puree finely. Now add ⅞ cup **whipping cream** and the asparagus heads, and simmer for 8 minutes. Season with salt, pepper, sugar, and **lemon juice**. **3** Cut the 2 slices **prosciutto** into three and fry in 1 tbsp oil in a non-stick pan until crisp. Cut 8 **basil leaves** into thin strips. Serve with the ham and basil.

Preparation time: 55 minutes. **Per serving:** 7 g P, 25 g F, 16 g C = 312 kcal (1313 kJ).

Asparagus Gratin

*Green asparagus is particularly popular in Italy
where it is usually served with a fruity tomato and basil sauce.*

Serves 2: 1 Mince 1 **onion** and fry in 2 tbsp **oil** with ½ tsp **sugar**. Add
1 can minced **tomatoes** (14 oz drained weight), season with salt and
pepper, and simmer uncovered for 5–7 minutes. Strip 10 **basil leaves**
from their stems and cut into thin strips. Peel the bottom third of the
stems of 2¼ lb **green asparagus** and cut off the woody ends. **2** Precook
the asparagus in boiling salted water with 1 tsp sugar and 1 tsp **butter**
for 5 minutes. Drain, pat completely dry and arrange in 2 oven-proof
ramekins (about 8 in long). Add the basil to the tomato sauce and season
again if necessary. Pour the sauce over the asparagus and sprinkle
4 tbsp grated **Parmesan** on top. **3** Brown in the oven, preheated to
430 degrees (fan oven not recommended) on the second shelf from the
top for 10 minutes. Garnish with a few basil leaves before serving.

* **Preparation time:** 35 minutes. **Per serving:** 14 g P, 18 g F, 13 g C = 270 kcal (1140 kJ).

Asparagus-Spinach Salad

The dressing makes this salad so sophisticated: made from goat's cheese and white balsamic vinegar. And then there is the fried asparagus!

Serves 4: 1 Bring to the boil 4 tbsp **white balsamic vinegar** in a small pan with 4½ oz **goat's cheese**, 5 tbsp water, 4 tbsp olive oil, salt, and pepper. Stir to make a fine puree. Put to one side. **2** Peel 18 oz **white asparagus** and cut off the woody ends. Cut the asparagus into four lengthways. Heat 1 tbsp oil in a non-stick pan, add the asparagus and fry over a high heat for 2–3 minutes. Season with salt and pepper, and 1 pinch sugar. **3** Briefly wash 9 oz **spinach salad** (pre-prepared in a bag from the supermarket, or made from 14 oz **raw leaf spinach**) and spin dry. Arrange the spinach on 4 plates, put the asparagus on top, and pour the dressing over the spinach and asparagus.

* **Preparation time:** 35 minutes.
  Per serving: 6 g P, 72 g F, 6 g C = 252 kcal (1057 kJ).

Quick Potato Soufflé

Light and very easy to make, this recipe uses mashed potato from a packet.
Served with salad, this soufflé is an ideal light evening meal.

Serves 2: 1 Prepare 1 packet **mashed potato**, following the instructions
on the packet. Season with a little **nutmeg** and pepper. **2** Separate 1 **egg**.
Stir the egg yolk into the mashed potatoes. Beat the egg white stiff with
1 pinch of salt, then fold into the mashed potatoes together with 4 tbsp
Parmesan. **3** Spoon the mixture into two small, greased, oven-proof
bowls or cups, and bake in the oven, preheated to 410 degrees (fan oven
375 degrees) on the second shelf from the bottom for 15 minutes.
Serve immediately.

Preparation time: 40 minutes. **Per serving:** 15 g P, 11 g F, 36 g C = 298 kcal (1250 kJ).

Cod with a Crumbly Crust

This dish is a perfect combination: the delicious crispy crust contrasts beautifully with the tender, juicy fish fillet underneath.

Serves 2:

2 tbsp herb butter

¾ cup breadcrumbs

2 tbsp olive oil
(plus olive oil for sprinkling)

1 tbsp minced parsley

1 tsp minced chervil

1 tsp minced dill

2 cloves of garlic

2 cod fillets (6 oz each)

salt

½ cup white wine

1 Melt the butter. Transfer to a bowl and add the breadcrumbs, olive oil, and herbs. Add a crushed clove of garlic to the mixture.

2 Season the cod fillets with some salt and place in a greased, oven-proof dish. Add the white wine and spread the breadcrumbs mixture on the cod fillets.

3 Bake in the oven, preheated to 410 degrees (fan oven 375 degrees) on the second shelf from the bottom for 20 minutes. Remove the cod fillets from the dish and put on 2 plates. Sprinkle with olive oil.

Preparation time: 40 minutes.
Per serving: 33 g P, 27 g F, 20 g C = 464 kcal (1942 kJ).

SQUARE, PRACTICAL, TASTY!
Practical when the fishmonger is a long way away or there isn't one: cod fillets, freshly caught, packed, and frozen in family packs or portions for two. Each fillet usually weighs about 6 oz. After defrosting, the boneless fillet can be steamed, fried or baked. Why not boiled? Because fish should never be boiled!

Fried Potatoes with Walnuts

A simple but classy dish, made with only a few ingredients. In this recipe the walnuts are fried with the potatoes.

Serves 2: 1 Scrub 14 oz small **potatoes** under running water and cook in boiling salted water. Mince 1 **red onion**. Coarsely mince 2 oz **walnuts**. **2** Run the potatoes under cold water and peel. Melt 2 tbsp **clarified butter** in a pan. Add the potatoes and fry until crisp and golden brown. Add the onions and walnuts and fry briefly. Season with salt and pepper, and sprinkle 2 tbsp coarsely minced **parsley** on top.

Preparation time: 45 minutes.
Per serving: 7 g P, 31 g F, 22 g C = 393 kcal (1646 kJ).

Pasta Gratin

While Italy is the country we associate with pasta dishes, we should not forget that other countries have their own pasta recipes. This one comes from Swabia in Germany!

Serves 2: 1 Peel 10 oz **onions**, cut in half and then into rings. Heat 2 tbsp melted **butter** and 1 tbsp **oil**, add the onions and fry over medium heat until golden brown. Season with salt, pepper, and **nutmeg**. Cook 8 pieces of ravioli (2 oz each), following the instructions on the packet. **2** Put half the onions in 2 ramekins (approximately 6 x 6 in) and arrange the pasta cases and the rest of the onions on top. Sprinkle ½ cup grated **Emmental** or other semi-hard cheese on top. Bake in the oven, preheated to 430 degrees (fan oven 390 degrees) on the second shelf from the top for 10 minutes. Sprinkle with **minced chives**.

Preparation time: 30 minutes. Per serving: 26 g P, 45 g F, 61 g C = 756 kcal (3164 kJ).

Pork Chops with a Crispy Onion Crust

*This transforms what can be a rather boring dish
into a really mouth-watering recipe.*

Serves 2: 1 Cut 1 **onion** into thin strips. Add 1 tbsp **oil** and 1½ tbsp **butter**
to a pan and fry the onion until golden brown. Season with salt and add
1 tbsp **green peppercorns** (from a jar) and 1 tbsp **parsley**. Mix together
2 tbsp freshly grated **Parmesan** and 1 tbsp **breadcrumbs**. **2** Season
2 **pork chops** (4 oz each) with salt and fry briskly on both sides in 1 tbsp
oil, place in an oven-proof dish and spread the onion mixture on top.
Sprinkle the grated cheese and breadcrumbs on top. **3** Brown in the
oven, preheated to 390 degrees (fan oven 355 degrees) for 12 minutes.

* **Preparation time:** 30 minutes. **Per serving:** 43 g P, 31 g F, 10 g C = 490 kcal (2054 kJ).

Sausage Shashlik

In theory this is a dish for children but there are plenty of adults who wouldn't say no to a tasty shashlik.

Serves 2: 1 Cut 2 **sausages** (4½ oz each) into 10 slices. Peel 1 **red onion** and cut into large cubes. Cut 1 **yellow bell pepper** into four, remove the seeds and cut into ¾ in pieces. Thread the sausages, onions, and peppers alternately on 4 kebab sticks. **2** Fry the sausage kebabs on all sides in 2 tbsp oil over medium heat for 6–7 minutes in all. When cooked, sprinkle some **powdered paprika** on top.

* **Preparation time:** 30 minutes.
  Per serving: 27 g P, 43 g F, 3 g C = 507 kcal (2123 kJ).

Colorful Crumble Cake

One cake, four different toppings: this is the solution for all those who want to offer their guests some choices of dessert without having to cook all day.

For 24 pieces: 1 Knead together 1 packet of **yeast dough cake mix** (12 oz) and **yeast** from the packet with 4 tbsp softened **butter**, 1 medium **egg**, and ⅝ cup lukewarm **milk**, following the instructions on the packet. Leave to rise. Work together 1½ cups **flour**, ⅜ cup **sugar**, ½ tsp **cinnamon**, and 7 tbsp softened butter, using your hands. Refrigerate. Wash and prepare 10 oz **rhubarb**, cut into 1¼-in pieces and add 4 tbsp sugar, stirring well. **2** Peel 14 oz **apples**, cut into quarters, core, cut into slices lengthways and stir in 2 tbsp lemon juice. Knock the dough back again, put on a greased cookie sheet (16 x 12 in), and press down to spread evenly on the cookie sheet with generously-floured hands. **3** Cover each quarter of the cookie sheet with respectively 9 oz **cherries** (from a jar), 9 oz **apricots** (from a can), the rhubarb, and the apples. Spread the crumble evenly on top. Leave to stand for 10 minutes. Bake in the oven, preheated to 390 degrees (fan oven 355 degrees) on the second shelf from the bottom for 30–35 minutes. When lukewarm sprinkle confectioners' sugar on top.

Preparation time: 1 hour 15 minutes. **Per serving:** 3 g P, 8 g F, 29 g C = 200 kcal (842 kJ).

Strawberry Jelly with Woodruff

This delicious wobbly jelly has been made more refined by the addition of wine and fresh strawberries. But it still wobbles as well as ever!

Serves 4: 1 Prepare 1 packet of <u>**woodruff jello**</u> (or if not available, lime jello cubes) with 1 cup <u>**apple juice**</u>, 1 cup <u>**white wine**</u> (for children, use apple juice), and ⅓ cup <u>**sugar**</u>, following the instructions on the packet. Put the jello in a bowl and refrigerate until the mixture begins to set (about 1 hour). Wash and prepare 14 oz small <u>**strawberries**</u> and cut in half. **2** Arrange the strawberries and jello in 4 glasses and refrigerate for another 2–3 hours. This is delicious served with vanilla custard.

* **Preparation time:** 30 minutes (plus cooling time).
  Per serving: 3 g P, 1 g F, 32 g C = 197 kcal (826 kJ).

Curried Asparagus

The traditional taste of asparagus and carrots is enhanced by the oriental aromas of curry and coconut.

Serves 2:

18 oz white asparagus

9 oz carrots

1 onion

1 red chili pepper

1½ tbsp butter

2 tbsp curry powder

½ cup vegetable stock

⅞ cup coconut milk

1–2 tbsp lime juice

salt

white pepper

4 pork tenderloin medallions (2 oz each)

1 tbsp oil

1 Peel the asparagus and carrots. Cut off the woody ends of the asparagus. Mince the onion. Cut the chili pepper in half, remove the seeds and mince.

2 Melt the butter in a pan, add the onions and chili pepper, and fry until transparent. Add the asparagus and carrots and fry briefly. Sprinkle the curry powder on top. Add the stock. Cover and cook the vegetables over medium heat for 12 minutes. Now add the coconut milk and cook for 3 minutes without the lid.

3 Meanwhile season the pork medallions with salt and pepper, and thread on a kebab if you like. Fry in hot oil in a pan for 3–4 minutes on each side and serve with the asparagus.

* **Preparation time:** 40 minutes.
Per serving: 32 g P, 33 g F, 11 g C = 469 kcal (1966 kJ).

IT'S THE COMBINATION THAT DOES IT: CURRY
This aromatic yellow powder contains 20 or more spices such as turmeric, ginger, cardamom, pepper, allspice, paprika, cinnamon, mace, cumin, and fenugreek. Depending on the composition, curry varies from mild to hot.

Baked Monkfish

The chef's ideal Sunday lunch: put all the ingredients together in a dish, put the dish in the oven, then go and read the newspapers.

Serves 4: 1 Cut 14 oz **tomatoes** into quarters, remove the seeds, and mince coarsely. Wash and prepare 7 oz **zucchinis**, cut in half lengthways, and cut into slices. Drain 1 oz **ripe olives**. Strip the leaves of 1 bunch **parsley** and ½ bunch **thyme**. Season 1¾ lb **monkfish fillets** (ready to cook) with salt and pepper. Put in an oven-proof dish (about 14 in long). **2** Cover with thin slices of ½ **lemon (untreated)** and sprinkle thyme and parsley on top. Arrange the tomatoes and zucchinis round the fish. Season with salt and pepper, and 1 **clove of garlic**, thinly sliced. Sprinkle with 6 tbsp each **white wine** and **olive oil**. Bake in the oven, preheated to 390 degrees (fan oven not recommended) on the second shelf from the bottom for 25–30 minutes.

Preparation time: 50 minutes. **Per serving:** 32 g P, 21 g F, 4 g C = 340 kcal (1427 kJ).

Tagliatelle with Smoked Trout

This is a very elegant dish: the refined, creamy lemon juice served with the tagliatelle combines beautifully with the smoky aroma of the trout.

Serves 2: 1 Peel only the bottom third of 9 oz **green asparagus**. Cut off the woody ends. Cut the asparagus stems into slices. Mince 1 **onion** and fry in 1 tbsp melted **butter**. Add ½ cup **white wine**, 1 pinch **sugar**, ½ tsp grated **lemon zest**, and ½ tsp **lemon juice**. Cook without a lid for 3 minutes. **2** Add 4 tbsp **crème fraîche** and ½ cup **vegetable stock** and cook without a lid for 5 minutes. Cook 7 oz **tagliatelle** in boiling salted water, following the instructions on the packet. Add the asparagus 4 minutes before the end of the cooking time and cook with the tagliatelle. **3** Cut 5 oz smoked **trout fillets** into pieces. Strip the leaves of ½ bunch **dill**, mince, add to the sauce and season generously. Drain the tagliatelle and asparagus and arrange with the sauce and trout fillet. Garnish with **lemon slices** if desired.

Preparation time: 25 minutes. **Per serving:** 32 g P, 27 g F, 76 g C = 692 kcal (2897 kJ).

Spaghetti with Vegetables and Pernod

Tender spring vegetables,
chervil, lemon zest and a dash of Pernod – pure heaven!

Serves 4: 1 Peel 18 oz **white asparagus** and cut the woody ends. Cut the stems into thin slices. Cut 5 oz **snow peas** into half. Peel 7 oz **carrots** and cook in boiling salted water for 5 minutes. After 3 minutes add the asparagus and snow peas and continue cooking. Drain the vegetables and reserve ⅞ cup of the cooking liquid. **2** Cook 14 oz **spaghetti** in plenty of boiling salted water, following the instructions on the packet. Mince 1 **onion** and fry in 2 tbsp **butter**. Add the ⅞ cup cooking liquid, 1 tsp grated **lemon zest (untreated)**, and 5 tbsp **lemon juice**. Cook without a lid for 3 minutes. Add 5 oz **crème fraîche** and cook for a further 3–5 minutes without a lid. Season with salt and pepper, and 3–4 tbsp **Pernod**. **3** Drain the pasta and stir into the sauce and vegetables. Sprinkle with 4 tbsp **chervil leaves** and perhaps a few strips of lemon zest.

Preparation time: 35 minutes.
Per serving: 15 g P, 20 g F, 78 g C = 574 kcal (2406 kJ).

Asparagus Risotto

Asparagus risotto is a very sophisticated appetizer, served with salad it is a pleasant evening meal, and accompanied by meat it is a delicious main course. Versatile or what?

Serves 2: 1 Mince 1 **onion** and fry together with ⅝ cup **short-grain rice** in 1 tbsp melted **butter** until transparent. Bring 2¼ cups **vegetable stock** to the boil. Add 4 tbsp **white wine** to the rice and enough stock to cover the rice. Cook without a lid over medium heat until all the stock has been absorbed, stirring occasionally. **2** Continue adding some stock until the rice is cooked (about 25 minutes). Peel 9 oz **white asparagus** (the complete stem), and only the bottom third of 9 oz **green asparagus**. Cut off the woody ends and cut the stems into pieces. Fry in 2 tbsp **butter** and a little **sugar** for 5 minutes. Season with salt and pepper. Toast 2 tbsp **pine nuts** in a pan without fat. **3** Stir the asparagus together with 3 tbsp grated **Parmesan** and 2 tbsp minced **chervil** into the rice. Sprinkle pine nuts and 2 tbsp Parmesan on top before serving.

* **Preparation time:** 40 minutes.
  Per serving: 18 g P, 32 g F, 67 g C = 631 kcal (2647 kJ).

Gnocchi with Wild Garlic Pesto

So tasty, and it only takes 30 minutes!

Serves 2: 1 Toast 1 oz **pine nuts** in a pan without fat, leave to cool. Wash 3½ oz **wild garlic**, dab dry and mince. Coarsely mince ¾ oz pine nuts and finely grate 1 oz **Parmesan**. Puree everything together with 6 tbsp **olive oil** and a little salt and pepper in a blender until very smooth. Adjust the seasoning if necessary. **2** Cook 14 oz fresh **gnocchi** in plenty of boiling salted water, following the instructions on the packet. Then drain and reserve 5–6 tbsp of the cooking liquid. Stir in the pesto, previously diluted with a little cooking water. Sprinkle with ¾ oz Parmesan shavings, ⅓ oz pine nuts and, if you like, some wild garlic.

* **Preparation time:** 25 minutes. **Per serving:** 19 g P, 48 g F, 74 g C = 802 kcal (3374 kJ).

Home-Made Style Roll Mops

A classic dish that is always popular: roll mops with sour cream sauce, apple, onion, gherkins, and plenty of dill.

Serves 2: 1 Mix together ⅝ cup **whipping cream**, 2 tsp **vinegar essence**, a little salt and pepper, ½ tsp **marjoram**, ½ tsp **sugar**, and 5 tbsp minced **dill**. Season again if necessary. Wash 1 red **apple**, cut into four, core, and cut diagonally into very thin slices. Stir immediately into the sauce. **2** Soak 4 **roll-mops fillets** (2 oz each) for 10 minutes in ⅝ cup **mineral water**. Cut 1 **onion** in half and cut into very fine rings, cut 3½ oz **pickled gherkins** into very thin slices and add both to the sauce. Serve with the roll-mops. The dish is delicious served with fried potatoes.

Preparation time:
25 minutes.
Per serving: 25 g P, 50 g F,
17 g C = 620 kcal (2596 kJ).

May Minestrone

Italian vegetable soups are the best in the world. Why?
Because Italians always make sure that their soups match the seasons.

Serves 2: 1 Peel and mince 2 **carrots**. Rinse 8 oz frozen **fava beans** under hot water and remove the outer skin, divide 10 oz **cauliflower** into florets. **2** Crush 1 **clove of garlic** through a press. Mince 1 **onion** and fry with the garlic in 2 tbsp **olive oil**. Add the vegetables, 3½ cups **chicken stock** (from a cube), and ¼ cup **easy-cook rice**. Cook for 10 minutes. **3** Shortly before the end of the cooking time, add 6 oz coarsely minced **smoked chicken breast** to the soup. Serve with pesto (in a jar).

Preparation time: 35 minutes. **Per serving:** 50 g P, 13 g F, 31 g C = 447 kcal (1869 kJ).

Strawberry Gratin

A most refined dessert: the marzipan mousse is light and airy, while the strawberries are fragrant and hot but not soft.

Serves 4: 1 Wash and prepare 14 oz **strawberries** and stir in 2 tbsp **straw-berry liqueur**. Spoon into 4 small gratin dishes (or a large gratin dish about 12 in long). Coarsely mince 3½ oz **marzipan** and mix together with 2 medium **egg yolks** and 1 tbsp **sugar**, using the whisk attachment of the hand-held mixer, until the mixture is very creamy. **2** Beat 2 **egg whites** stiff with 1 pinch of salt, carefully beat in 2 tbsp sugar and continue whisking for another 2 minutes. Now fold the beaten egg white into the marzipan mixture. Spoon over the strawberries. Brown in the oven, preheated to 390 degrees (fan oven not recommended) on the second shelf from the top for 8–10 minutes. Sprinkle with **confectioners' sugar**.

Preparation time: 25 minutes. **Per serving:** 8 g P, 12 g F, 36 g C = 298 kcal (1250 kJ).

Chicken Wings with Barbecue Sauce

The most popular sauce for steaks – sweet and sour tomato ketchup – is here used to brown the chicken wings.

Serves 2–4:

12 chicken wings

salt

pepper or cayenne pepper

1 tbsp oil

3 ½ oz tomato ketchup

3 tbsp orange juice

2–3 tbsp honey

1 tbsp red wine vinegar

Tabasco sauce

1 tbsp hot mustard

1 Cut the wings through at the joints, season with salt and pepper and coat in oil in a bowl. Put on a cookie sheet lined with aluminum foil. Bake in the oven, preheated to 450 degrees (fan oven 430 degrees) on the second shelf from the bottom for 10 minutes, turn, and continue cooking for another 7 minutes.

2 Mix together the ketchup, orange juice, honey, vinegar, and a few dashes of Tabasco and mustard. Dip the hot wings in this mixture and return to the cookie sheet. Bake for another 10 minutes as described above.

* **Preparation time:** 35 minutes.
Per serving (based on 4 servings):
16 g P, 17 g F, 14 g C = 276 kcal
(1155 kJ).

THE IDEAL SAUCE TO ACCOMPANY CHICKEN

The more honey you add to the sauce, the crisper the sweet and sour sauce becomes when browned under the broiler. But be careful, this sauce should not only taste sweet!

Strawberry Mousse

It may look like one of grandma's desserts but it tastes like a gourmet dish: light, airy strawberry mousse with strawberry puree.

Serves 6–8: 1 Soak 5 leaves **gelatin** in cold water. Wash and prepare 18 oz **strawberries** and puree together with 2 tbsp **lemon juice**, and ⅓ cup **sugar**. Bring ⅞ cup **milk** and the pulp of 1 **vanilla bean** to the boil. Mix together 2 tbsp **cornstarch**, 2 medium **egg yolks**, and 3 tbsp **milk**, stir this mixture into the hot milk and bring to the boil again. **2** Pour into a bowl. Squeeze the gelatin to get as much water out as possible and dissolve in the bowl. Stir in 10 oz strawberry puree and put the bowl in the refrigerator. When the mixture begins to set, beat 1 cup **whipping cream** with 1 tbsp **vanilla sugar** and fold into the setting mixture. Now spoon the mixture in 6–8 ramekins or cups (each about ½ cup) and keep in the refrigerator for 4 hours. **3** Briefly dip the ramekins or cups into hot water, loosen the edges with the tip of a knife and turn out onto a plate. Garnish with the rest of the puree and a few more strawberries.

Preparation time: 45 minutes (plus cooling time). **Per serving:** 4 g P, 12 g F, 19 g C = 206 kcal (865 kJ).

Cauliflower Gratin with Curry

*It is amazing how interesting cauliflower, potatoes, and boiled ham
can become when curry is added.*

Serves 4: 1 Wash and prepare 1 small **cauliflower** (about 2 ¼ lb) and
divide into florets. Peel 1 large **potato** (about 7 oz), wash, and cut into ⅝-in
cubes. Put the cauliflower and potato in a pan and add just enough water
to cover. Add 5 tbsp **milk** and ½ tsp salt to the cooking water, bring to
the boil, and cook for about 5–8 minutes. Drain. **2** Melt 2 tbsp **butter** in
a small pan. Add 2 tbsp **flour**, stir into the butter, and brown lightly over
medium heat for 2–3 minutes. Add 1 ½ tbsp **mild curry powder** and
fry briefly. Now add 1 ¼ cups milk and ⅞ cup **chicken stock** and stir until
smooth. Cook over medium heat for 5 minutes. Season with salt and
pepper and 1 tbsp **lemon juice**. Put the sauce to one side. **3** Coarsely
mince 5 oz **boiled ham**. Grease a gratin dish (10 x 6 in). Stir together the
ham, potatoes, cauliflower, and 3 ½ oz **frozen peas**, and transfer to the
gratin dish. Pour the curry sauce on top and bake in the oven, preheated
to 355 degrees (fan oven 320 degrees) on the second shelf from the
bottom for 20–25 minutes.

* **Preparation time:** 45 minutes.
  Per serving: 16 g P, 11 g F, 20 g C = 243 kcal (1020 kJ).

Pork tenderloin with Red Onion Sauce

A dish worthy of modern bistro cuisine with plenty of red onions, port, and rosemary. Sustaining and quick to prepare but very refined.

Serves 4:

18 oz red onions

3 long sprigs rosemary

3 pork tenderloins (about 1 ¾ lb in all)

salt

black pepper

2 tbsp oil

¾ cup white port

½ cup veal stock

1–2 tsp liquid honey

1 tbsp minced parsley

1 Cut the onions into slices ¾-in thick, break the rosemary twigs in half, and place on the pork tenderloins (see photograph below). Season with salt and pepper. Heat oil in a pan, add the pork tenderloins, and fry briskly on all sides.

2 Remove the fillets. Add the onions and fry for 3 minutes while stirring. Add the port and the stock. Return the pork tenderloins to the pan and cook in the oven, preheated to 390 degrees (fan oven not recommended) on the second shelf from the bottom for 20 minutes.

3 Take the meat out, wrap in aluminum foil and allow to rest for 5 minutes. Season the onions with salt, pepper, and honey. Stir in the parsley, cut the pork tenderloins into slices, and serve with the onions.

* **Preparation time:** 45 minutes.
Per serving: 46 g P, 9 g F, 8 g C = 312 kcal (1308 kJ).

DIRECT SEASONING
Cooked in this way the rosemary is in direct contact with the meat: arrange the twigs lengthways on the fillets, and secure with string.

Summer has finally arrived

The 21st of June is the summer solstice: the official start of the summer. This event is celebrated very widely in northern Europe. In Sweden, for instance, it is the day when the first new potatoes are eaten. Naturally, we too have new potatoes but we also have many other delicious things, so the whole month is transformed into a culinary event.

Strawberry Swiss Roll

One of the best things at teatime on a Sunday: sitting together round a Swiss roll with cream and strawberries.

For 12 pieces:

3 medium eggs (separated)

salt

⅔ cup sugar plus sugar for the dish towel

1 tsp grated untreated lemon zest

1 cup 2 tbsp flour

¾ oz cornstarch

½ tsp baking powder

1¼ lb strawberries

2¼ cups whipping cream

1 tbsp vanilla sugar

2 pkts cream thickener

SUGAR ON THE DISH TOWEL
Sugar sprinkled on the dish towel ensures that the dough does not stick.

1 Line a cookie sheet with grease-proof paper. Beat the egg whites with 1 pinch of salt, and 3 tbsp cold water using a hand-held mixer. Add ⅝ cup sugar little by little while whisking, and continue whisking for 3 minutes. Stir in the lemon zest and egg yolk briefly on the lowest setting. Sift the flour, cornstarch, and baking powder, and fold in carefully.

2 Spread the dough on the cookie sheet. Bake in the oven, preheated to 410 degrees (fan oven 375 degrees for 7 minutes) on the second shelf from the bottom for 8 minutes. Turn the pastry immediately onto a dish towel thinly covered with sugar. Brush the paper with a little cold water and pull the paper off. Roll up the pastry with the help of the dish towel and allow to cool.

3 Wash and prepare 14 oz strawberries and cut into thin slices. Beat the cream, vanilla sugar, and 2 tbsp sugar until stiff. Unroll the pastry, spread ⅔ of the whipped cream on the pastry. Then arrange the sliced strawberries overlapping and press lightly into the cream.

4 Roll up the pastry with the strawberries using the dish towel and cover with the remaining cream. Wash and prepare 7 oz strawberries, and cut into half. Garnish the Swiss roll with strawberries.

* Preparation time: 50 minutes.
 Per piece: 4 g P, 14 g F, 28 g C = 260 kcal (1090 kJ).

Cassis and Berries Sorbet

Quick but extremely festive: frozen, pureed red currants, steeped in sparkling wine.

Serves 4: 1 Mix together 7 oz **frozen red currants** or **frozen strawberries** with 2 tbsp **Cassis**, 1 tbsp **vanilla sugar** and 3 tbsp **confectioners' sugar**. Leave to defrost lightly for 10 minutes. Then puree with a blender until very smooth. **2** Scoop out 8 balls from the mixture, put them on a plate lined with Saran wrap and freeze for 1 hour. Then arrange two scoops in 4 champagne goblets and pour ⅝ cup ice cold, **dry sparkling wine** in each bowl. Serve at once.

* **Preparation time:** 15 minutes (plus defrosting and freezing time).
Per serving: 1 g P, 0 g F, 20 g C = 189 kcal (791 kJ).

Shrimp Omelet with Sorrel

A perfect combination: an omelet filled with sorrel, shrimp, and scallions.

Serves 2: 1 Beat 5 **eggs** in a bowl, stir in 2 tbsp **whipping cream**. Wash 3 oz (1 bunch) sorrel, spin dry, and cut into fine trips. Cut the light green and white parts of 2 **scallions** into thin slices. **2** Heat the **butter** in a non-stick pan. Add the eggs and let them thicken over medium heat while shaking the pan. **3** Spread half the sorrel, scallions and 3 oz **shrimp** on the omelet. Roll up the omelet and sprinkle the rest of the sorrel on top.

* **Preparation time:** 25 minutes. **Per serving:** 28 g P, 29 g F, 5 g C = 388 kcal (1624 kJ).

Pork tenderloin with Herbs

Visually pleasing, this is also very tender and full of fragrance: pork tenderloin, wrapped in bay leaves, thyme, and rosemary.

Serves 2–4: 1 Pat the **pork tenderloin** (18 oz) dry and season with salt. Cover the meat with 5 **bay leaves**, 5 sprigs of **thyme**, and sprigs of **rosemary**, and secure with string. **2** Cut 4 **onions** into quarters. Cut 4 **cloves of garlic** in half. Heat 2 tbsp **oil**, add the meat, onions, and garlic, and brown. **3** Add ½ cup **white wine** and ¾ cup **chicken stock**, and bring to the boil. **4** Bake in the oven, preheated to 390 degrees (fan oven not recommended) on the second shelf from the bottom for about 25 minutes. Wrap the meat in aluminum foil, and allow to rest for 3–4 minutes. Bring the cooking juices back to the boil and season with salt and pepper. Slice the meat and serve with the sauce.

* **Preparation time:** 45 minutes. **Per serving:** 28 g P, 8 g F, 3 g C = 200 kcal (840 kJ).

Vegetables baked in a roasting pan

Delicious as an accompaniment to meat, fish, or simply with a baguette. Nothing is more healthy and crisp than colorful, roast vegetables.

Serves 2: 1 Divide 9 oz <u>cauliflower</u> into florets. Peel 5 oz <u>carrots</u> and cut them into six lengthways. Cut 1 <u>red</u> and 1 <u>yellow bell pepper</u> into quarters, remove the seeds and cut into 1¼-in pieces. Thinly slice 2 <u>cloves of garlic</u>. **2** Arrange the vegetables in a roasting pan with 2 twigs of <u>rosemary</u>, 3 sprigs of <u>parsley</u>, 4 sprigs <u>thyme</u>, and 2 <u>bay leaves</u>, season with salt and pepper. **3** Pour ⅝ cup <u>white wine</u> and 4 tbsp <u>olive oil</u> over the vegetables. Bake in the oven, preheated to 390 degrees (fan oven not recommended) on the second shelf from the bottom for 20–25 minutes. After 15 minutes add 7 oz cherry tomatoes.

* **Preparation time: 50 minutes.**
  Per serving: 6 g P, 21 g F, 14 g C = 283 kcal (1186 kJ).

Penne, Fava Beans and Bacon

This is a simple, delicious pasta dish, well worth trying for a change.

Serves 2: 1 Cook 12 oz **frozen fava beans** in salted water for 4 minutes, drain, and run under cold water. Remove the outer skins and put to one side. **2** Cook 8 oz **penne pasta** *al dente* in plenty of salted water, following the instructions on the packet, then drain. **3** Mince 2 **cloves of garlic** and cut 3 slices of **bacon** into wide strips. Put the bacon in a cold pan and fry over medium heat until crisp. Add the garlic and beans and fry for about 2 minutes. Season with salt and pepper, and 1–2 tsp lemon juice. Stir into the penne and put on plates.

* **Preparation time:** 25 minutes. **Per serving:** 52 g P, 6 g F, 121 g C = 756 kcal (3167 kJ).

Sirloin Steak with Salsa Verde

This Italian green sauce made from pickled gherkins, garlic, basil, chervil, and parsley is an excellent accompaniment to fried meat.

Serves 2:

1 egg

1 bunch basil

1 bunch flat-leaved parsley

½ bunch chervil

2 oz pickled gherkins

2 shallots

4 small cloves garlic

1 tbsp capers (drained weight)

7–8 tbsp olive oil

1 tbsp lemon juice

salt

pepper

1 tbsp oil

2 sirloin steaks (7 oz each)

2 sprigs rosemary

2 bay leaves

1 Hard-boil the egg, run under cold water, shell, and mince. Strip the leaves off the stems of basil, parsley, and chervil, and mince them finely. Mince the gherkins, shallots, and 2 cloves of garlic very finely. Mince the capers.

2 Put everything in a bowl, add the olive oil and lemon juice, and mix well. Season with salt and pepper.

3 Heat the oil in a pan. Season the sirloin steaks with salt and pepper, and fry in hot oil for 4–5 minutes on each side with rosemary, bay leaves, and 2 cloves of garlic. Wrap in aluminum foil and leave to rest for 2 minutes. Serve with the green sauce.

* **Preparation time:** 35 minutes.
  Per serving: 50 g P, 52 g F, 6 g C = 693 kcal (2906 kJ).

HERB SAUCE WITH CRÈME FRAÎCHE
If you prefer the sauce to be creamier, use crème fraîche instead of oil in the salsa verde.

Asparagus Soup with Vanilla

At a first glance, a rather bold combination. But one spoonful is sufficient: asparagus and vanilla are a marriage made in heaven, like Fred and Ginger.

Serves 4: 1 Peel 1½ lb **white asparagus** and cut off the woody ends. Cut off the asparagus tips, cut in half lengthways and put to one side. Cut the stems into pieces and mince 1 **onion**. Melt 1 tbsp **butter** in a pan, add the onion and pieces of asparagus, and fry lightly over low heat. Season with salt, pepper, and ¼ tsp **sugar**. Add 3½ cups **vegetable stock**, bring to the boil, cover, and simmer for 15–20 minutes. **2** Puree finely, add ⅝ cup **whipping cream**, and bring briefly to the boil again. Season with salt and pepper, and 1–2 tbsp **orange juice**. Melt 1 tbsp butter in a pan, add the asparagus tips, the pulp of ½ **vanilla bean**, and 1 tsp of **strips of orange zest (untreated)**. Fry for 3–4 minutes. Season with salt, pepper, and 1 pinch of sugar. Garnish the soup with the asparagus tips and 2 tbsp **chervil leaves**.

Preparation time: 35 minutes.
Per serving: 4 g P, 15 g F, 7 g C = 189 kcal (783 kJ).

Rabbit in a Cream Sauce

A perfect party piece: braised rabbit in a creamy mustard-tarragon sauce.

Serves 4: 1 Cut 2 **onions** into thin strips. Squeeze 2 **cloves of garlic** in a garlic press. **2** Heat the oil in a wide pan. Season 4 **rabbit pieces** (legs/thighs, 9 oz each) with salt and coat in **flour**. Add to the pan and fry in the hot oil until golden brown, then remove from the pan. Now add the onions and garlic and fry over medium heat for 3–4 minutes until transparent. **3** Add ½ cup **white wine** and ⅝ cup **chicken stock**. Return the rabbit to the pan, cover, and cook in the oven, preheated to 375 degrees (fan oven 170 degrees) on the second shelf from the bottom for 40 minutes. **4** At the end of the cooking time, take out the rabbit and keep in a warm place. Pass the sauce through a strainer, add 5 oz **crème fraîche** and 2 tbsp minced **tarragon**, then bring to the boil. Stir in 2 tbsp **Dijon seed mustard**, season with salt and pepper and serve with the rabbit.

Preparation time: 1 hour. **Per serving:** 43 g P, 21 g F, 7 g C = 400 kcal (1671 kJ).

Three-Cheeses Spaghetti

Mild mascarpone, tangy gorgonzola and sharp Parmesan in perfect harmony make a delicious accompaniment to pasta.

Serves 2: 1 Cook 7 oz **spaghetti** in boiling salted water, following the instructions on the packet. **2** In the meantime coarsely mince ½ bunch **parsley**. Melt 3 oz **mascarpone** in a non-stick pan. Crumble the **gorgonzola** and add to the mascarpone. **3** Drain the spaghetti and reserve some of the cooking water. Add the spaghetti to the pan with the cheeses, season with salt and pepper, and stir in a little cooking water if necessary. Add the grated **Parmesan** and parsley, and serve immediately.

Preparation time: 20 minutes. **Per serving:** 29 g P, 41 g F, 70 g C = 768 kcal (3218 kJ).

Kohlrabi with a Lemon and Cream Sauce

The fresh aromatic fragrance of the lemon zest and the sharpness of the cress perfectly complement the crisp kohlrabi.

Serves 2: 1 Peel 14 oz <u>**kohlrabi**</u>, cut into sticks ⅜-in wide and fry lightly in 1 tbsp <u>**butter**</u>. Season with salt and pepper and ¼ tsp <u>**sugar**</u>. Add ½ cup <u>**vegetable stock**</u>, cover, and cook over medium heat for 5 minutes.
2 Now add 2 tbsp <u>**crème fraîche**</u> and cook without a lid for 3–5 minutes. Add 1 tsp grated <u>**lemon zest (untreated)**</u> and 1–2 tbsp <u>**lemon juice**</u>. Season with salt and pepper if necessary. Add 6 tbsp <u>**cress**</u> to the kohlrabi and mix well.

* Preparation time: 20 minutes. Per serving: 4 g P, 14 g F, 9 g C = 178 kcal (745 kJ).

Semolina Cake

The simplest is often the best: plain, very moist sponge cake,
made with semolina and creamy yoghourt, soaked in orange syrup.

For 14 pieces: 1 Grate the zest of 1 **orange** and 1 **lemon** and squeeze
4 tbsp of juice from each of them. Melt 7 tbsp **butter**. Beat together
4 medium **eggs**, 1 pinch of salt, and ¾ cup **sugar**, using a hand-held
mixer, for 8 minutes until creamy. Stir in 14 oz **creamy yoghourt**, the
orange and lemon zest, and the orange and lemon juice as well as the
butter. **2** Mix together 11 oz **semolina** and 3 tbsp **baking powder** and
fold in carefully, using a spatula. Transfer to a well-greased and floured
fluted cake pan (10 in in diameter, or a springform mold). Bake in the
oven, preheated to 355 degrees (fan oven 320 degrees) on the second
shelf from the bottom for 35 minutes. **3** Bring to the boil ⅞ cup **orange juice**, the pulp of 1 **vanilla bean**, and ⅝ cup sugar, and cook for
2 minutes. Leave to cool until lukewarm. Turn out
the cake onto a deep plate, prick several
times, and pour the syrup over the cake.
Leave to stand for 30 minutes.

Preparation time: 1 hour (plus standing time).
Per serving: 6 g P, 12 g F, 40 g C = 288 kcal (1204 kJ).

Vanilla Tarts

Best eaten straight from the oven because the puff pastry will still be deliciously crisp and the vanilla custard so very creamy!

For 12 pieces: 1 Defrost 10 oz **frozen puff pastry**. Bring to the boil 1 cup **whipping cream**, ⅞ cup **milk** with the pulp of 1 **vanilla bean**. Now stir together 3 tbsp milk, 1 tbsp **vanilla-flavored custard powder**, 2 medium **egg yolks**, and ¼ cup **sugar**. Add to the boiling milk-cream mixture. Bring the whole to the boil again. Pour into a bowl and to cool until lukewarm. **2** Put the sheets of puff pastry on top of each other and roll out onto a floured surface to make a rectangle of 18 x 14 in. Then cut out 12 circles each 4 ½ in in diameter. Put into the greased hollows of a muffin pan and press down. Stir the custard thoroughly and spoon onto the puff pastry in the hollows. **3** Bake the tarts in the oven, preheated to 450 degrees (fan oven not recommended) on the lowest shelf for 20 minutes. Leave to cool, and sprinkle with **confectioners' sugar**.

* **Preparation time:** 50 minutes (plus cooling time).
  Per piece: 3 g P, 13 g F, 18 g C = 200 kcal (839 kJ).

Light Chicken Fricassée

Translated fricassée means nothing more than "hotchpotch"! But with chicken, asparagus, and yoghourt, it becomes a particularly delicious dish.

Serves 2:

5 oz mushrooms

9 oz green asparagus

10 oz chicken breasts

2 tbsp oil

salt

pepper

2 tbsp butter

⅞ cup chicken stock

3½ oz creamy yoghourt

1 scant tbsp flour

4–5 sprigs tarragon

nutmeg

1–2 tsp lemon juice

1 Wash and prepare the mushrooms, and cut the larger ones in half. Peel the bottom third of the asparagus and cut off the woody end. Cut the stems diagonally into pieces and cut the asparagus tip in half lengthways. Cut the chicken into 1¼-in cubes. Heat 1 tbsp oil in a pan, add the mushrooms and fry until golden-brown. Season with salt and pepper and take out of the pan.

2 Heat the oil and butter. Add the chicken and asparagus and fry until golden-brown. Season with salt and pepper. Add the chicken stock and bring to the boil. Stir together the yoghourt and add to the pan. Cover and simmer for 5 minutes. Strip the tarragon leaves off the stems and mince. Add together with the mushrooms to the fricassée and reheat. Season with salt, pepper, nutmeg, and lemon juice.

* **Preparation time:** 35 minutes.
Per serving: 40 g P, 37 g F, 8 g C = 537 kcal (2242 kJ).

GRANDMA'S TIP

It is essential that you stir the yoghourt into the flour before you add it to the hot liquid. Why? The starch molecules in the flour prevent the yoghourt from curdling in the hot mixture. If you are using cream or crème fraîche, there is no need to add flour because they have a higher fat content.

Salmon and Cucumber in a Creamy Sauce

Fried cucumber? You should try it! With cubed salmon, a dash of cream, and a little mustard, it's pure heaven.

Serves 2: 1 Peel 1 <u>cucumber</u> (about 18 oz), cut in half lengthways, scoop out the seeds with a spoon and cut into half-rings ⅜-in wide. Mince 1 small <u>onion</u>. Heat 1 tbsp <u>oil</u> in a pan and fry the onion lightly, add the cucumber and fry for another 2 minutes. Sprinkle 2 tbsp <u>flour</u> over the onion and cucumber, and fry briefly. **2** Add ⅝ cup <u>whipping cream</u>, 1 cup <u>vegetable stock</u>, and 2–3 tsp <u>seed mustard</u>, cover and cook over medium heat for 8 minutes. Cut 12 oz <u>salmon fillets</u> (without skin) into cubes 1 x1 in. Add to the cucumber and cook for another 7–8 minutes. Season with salt and pepper, and a little <u>lemon juice</u>. **3** Mince ½ bunch <u>flat-leaved parsley</u> and add to the salmon before serving.

* Preparation time: 25 minutes. Per serving: 37 g P, 39 g F, 12 g C = 546 kcal (2282 kJ).

Stuffed Baguette

Hot from the oven and ready to eat: a baguette filled with herb butter, tomatoes and basil.

Serves 2: 1 Cut 3 small <u>**tomatoes**</u> into slices. Strip 16 <u>**basil leaves**</u> off their stems. Take half a <u>**baguette**</u> (about 3 ½ oz) and make cuts at ⅝-in intervals, but without cutting all the way through. Spread 2 oz herb butter into these cuts and stuff each one with 1 slice of tomato and 1 basil leaf.
2 Put the baguette on a cookie sheet and bake in the oven, preheated to 390 degrees (fan oven 355 degrees) on the second shelf from the bottom for 8–10 minutes.

* **Preparation time:** 30 minutes. **Per serving:** 5 g P, 22 g F, 28 g C = 322 kcal (1352 kJ).

Calf's Liver with Cherries

*If you have your doubts about liver, we ask you to trust us
... you will be amazed!*

Serves 4: 1 Cut 3 ½ oz <u>**onions**</u> into thin strips and press 1 <u>**clove of
garlic**</u> through a garlic press. Heat 1 tbsp oil, add the onions, and
garlic, and fry until brown. Add 1 tbsp <u>**cherry jelly**</u>, 9 oz <u>**beef stock**</u>,
and 2 tbsp <u>**balsamic vinegar**</u>, and cook without a lid for 5 minutes over
medium heat. Wash and prepare 5 oz <u>**sweet cherries**</u>, cut in half and
remove the pits (or use 3 ½ oz <u>**cherries**</u> out of a jar), add to the sauce
and simmer for another 3 minutes. **2** Coat 4 slices of <u>**calf's liver**</u> (5 oz,
ready to cook) in 4 tbsp <u>**flour**</u>. Tap off the excessive flour. Heat 1 tbsp
<u>**butter**</u> and 2 tbsp oil in a large non-stick pan. Add the liver and fry for
2 minutes on each side. Season with salt and pepper. Add 8 <u>**sage leaves**</u>
after 2 minutes and fry. Season the sauce with salt and pepper; optionally
add a little cherry jelly, then serve it with the liver.

Preparation time: 25 minutes. Per serving: 32 g P, 16 g F, 20 g C = 380 kcal (1589 kJ).

Turkey and Rosemary Kebab

It looks fun and tastes delicious: pieces of turkey and cherry tomatoes threaded on a stem of rosemary and fried until golden yellow.

Serves 2: 1 Finely dice 1 **onion**. Cut 10 oz **turkey fillet** into 12 cubes. Make some holes in the cubes of turkey and **cherry tomatoes**, using a wooden skewer. then thread alternately 3 cubes of turkey and 3 cherry tomatoes on 4 sprigs of **rosemary**. Season with salt and pepper. Fry briefly but briskly on all sides in 2 tbsp hot **olive oil**. **2** Arrange the kebabs in an oven-proof dish. Cook in the oven, preheated to 390 degrees (fan oven 355 degrees) on the second shelf from the bottom for 10 minutes. Briefly brown the onions in the cooking juices. Add ⅝ cup **vegetable stock** and cook without a lid for 3–4 minutes. Thicken with 1–2 tbsp **dark gravy thickener**. Serve with the kebabs.

* **Preparation time:** 25 minutes.
  Per serving: 37 g P, 12 g F, 5 g C = 274 kcal (1147 kJ).

Stuffed Veal Escalope

It could be said that thin schnitzel is made to be stuffed: here we suggest four exciting variations with Mozzarella. Choose your favorite!

Serves 2: 1 Drain 1 ball of <u>**Mozzarella**</u> (4½ oz) and cut into thin slices, cut 2 <u>**tomatoes**</u> (about 5 oz) into slices. Season with salt and pepper. Cover half of each of the 4 <u>**veal escalopes**</u> (3 oz each) with the Mozzarella and tomato slices. Put 4 <u>**basil leaves**</u> on top of each one. **2** Fold the other half over the filling and secure with cocktail sticks. Heat 3 tbsp <u>**oil**</u> in a pan. Add the meat and fry for 2 minutes on each side over medium to high heat until brown, then season with salt and pepper. Remove from the pan, wrap in aluminum foil and keep warm. **3** Add ½ cup <u>**white wine**</u> in the pan and cook to loosen the cooking residue. Add ½ cup <u>**veal stock**</u> and thicken with 1 tbsp <u>**dark gravy thickener**</u>. Season with salt and pepper. Serve with the meat and garnish with basil.

*** Preparation time:** 35 minutes. **Per serving:** 47 g P, 30 g F, 4 g C = 488 kcal (2045 kJ).

Salami	Spinach	Mango
1 **Mozzarella** (4½ oz) in slices, 2 oz **salami** in thin slices and, if you like, use 8 sliced **olives stuffed with peppers** as filling.	8 oz **frozen spinach**, defrost, squeeze well, fry with 1 minced **onion** and 1 **clove of garlic** in 1 tbsp **butter**, season with salt and pepper and use with 1 **Mozzarella** (4½ oz) in slices as filling.	Use 7 oz **mango** cut into segments, 1 **Mozzarella** (4½ oz) in slices, 2 tsp **curry powder**, and 1 tbsp **cilantro** or **parsley leaves** as filling.

Zucchinis with Feta

The pinnacle of Greek culinary art: this variation with zucchinis is also ideal for broiling but covered in aluminum foil.

Serves 2: 1 Mince 3 ½ oz **ripe olives** (pitted) and 2 oz **almonds**. Puree both together with 1 tbsp **capers**, 3 tbsp **olive oil**, and 1 crushed **clove of garlic** in a blender to make a paste. Season with pepper, **Tabasco**, and a little salt if necessary. Add 2 tbsp **flat-leaved parsley**. **2** Wash and prepare 2 medium-sized **zucchinis** (about 7 oz) and cut lengthways in about slices ⅛-in thick. Spread the olive mixture loosely on the sliced zucchinis, then arrange the zucchinis in a gratin dish (12 x 8 in), greased with olive oil, in such a way that they overlap. Add 3 ½ oz halved **cherry tomatoes** and sprinkle 5 oz coarsely crumbled **Feta** on top of all. Sprinkle 2 tbsp olive on top. **3** Bake in the oven, preheated to 430 degrees (fan oven 390 degrees) on the bottom shelf for 20 minutes.

* **Preparation time:** 40 minutes.
  Per serving: 21 g P, 59 g F, 8 g C = 664 kcal (2752 kJ).

Beef Steaks Coated in Breadcrumbs

A Mediterranean delight: Italian herbs enhance the taste of the coating while thyme adds a touch of the south to the tomatoes.

Serves 2: 1 Cut 14 oz **tomatoes** into eight segments and remove the seeds. Cut 1 **onion** into thin slices. Heat 2 tbsp **oil**. Add the onion and fry for 3–5 minutes over medium heat. Add the tomatoes and 2 tbsp **thyme leaves** and fry for another 3–4 minutes. Season generously with salt and pepper. **2** Cut 10 oz **beef tenderloin** into 6 slices. Mix together 3 oz **breadcrumbs** and 1 tsp dried **Italian herbs**. Beat 1 **egg** with a little salt and pepper. Coat the meat first in **flour**, then roll it in the beaten egg and finally in the breadcrumbs mixture. **3** Heat 6 tbsp oil in a pan. Add the meat and fry for 1 minute on each side until crisp. Drain on kitchen paper. Serve the meat with the tomatoes.

* **Preparation time:** 25 minutes. **Per serving:** 42 g P, 40 g F, 37 g C = 680 kcal (2854 kJ).

Rhubarb Gratin

Rhubarb caramelized in vanilla sugar in a light curd mixture, gratinéed in the oven. We are really grateful for this recipe.

Serves 2: 1 Finely grate 2 oz **marzipan**. Beat together the marzipan, 3½ oz **curd**, 2 medium **egg yolks**, 2 tbsp melted **butter**, 2–3 tbsp **white wine**, 1 tbsp **vanilla sugar**, 2 tbsp **sugar**, and 1 heaping tbsp **cornstarch**, using the whisk attachment of the hand-held mixer, until creamy. Beat 2 medium **egg whites** with 1 pinch salt until stiff. Stir in 1 tbsp sugar and continue whisking for 1–2 more minutes. Carefully fold into the curd mixture. **2** Wash and prepare 14 oz **rhubarb**, and cut diagonally into pieces 2 in long. Heat 1 tbsp butter in a non-stick pan, add the rhubarb and vanilla sugar and caramelize over high heat for 3–5 minutes. **3** Put the curd mixture and rhubarb in a gratin dish (about 9 in in diameter). Then sprinkle with 1 oz flaked **almonds**. Bake in the oven, pre-heated to 390 degrees (fan oven not recommended) on the second shelf from the bottom for 20–25 minutes. Sprinkle with 1 tbsp **confectioners' sugar**.

* **Preparation time:** 25 minutes. **Per serving:** 21 g P, 38 g F, 66 g C = 711 kcal (2965 kJ).

Salzburg Dumpling Soufflé

This light, airy egg mixture collapses like a soufflé if it is not served immediately. Delicious served with a strawberry coulis.

Serves 2: 1 Melt 1 tbsp **butter** in a shallow oven-proof dish (about 8 in long) in the oven, preheated to 390 degrees (fan oven not recommended) on the second shelf from the bottom for 40 minutes. Beat 2 medium **egg whites** and 1 pinch of salt until stiff. Carefully add ¼ cup **sugar** and continue whisking for another 3 minutes. **2** Mix together the pulp of 1 **vanilla bean** and 2 medium **egg yolks**, then carefully fold into the stiffly beaten egg whites with 2 tbsp **flour**. Put the mixture in the gratin dish as 2 large dumplings. Bake in the oven, preheated to 390 degrees (fan oven not recommended) on the second shelf from the bottom for 12–14 minutes until gold-yellow (fan oven). **3** Wash and prepare 9 oz **strawberries** and puree with 1 tbsp **lemon juice** and 2 tbsp sugar. Sprinkle with **confectioners' sugar** and serve the dumpling soufflé immediately with the strawberry coulis.

Preparation time: 30 minutes. **Per serving:** 9 g P, 13 g F, 58 g C = 395 kcal (1656 kJ).

Italian Asparagus Salad

Any dish with the colors of Italy can only mean good things: the tomatoes, Mozzarella and avocado are full of vitamins.

Serves 2:

18 oz white asparagus

4 ½ oz Mozzarella

4–5 sprigs basil

4 tbsp white balsamic vinegar

5–6 tbsp olive oil

sugar

salt

pepper

1 avocado (about 5 ½ oz)

1 Peel the asparagus and cut off the woody ends. Cook for 10–14 minutes in salted water with 1 pinch of sugar, then drain. Cut the cherry tomatoes in half. Drain the Mozzarella and cut into thin slices.

2 Mince the basil leaves and mix together with the vinegar, olive oil, 1 pinch of sugar, salt, and pepper.

3 Cut the avocado in half, remove the pit, peel the avocado, and cut diagonally into thin slices. Cut thick asparagus stems in half lengthways. Arrange the asparagus, Mozzarella, and avocado on a dish, and garnish with the cherry tomatoes. Pour the vinaigrette on top and sprinkle with a few basil leaves.

* **Preparation time:** 40 minutes.
  Per serving: 17 g P, 52 g F, 12 g C = 576 kcal (2418 kJ).

FRY THE BACON SLOWLY
Those who prefer a more nourishing salad can add some bacon. To ensure that as much fat as possible is rendered, put the bacon in a cold pan and fry very slowly. Then allow the bacon to drain to remove all excess fat.

Potato and Herb Salad

The seven herbs of Frankfurt green sauce give this elegant potato salad an attractive appearance. The dish is enhanced with a chicken-flavored vinaigrette.

Serves 2: 1 Wash 18 oz small **salad potatoes** and boil for 18 minutes in salted water. Drain, peel, and allow to cool a little. **2** Wash and mince ½ bunch **Frankfurt green-sauce herbs** (parsley, borage, chives, sorrel, chervil, burnet, and lemon balm), and mince. Finely dice 2 small **onions**. Stir together ½ cup cold **chicken stock**, 2 tbsp **white wine vinegar**, and 2 tbsp **sunflower oil**, and season with salt, pepper, and 1 pinch of sugar. **3** Cut the still-warm potatoes into slices. Add the onions, vinaigrette, and herbs. Mix well and leave to stand for 15 minutes. Season with salt and pepper.

* **Preparation time:** 25 minutes.
  Per serving: 9 g P, 11 g F, 40 g C = 303 kcal (1284 kJ).

Frankfurt Herb Soup

It would be impossible to be any greener: a quick, refreshing summer soup made with Frankfurter herbs. Perfect as a appetizer or main dish.

Serves 2: 1 Mince 2 small **onions**. Fry in 2 tbsp **butter** until transparent. Sprinkle ½ cup **flour** into the pan and brown briefly. Add 3½ cups **vegetable stock** while stirring and cook for 15 minutes. **2** Remove the stems from 1 bunch of **Frankfurt green-sauce herbs** (parsley, borage, chives, sorrel, chervil, burnet, and lemon balm). Wash and mince coarsely. **3** Add the herbs and 2 oz **crème fraîche** to the soup, and puree finely. Season with salt, pepper, and a little **lemon juice**.

* **Preparation time:** 35 minutes. **Per serving:** 7 g P, 21 g F, 24 g C = 307 kcal (1284 kJ).

Gooseberry Cake

In the UK people are so fond of gooseberries that they organize gooseberry competitions. The record for the largest single gooseberry is over 2 ounces!

For 14 pieces:

1 cup milk

½ cup sugar

salt

good ¾ cup flour

5 medium eggs (separated)

10 oz gooseberries

⅝ cup light grape juice (or apple juice)

2 kiwi fruit

1 tbsp confectioners' sugar

1 Mix together the milk, ¼ cup sugar, 1 pinch salt, and flour in a pan, and bring to the boil while stirring continuously and vigorously. Transfer to a bowl and leave to cool. Beat in the egg yolks, one by one, using a hand-held mixer. Beat the egg whites stiff using a clean whisk, slowly stirring in ¼ cup sugar, and continue whisking for another 2 minutes. Fold the stiffly beaten egg whites into the pastry mixture.

2 Spread the pastry mixture in a spring-form mold (9 in diameter) lined with waxed paper. Bake in the oven, preheated to 355 degrees (fan oven 320 degrees) on the lowest shelf for 1 hour. Cover with waxed paper after 30 minutes. Leave to cool in the mold.

3 Wash and prepare the gooseberries for the compote. Bring the grape juice or apple juice to the boil while stirring. Stir in the gooseberries, cover, and simmer for 3–5 minutes until the gooseberries are soft but do not disintegrate. Peel the kiwi fruit, cut in half lengthways, and cut into slices, then stir into the compote. Pour the compote into the hollow in the top of the baked pastry mixture and leave to set. Sprinkle with confectioners' sugar.

NOT JUST HOT AIR
At first the pastry mixture rises in the oven and then sinks again. But do not panic: this collapsed middle or hollow is the secret of this sunken fruit cake.

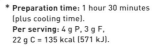

*** Preparation time:** 1 hour 30 minutes (plus cooling time).
Per serving: 4 g P, 3 g F, 22 g C = 135 kcal (571 kJ).

Green Salad with Citrus Dressing

Very simple, very quick, and yet so stylish: the tomato and oak-leaf lettuce salad is enhanced by the addition of toasted pine nuts and orange juice.

Serves 2: 1 Wash, dry, and prepare 1 <u>light-colored oak-leaf lettuce</u>.
2 Toast 2 tbsp <u>pine nuts</u> in a pan without fat. Cut 4 small <u>tomatoes</u> into slices. Mince 1 <u>shallot</u> and stir together with ½ tsp <u>lemon zest</u>, 2 tbsp <u>lemon juice</u>, 4 tbsp <u>orange juice</u>, some salt, pepper, 1 pinch <u>sugar</u>, and 4 tbsp <u>olive oil</u>, and mix well. **3** Stir the vinaigrette into the lettuce and tomato salad, and sprinkle pine nuts on top.

* **Preparation time:** 15 minutes. **Per serving:** 4 g P, 25 g F, 20 g C = 287 kcal (1203 kJ).

Mashed Potatoes

This is the ultimate mashed potato dish: with fried bacon, chives, and a generous dollop of cream.

Serves 2: 1 Peel 14 oz floury **potatoes**, mince coarsely and cook in boiling water. **2** Meanwhile fry 1 oz **diced bacon** in a pan without fat until crisp. Mince ½ bunch **chives**. **3** Stir together 4 tbsp **cream**, a little salt, pepper, **nutmeg**, and ⅔ of the minced chives. Drain the potatoes and return to pan to the cooker with the heat turned off until all the liquid has evaporated. Mash the potatoes coarsely together with 1 tbsp cream. Serve with the rest of the cream, chives, and diced bacon.

* **Preparation time:** 30 minutes.
  Per serving: 7 g P, 16 g F, 26 g C = 283 kcal (1187 kJ).

233

Cannelloni with Ricotta and Swiss Chard

Usually cannelloni is stuffed with ground meat but our vegetarian variation is stuffed with ricotta and Swiss chard – heaven!

Serves 4:

9 oz ricotta

10 oz Swiss chard (or spinach)

salt

2 egg yolks

salt

pepper

nutmeg

8 canelloni cases

1 ¼ cups tomato sauce

3 ½ oz Mozzarella

1 Drain the ricotta in a strainer. Meanwhile wash the Swiss chard, cut off the stems, and mince. Cut the leaves into thin strips. Cook together in boiling salted water for 3 minutes, drain, run under cold water. Put in a cloth and squeeze to remove all the water then mince.

2 Mix together the ricotta, egg yolks, salt, pepper, and nutmeg. Fold in the Swiss chard.

3 Put the ricotta mixture in a pastry bag and stuff the cannelloni. Arrange the cannelloni in an oven-proof dish and pour the tomato sauce on top.

4 Cook in the oven, preheated to 390 degrees (fan oven 355 degrees) on the second shelf from the bottom for 35 minutes. 15 minutes before the end, sprinkle with pieces of Mozzarella.

* **Preparation time:** 50 minutes.
Per serving: 18 g P, 20 g F, 29 g C = 377 kcal (1576 kJ).

READY-MADE TOMATO SAUCE
It could not be easier: a ready-made tomato sauce, flavored with herbs is ideal as a topping for cannelloni.

Not only cake

The French queen Marie-Antoinette allegedly told her hungry citizens: "If you have no bread, you should eat cake." This advice had serious repercussions: on 14 July 1789 the people stormed the Bastille and the French Revolution began. Our tips are much more useful: delicious recipes which will prevent any revolutionary tendencies in your family. And you can make cake…

Risotto Flavored with Lemon and Herbs

Tender chervil and plenty of grated lemon zest add a refreshing summery touch to this carrot risotto.

Serves 2:

1 clove of garlic

2 carrots (about 5 oz)

1 untreated lemon

½ bunch chervil

2 ½ cups vegetable stock

2 tbsp olive oil

½ cup short-grain rice

2 oz grated Parmesan

salt

pepper

1 Mince the garlic. Peel the carrots and mince into ⅙-in cubes. Peel the lemon zest, avoiding the white pith, and squeeze. Cut the zest into thin strips. Bring the vegetable stock to the boil and keep warm over medium heat.

2 Heat the olive oil in a pan. Add the carrots, rice, and garlic, and fry lightly for 2–3 minutes while stirring. Add half the hot vegetable stock. Cook over medium heat until all the liquid has been absorbed by the rice, stirring constantly. Now add the rest of the vegetable stock and continue cooking while stirring.

3 As soon as all the liquid has been absorbed, remove the pan from the heat and stir in the grated Parmesan, chervil, and 2 tsp lemon zest. Season with salt, pepper, and lemon juice. Sprinkle with chervil before serving.

* **Preparation time:** 35 minutes.
Per serving: 14 g P, 19 g F, 51 g C = 435 kcal (1821 kJ).

FOR LEMON ZEST, GINGER, AND NUTMEG
Usually half the lemon zest remains stuck in the grater: but this does not happen with this model: the grated zest is stuck on the front of the grater and can easily be wiped off.

Pork Chop with Scallions and Apples

A pork chop will often benefit from a little variation: why not try it with scallions, apples, and marjoram.

Serves 2: 1 Wash and prepare 5 oz **scallions**, and cut into thin rings. Cut 1 **red apple** in half, core, and cut into thin segments. Season 2 **Pork chops** (7 oz each) with salt and pepper. Heat 3 tbsp **oil** in a large pan, add the chops, and fry briskly for 1 minute on both sides. Put the chops in an oven-proof dish, place 2 sprigs of **marjoram** on top (or sprinkle with ½ tsp dried **marjoram**). **2** Cook in the oven, preheated to 355 degrees (fan oven not recommended) on the second shelf from the bottom for 12–14 minutes. Lightly fry the scallions and apples in the cooking fat for 3–4 minutes. Pull the leaves off 2 sprigs of marjoram, mince, and add to the pan. Season with salt, pepper, **nutmeg**, and a little **sugar**, and serve with the Chops.

Preparation time: 25 minutes. **Per serving:** 39 g P, 24 g F, 16 g C = 440 kcal (1840 kJ).

Greek Stuffed Peppers

A fantastic filling for a traditional summer dish: rice, pine nuts, peppers, garlic, and Feta.

Serves 2: 1 Cook bare ½ cup **long-grain rice** in salted water, following the instructions on the packet. Wash and prepare 3 oz **scallions** and 1 **yellow bell pepper**. Heat 2 tbsp **olive oil** in a pan, add the peppers, and fry with 1 minced **clove of garlic**. Season with salt and pepper. Toast 2 tbsp **pine nuts** in a pan without fat. Stir in the drained rice, onion mixture, pine nuts, 3 oz crumbled **Feta**, 4 tbsp **cream**, and 1 **egg yolk**. Season to taste. **2** Wash and prepare 2 **red bell peppers**, cut in half, and remove the seeds. Fill with the rice mixture and put in an oven-proof dish. Add ⅝ cup **vegetable stock**. Cook in the oven, preheated to 355 degrees (fan oven not recommended) on the second shelf from the bottom for 30 minutes.

Preparation time: 45 minutes.
Per serving: 19 g P, 39 g F, 51 g C = 632 kcal (2649 kJ).

240

Sliced Beans

A dish truly worthy of summer. The addition of cream further enhances the delicate taste of the beans.

Serves 2: 1 Wash and prepare 14 oz **green beans**, and cut diagonally into thin strips. Mince 1 **onion**. Heat 1 tbsp melted **butter** in a pan, add the beans and minced onion, and fry lightly. Sprinkle 1 tbsp **flour** into the pan, stir, and fry briefly. Add ⅜ cup **vegetable stock**. Season with salt and pepper, cover, and cook for 8–10 minutes until the beans are *al dente*. **2** Mince 2 tbsp **savory** or **parsley**. Add to the beans together with 6 tbsp **whipping cream** and heat briefly. Season with 1–2 tsp **prepared mustard**, salt, pepper, and **sugar**. Sprinkle minced savory or parsley on top.

* **Preparation time:** 20 minutes. **Per serving:** 6 g P, 16 g F, 12 g C = 218 kcal (914 kJ).

Cherry Soufflé

A summer favorite! In season you can also make this dish with fresh cherries. If you do, wash 14 oz sour cherries and remove the pits.

Serves 4:

6 stale milk rolls
(9 oz, or stale bread)

1 cup milk

½ tsp ground cinnamon

7 tsp butter

⅓ cup sugar

1 ½ tsp vanilla sugar

3 medium eggs (separated)

4 ½ oz crème fraîche

salt

2 oz minced almonds

2 oz chocolate drops

10 oz Bing cherries
(from a jar)

1–2 tbsp confectioners' sugar

1 Cut the rolls into small cubes, stir together the milk and cinnamon, pour over the diced rolls and leave to soak for 10 minutes. Beat together softened butter, 3 tbsp sugar, and vanilla sugar, using a hand-held mixer, until creamy. Add the egg yolks one by one. Stir in the cream. Beat the egg whites stiff with 1 pinch of salt, carefully stir in the rest of the sugar, and continue whisking for another 2 minutes. Fold the stiffly beaten egg whites into the milky bread mixture together with the almonds and chocolate drops.

2 Thoroughly drain the cherries and place in a greased soufflé dish (12 in long) together with the bread mixture. Bake in the oven, preheated to 340 degrees (fan oven 300 degrees) on the second shelf from the bottom for 45 minutes. If necessary, cover after 25 minutes. Allow to rest briefly and sprinkle with confectioners' sugar. This is delicious served with vanilla custard.

 * **Preparation time:** 75 minutes.
 Per serving: 17 g P, 46 g F, 80 g C = 807 kcal (3382 kJ).

FRUITY VARIATION
Vanilla custard with orange: bring 1 cup milk to the boil. Stir together ¼ orange juice, 1 packet vanilla custard and ¼ cup sugar. Add to the milk together with 1 tsp grated orange zest (untreated) and bring to the boil again.

Flattened Chicken with Paprika

A very unusual chicken dish: very spicy, very crisp, and very juicy.

Serves 4: 1 Mince or crush 1 **clove of garlic**. Mix together with 1 tbsp **hot paprika powder** and 1 tbsp **sweet paprika powder** in a bowl. **2** Remove the backbone of 1 **chicken** (3 lb 5 oz) with sharp scissors and press the chicken to flatten it. Season with salt and pepper, and rub with **oil**. Spread the garlic and paprika over the chicken. **3** Pour ⅝ cup **chicken stock** and ½ cup **white wine** in a deep roasting pan. Put the chicken on a roasting grid over the roasting pan. Roast in the oven, preheated to 410 degrees (fan oven not recommended) on the lowest shelf for 50 minutes. Cut 1 **lemon** into slices and place on the chicken with 4 **sprigs of rosemary** after 20 minutes.

* **Preparation time:** 1 hour.
  Per serving: 55 g P, 26 g F, 0 g C = 457 kcal (1912 kJ).

Quick Carpaccio with Beet

The ideal combination: pickled gherkins and beet served as a delicious appetizer.

Serves 4: 1 Mince 3 oz **pickled gherkins**. Mince 1 **onion**. Stir both with 2 tbsp **white wine vinegar**, 5 tbsp **oil**, salt, pepper, and **sugar**. Add 1 tbsp minced chives. **2** Wash and peel 7 oz beet. Grate into thin strips. In a bowl mix together 1 tbsp oil, 1 tsp vinegar, salt an pepper. **3** Arrange 7 oz cold roast pork (8 slices) on 4 plates. Arrange the beet on top and pour the gherkin vinaigrette on top.

Preparation time: 40 minutes. **Per serving:** 15 g P, 21 g F, 4 g C = 264 kcal (1106 kJ).

245

Curd Gazpacho

Gazpacho is famous as a refreshing cold soup but in curd the cucumber, peppers, tomatoes, and garlic are a real revelation!

Serves 2: 1 Stir together 500 g **buttermilk curd** (otherwise low-fat curd) with 4–5 tbsp **milk** until smooth. Season with salt and pepper. Peel 10 oz **cucumber**, remove the seeds, and mince. Cut 10 oz **tomatoes** into four, remove the seeds, and mince. Wash and prepare 1 **yellow bell pepper**, and mince. **2** Mince 1 **clove of garlic** and stir into the curd mixture together the other minced vegetables. Wash and prepare 1 **scallion**, cut into fine rings, and sprinkle over the curd.

Preparation time: 15 minutes. Per serving: 38 g P, 2 g F, 20 g C = 262 kcal (1100 kJ).

Cajun Burger

Garlic, paprika, and chili add sharpness and spiciness to the meatballs.
And it is also delicious with crisp bacon!

Serves 2: 1 Stir 4 tbsp **mayonnaise** with 1 crushed **clove of garlic**, and
2–3 tsp **lime juice**. Season with salt and pepper. **2** In a bowl, mix
together 18 oz **ground beef** with 2 tbsp **barbecue sauce**. Shape
into 4 burgers of equal size and broil under a medium heat for
4 minutes on each side. **3** Put the burger on the bottom half
of the hamburger bun and garnish with 1 slice of **tomato**,
raw **onion**, and a little **lettuce**. Put the other half on top
and serve with the garlic mayonnaise.

Preparation time: 15 minutes.
Per serving: 57 g P, 77 g F, 50 g C = 1116 kcal (4673 kJ).

Potatoes in a Salt Crust

Finally a salted potatoes dish that deserves its name: these Spanish bakes are a salty revelation.

Serves 2: 1 Dissolve 4 oz **salt** in 2¼ cups hot water. Thoroughly scrub 18 oz small **potatoes**. Put in a pan with the salted water, bring to the boil, and cook for 15–20 minutes without a lid. Drain the potatoes and put them wet on a cookie sheet. Put them immediately in the oven, preheated to 390 degrees (fan oven 355 degrees), and allow to dry on the second shelf from the bottom for about 12 minutes until a fine crust of salt forms on the skin. **2** Mix together ½ cup **hot chili sauce**, 3 strips of **pickled peppers**, and 2 tbsp minced **parsley**, and serve with the potatoes.

Preparation time: 40 minutes.
Per serving: 5 g P, 0 g F, 46 g C = 212 kcal (894 kJ).

248

Thai Cucumber Salad

A completely different cucumber salad: exotic, spicy, and yet very refreshing.

Serves 2: 1 Cut open 1 **red chili pepper**, remove the seeds and cut into thin strips. Remove the leaves from 3 sprigs of **cilantro** (or **parsley**), and mince. Add both to 2 tbsp **lime juice**, 1 tbsp **soy sauce**, 1 tsp **sugar**, and 2 tbsp **oil**, and stir well. Wash and trim the **cucumber** and cut in half diagonally. Using a potato peeler, cut long spirals lengthways round the soft flesh but do not use the soft inner part. **2** Carefully stir the cucumber spirals into the sauce and sprinkle 3 tbsp **salted peanuts** on top. Serve immediately.

* **Preparation time:** 15 minutes.
  Per serving: 5 g P, 18 g F, 10 g C = 226 kcal (944 kJ).

249

Oriental Noodle Dish

An exotic variation: spaghetti with plenty of vegetables and amazing sweet yet sharp seasoning.

Serves 2:

3 ½ oz spaghetti

salt

5 oz carrots

3 ½ oz scallions

3 ½ oz small mushrooms

3 oz snow peas

2 tbsp oil

1 tbsp sesame oil
(or a neutral oil)

½ cup vegetable stock

3 tbsp sweet soy sauce

1 tsp Sambal Oelek

2 tbsp salted cashew nuts

1 Cook the spaghetti in plenty in boiling salted water, following the instructions on the packet, run under cold water and drain thoroughly. Grate or cut the carrots into sticks. Wash and prepare the scallions and cut into strips. Wash and prepare the mushrooms and cut in half. Cut the snow peas in half.

2 Fry the carrots and mushrooms in hot oil and sesame oil for 2 minutes while stirring. Add the scallions and snow peas and fry briefly. Now add the vegetable stock, soy sauce, and a little Sambal Oelek. Cook for 3 minutes without a lid. Add the noodles, heat briefly, season again if necessary, and sprinkle cashew nuts on top.

Preparation time: 35 minutes.
Per serving: 12 g P, 22 g F, 45 g C = 424 kcal (1777 kJ).

SWEET AND SHARP
The mixing of sweet soy sauce and sharp Sambal Oelek adds a sophisticated sweet-sharp taste to the spaghetti. If you cannot find sweet soy sauce, use 3 tbsp ordinary soy sauce and sweeten with 1 tbsp sugar.

Braised Cucumber

The best way to enjoy a cucumber: braised with dill.

Serves 2: 1 Peel 18 oz **cucumber**, cut in half and remove the soft middle with a spoon. Cut into ¾-in cubes. Peel 14 oz **firm potatoes** and mince coarsely. Mince 1 **onion** and fry lightly in 2 tbsp **oil**. Add the potatoes, cucumber, and 1 tsp **mustard seeds** (or 2 tsp **mustard**) and fry lightly. Stir together 3½ oz **sour cream** with 1 tsp **flour** and add to the potato mixture together with ⅝ cup vegetable stock. Season with salt and pepper and 1 pinch of **sugar**. **2** Bring to the boil, cover and cook over low heat for 13–15 minutes. Fry **sausages** (5–7 oz each) in 2 tbsp oil until crisp all round. Pull the leaves off ½ bunch **dill**, mince and add to the potatoes. If necessary, adjust the seasoning and serve with the sausages.

* **Preparation time:** 35 minutes. **Per serving:** 25 g P, 63 g F, 36 g C = 813 kcal (340 kJ).

Spicy Tortilla

A kind of Mediterranean breakfast of fried potatoes, scrambled eggs, and bacon. Very easy, especially if you still have some potatoes left over from the day before.

Serves 2: 1 Wash 14 oz firm **potatoes** and cook in boiling salted water. Wash and prepare 7 oz **zucchinis**, and cut into thin slices. Mince 1 **onion** and 1 **clove of garlic**. Beat together 3 medium **eggs**, ⅞ cup **milk**, a little salt, pepper and ½ tsp **hot paprika powder**. **2** Peel the potatoes and cut into slices. Heat 2 tbsp **olive oil** in an oven-proof non-stick pan (8 in diameter), add the zucchinis, onion, garlic, and 2 tbsp **flaked almonds** and fry. Season with salt and pepper and remove from the pan. Fry the potatoes in 2 tbsp olive oil and stir in the zucchinis mixture. **3** Add the egg mixture to the pan. Bake in the oven, preheated to 355 degrees (fan oven 320 degrees) on the second shelf from the bottom for 20–25 minutes. Leave to rest briefly and turn out of the pan.

* **Preparation time:** 45 minutes.
 Per serving: 22 g P, 39 g F, 32 g C = 571 kcal (2396 kJ).

Yellow Fruit Dessert

Made with apricots, nectarines, and melons: it is certainly a match for its better known sister, the red fruit dessert.

Serves 4: 1 Cut 9 oz **apricots** in half, remove the pits, and cut into segments. Cut 1 **nectarine** (7 oz) in half, remove the pit, and cut into segments. Remove the seeds of a 10 oz **Cantaloupe melon**, cut the flesh out of the skin, and cut into segments. Bring to the boil 1 cup **orange juice**, ½ cup **white wine** (or just orange juice), 1 **cinnamon stick**, 6 tbsp **sugar**, the peeled zest of ½ **lemon**, and 3 tbsp **lemon juice**. **2** Mix together 3 level tbsp **cornstarch** and 4 tbsp water, and stir until smooth. Add to the thickened juice, bring to the boil again. Add the fruit, bring back to the boil briefly, transfer to a bowl, and leave to cool down. Beat together ⅞ cup **whipping cream**, 1 tbsp sugar, and a little **ground cinnamon**, and serve with the dessert.

Preparation time: 20 minutes (plus cooling time).
Per serving: 3 g P, 15 g F, 63 g C = 415 kcal (1743 kJ).

Peach and Lady Finger Gratin

At least as delicious as the famous peach melba and far, far crispier.

Serves 4: 1 Make a cross-shaped cut in the top of 4 **peaches**, dip briefly in boiling water, then plunge into ice-cold water and peel. Cut the peaches in half and remove the pits. Arrange 3 ½ oz **lady fingers** in a greased gratin dish (about 10 x 6 in) with their sugary side facing upward. Pour 5 tbsp **almond liqueur** (for instance Amaretto, or for a alcohol-free dish, **orange juice**) over the lady fingers. Place the peaches with their rounded side upward on top. **2** Beat together ⅞ cup **milk**, 2 **egg whites**, and 2 medium **egg yolks**, 4 tbsp **sugar**, and 1 tbsp of **vanilla sugar**, and pour over the peaches. Bake in the oven, preheated to 355 degrees (fan oven 320 degrees) on the second shelf from the bottom for 40 minutes. Toast 1 tbsp **flaked almonds** in a pan without fat, sprinkle over the gratin, and serve. Delicious with ice-cream.

* **Preparation time:** 55 minutes. Per serving: 12 g P, 14 g F, 54 g C = 398 kcal (1672 kJ).

Chicken with Spinach

Very easy and very delicious. You can make these juicy, spicy chicken legs very economically.

Serves 2:

½ red chili pepper

1 onion

1 clove of garlic

4 chicken legs
(about 5 oz each)

salt

chili pepper

3 tbsp olive oil

5 tbsp white wine

⅝ cup chicken stock

½ untreated lemon

4 oz frozen leaf spinach

1 Cut open the chili pepper, remove the seeds, and cut into thin strips together with the onion and garlic. Season the chicken legs with salt and chili pepper. Fry them all on all sides in hot olive oil in a suitable pan until crisp. Add the onions, garlic, and pepper pods, and fry briefly. Now add the wine and the stock. Cook in the oven, preheated to 390 degrees (fan oven 355 degrees, and add an additional 3 tbsp chicken stock) on the second shelf from the bottom for 30 minutes.

2 Cut the lemon into segments. Defrost the spinach, following the instructions on the packet and press out as much water as possible. After 20 minutes add the spinach and lemon to the pan with the chicken. Adjust the seasoning if necessary and serve with bread or risotto.

* **Preparation time:** 45 minutes.
Per serving: 32 g P, 33 g F, 1 g C = 434 kcal (1814 kJ).

VERY PRACTICAL
These combination utensils are known as "sporks" because they combine the features of both spoon and fork. Ideal for dishes with a lot of sauce.

Sicilian Vegetable Sauce

How many vitamins can you fit in a pasta dish? Lots! This sauce from Southern Italy will show you how!

Serves 4: 1 Mince 1 **red bell pepper** and 1 **onion**. Cut 18 oz **beef tomatoes** in quarters, remove the seeds, and cut into small dice. Mince 9 oz **eggplants**. Heat 3 tbsp **olive oil**, add the eggplants, and fry briskly. Now add the minced pepper and onion, 1 crushed **clove of garlic**, and 2 tbsp **tomato paste**, and fry briefly. Season with salt and pepper. Add the minced tomatoes, cover, and cook for 10 minutes. **2** Meanwhile, cut 4 ribs of **celery** into thin slices. Add to the sauce together with 1 tbsp **capers** and 1 tsp **sugar**, and simmer for another 10 minutes. Cook 14 oz **pasta** (for instance penne), following the instructions on the packet. Season with salt and pepper, **red wine vinegar**, and sugar. **3** Strip the leaves off 2 sprigs of **oregano** and mince coarsely. Drain the pasta thoroughly. Add the sauce and the oregano to the pasta. Sprinkle with 3 oz grated **Parmesan**.

Preparation time: 40 minutes.
Per serving: 22 g P, 17 g F, 79 g C = 570 kcal (2390 kJ).

Tomato Pesto

Simple but heavenly: this is how happiness would taste if it were edible.

Serves 2: 1 Cook 2 oz **sun-dried tomatoes** (without oil) in boiling water with 1 tsp dried **thyme**. Drain, reserving ½ cup of the cooking water. Leave the tomatoes to drain. Toast 2 oz **pine nuts** in a pan without fat. Grate 1 ½ oz **Parmesan**. Mince the tomatoes coarsely and puree finely together with 1 ½ oz pine nuts, 2 tbsp **paprika paste**, the cooking water, 3 tbsp **olive oil** and the Parmesan. **2** Season with salt and pepper, and **sugar**. Cook 7 oz **pasta** (for instance spaghetti), following the instructions on the packet. Heat 2 tbsp olive oil in a pan, add 3 ½ oz **cherry tomatoes**, and fry. Add 1 tbsp thyme and fry briefly. Season with salt and pepper. Drain slightly and stir in the pesto. Garnish with tomatoes, thyme, and ¾ oz pine nuts.

* **Preparation time:** 30 minutes.
  Per serving: 27 g P, 43 g F, 76 g C = 804 kcal (3365 kJ).

Goat's Cheese and Figs

A couple of ingredients to create a sophisticated dish – so simple but so refined.

Serves 2: 1 Wash 4 fresh **figs** and dab dry very carefully. Make a cross-shaped incision at the pointed end halfway down and open up slightly. Season with a little pepper. Crumble 3 oz **goat's cheese** coarsely and press into the figs. **2** Arrange the figs on a greased cookie sheet and bake in the oven, preheated to 430 degrees (fan oven 390 degrees) on the second shelf from the top for 8–10 minutes. Sprinkle with freshly ground pepper before serving. Delicious with bread.

* **Preparation time:** 15 minutes.
Per serving: 5 g P, 12 g F, 16 g C = 200 kcal (843 kJ).

Puff Pastry Cones

Beautiful and tasty: these crisp puff pastry cones are filled with ground beef mixed with salted almonds and raisins.

Serves 10: 1 Defrost 1 packet **frozen puff pastry** (1 lb, 10 sheets). Mince 2 tbsp **raisins** and 2 tbsp **roasted salted almonds**. Add both to 14 oz **ground beef** together with 2 eggs and mix well. Season generously with salt, pepper, and **hot paprika pepper**. **2** Divide the ground beef mixture onto the sheets of puff pastry and fold to make triangles. Press the edges together tightly with a floured fork. Place the cones on a cookie sheet lined with waxed paper and sprinkle with 2 oz grated **Manchego** cheese (or **Gouda**). Bake in the oven, preheated to 430 degrees (fan oven 390 degrees) on the lowest shelf for 20–25 minutes.

* **Preparation time:** 40 minutes.
 Per serving: 14 g P, 21 g F, 19 g C = 324 kcal (1354 kJ).

Salmon Kebabs

This salmon dish is easy to make to say the least. It is delicious served with peppers and onions, braised in white wine with honey overtones.

Serves 2:

1 ¼ lb red and yellow bell peppers

2 cloves of garlic

1 bunch scallions

5 slices salmon fillet (each 3 oz, skinned)

3 tbsp oil

1 tbsp liquid honey

2 tbsp lemon juice

½ cup white wine

salt

pepper

1 Cut the peppers into 4, remove the seeds, wash, and cut into ¾-in cubes. Cut the cloves of garlic into thin slices. Cut both the white and green of the scallions into thin slices.

2 Roll up the slices of salmon into a snail shape and stick on a skewer. Put in the refrigerator.

3 Heat 2 tbsp oil in a pan, add the sliced garlic, and fry over low heat until transparent. Add the peppers and fry for another 4–5 minutes over low heat while stirring.

4 Add the honey, lemon juice, and white wine. Bring to the boil, half cover, and simmer for 7–8 minutes. Season with salt and pepper and add the scallions.

5 Season the salmon kebabs with salt and pepper. Heat 1 tbsp oil in a pan, add the salmon and fry for 2 minutes on each side. Garnish with the vegetables.

Preparation time: 35 minutes.
Per serving: 36 g P, 27 g F, 19 g C = 482 kcal (2016 kJ).

THIS IS HOW YOU TURN SALMON INTO SNAIL SHAPES
Simple and effective: rolled up and stuck on a skewer, the fish looks much more stylish.

Cold Strawberry Soup

A delicious combination: sweet strawberries and spicy basil. Try this quite unusual soup!

Serves 2: 1 Wash and prepare 1 ¼ lb **strawberries** and cut onto quarters. Finely puree 14 oz strawberries with ½ cup **red grape juice**, 1 pinch **powdered cinnamon**, ¼ cup **sugar**, and 2 tbsp **lemon juice**. Add the remaining 7 oz quartered strawberries and refrigerate for 2 hours. **2** Cut 3 ½ oz **brioche** into ⅜-in cubes. Heat 2 tbsp **butter** in a non-stick pan until foamy. Add the brioche cubes and fry until golden brown over low heat. Add 1 tbsp **vanilla sugar** and allow to melt briefly. Strip the leaves off 4 stems of **basil**, cut into strips, and add to the hot brioche cubes. Add these to the cold strawberry soup.

* **Preparation time:** 25 minutes.
  Per serving: 5 g P, 24 g F, 83 g C = 590 kcal (2470 kJ).

Apricot and Black-berry Focaccia

A delicious Italian way of preparing yeast dough.

For 16 pieces: 1 Knead 1 packet **yeast dough** mixture (12 oz) with 2 oz softened **butter**, ⅝ cup lukewarm **milk**, and 1 medium **egg** until you obtain a smooth dough. Cover and put in a warm place to rise for about 30 minutes. Cut 1 ¼ lb **apricots** in half, remove the pits, and cut into slices. Wash and prepare 9 oz **blackberries**. **2** Knead the dough again thoroughly on a floured cookie sheet. Divide into two amounts. Roll out 2 oblong pieces (each 14 x 10 in) on a floured surface. Then put on a cookie sheet lined with waxed paper. Spread 3 oz **apricot jelly** on each of the pieces, arrange fruit on top, and sprinkle with 1 tbsp **vanilla sugar**. **3** Bake in the oven, preheated to 390 degrees (fan oven 355 degrees), one after the other, on the lowest shelf for 20 minutes. Serve warm with **whipping cream** or **crème fraîche**.

Preparation time: 1 hour (plus cooking time).
Per serving: 3 g P, 3 g F, 26 g C = 156 kcal (660 kJ).

Beans with Walnut Butter

The season of runner beans! These big, fat green beans add a country note to a stew but are transformed into a sophisticated dish when served with walnut butter.

Serves 2: 1 Wash and prepare 18 oz **green beans**, and cook for 8–10 minutes in boiling salted water. **2** Meanwhile cut 1 **clove of garlic** into thin slices. Coarsely mince 2 oz **walnuts**. Cut 1 **red chili pepper** in half lengthways, remove the seeds, and mince. **3** Heat 4 tbsp **butter** until foamy. Add the garlic, walnuts, and chili pepper and fry for 1 minute over low heat. Add 1 tbsp **parsley**. **4** Drain the beans thoroughly and stir into the butter and walnut mixture. Season with salt and pepper.

Preparation time: 20 minutes.
Per serving: 9 g P, 37 g F, 10 g C = 406 kcal (1702 kJ).

Potato and Cheese Croquettes

Anyone who likes potatoes will adore these croquettes. With Camembert and rosemary, they may also be served as a main dish.

Serves 4: 1 Bring 1¼ cups water to the boil. Remove from the heat and leave the water to cool for 1 minute. Stir 1 packet of powdered **mashed potato** (with milk for 3 portions) into the water. Allow the mixture to thicken in a bowl while cooling a little. **2** Strip the leaves off 2 sprigs of **rosemary** and mince. Cut 2 oz **Camembert** into very small cubes. Add both to the lukewarm potato mixture. Shape into a roll 6½ in long and cut into 8 slices. Coat each slice with 4 tbsp **breadcrumbs**. Heat 2 tbsp **oil** and 2 tbsp **butter** in a pan. Add the croquettes and fry for 3–4 minutes on each side until golden brown.

Preparation time: 25 minutes (plus cooling time).
Per serving: 6 g P, 14 g F, 25 g C = 254 kcal (1064 kJ).

Mustard Meatballs

A spicy version of this favorite: as well as low-fat quark we have added a generous portion of hot mustard.

For 2 portions: 1 Finely chop 1 **<u>onion</u>** and 1 small **<u>clove of garlic</u>**. Heat 1 tbsp of oil in a pan, add the garlic and onion, then fry until transparent. Leave to cool. **2** Knead together with 14 oz **<u>mixed ground meat</u>**. Add 1 tbsp **<u>breadcrumbs</u>** and 2 tbsp **<u>low-fat quark</u>** and stir in well. Season with salt, pepper and 1–2 tbsp **<u>extra strong mustard</u>**. Make six meatballs from the mixture. **3** Heat 2–3 tbsp oil in a pan, add the meatballs, and brown briskly. Reduce the temperature and fry for 6 minutes on both sides over medium heat.

＊ **Preparation time:** 30 minutes.
  Per serving: 43 g P, 48 g F, 7 g C = 629 kcal (2636 kJ).

Romeo Salad

Not only for Juliet: this smooth dressing, made from red wine vinegar, honey, mustard, and eggs is simply irresistible.

Serves 4: 1 Put 2 **egg yolks** with 2 tbsp **Dijon mustard**, 1 **clove of garlic**, 2 tbsp **red wine vinegar**, 1 tbsp **liquid honey**, and ⅝ cup **oil** in a high-sided bowl. **2** Beat with a mixer at the highest setting until smooth. Season with salt and pepper. **3** Cut a **baguette** into slices, coat with **olive oil**, and bake on both sides under the oven broiler until gold yellow. **4** Cut 3 **romaine lettuce hearts** into slices and pour over the dressing. **5** Add small cubes of baguettes-croutons and 1 oz grated of **mountain cheese** (Manchego, or otherwise Edam).

* **Preparation time:** 30 minutes.
Per serving: 7 g P, 49 g F, 17 g C = 537 kcal (2247 kJ).

Fennel-Melon Salad

Raw fennel in salad? The beautiful bulb with its characteristic aniseed taste is perfect with watermelon and prosciutto!

Serves 4: 1 Wash and prepare 1 **fennel bulb** (1 ½ lb) and grate as finely as possible. **2** Put in a bowl and add salt, pepper, and 1 tbsp minced **basil**. Mix well and stir vigorously for 2–3 minutes. Add 2 tsp **lemon juice** and 2 tbsp **olive oil**. Allow to draw for 10 minutes. **3** Meanwhile remove the skin from 1 ¼ lb **watermelon** and remove as many seeds as possible. Cut the melon into cubes and add to the fennel mixture. **4** Arrange 8 slices of **prosciutto** on 4 plates and garnish with the salad. Sprinkle some pepper on top.

Preparation time: 30 minutes.
Per serving: 9 g P, 7 g F, 6 g C = 139 kcal (580 kJ).

Kohlrabi and Apple Salad

A summer salad as it should be: fruity, juicy, and crisp.

Serves 2: 1 Peel 10 oz **kohlrabi**, cut into quarters, and grate or cut into very thin slices. Sprinkle with ½ tsp **salt**, mix carefully, and leave to draw for 10 minutes. Roast 2 tbsp **pine nuts** in a pan without fat. Mince 2 tbsp **thyme leaves** and beat together with 2 tbsp **white wine vinegar**, 1–2 tsp **honey**, a little salt, pepper, and 4 tbsp **oil**. **2** Cut 1 **red apple** into quarters, core, and cut into very thin slices, and stir immediately into the sauce. Dab the kohlrabi dry and add to the sauce, mix well, and sprinkle pine nuts on top.

* **Preparation time:** 20 minutes. **Per serving:** 5 g P, 25 g F, 18 g C = 322 kcal (1349 kJ).

Redcurrant Yeast Cake

Acres of pure red-currant delight. Make sure you make two of them because they are absolutely irresistible!

For 12 pieces:

1¾ lb redcurrants

4 cups flour

1 tsp baking powder

1 tsp dried yeast

1 cup 2 tbsp sugar

1½ tsp vanilla sugar

salt

⅞ cup milk

6 tbsp butter or margarine

4 medium eggs

pulp of 1 vanilla bean

18 oz low-fat curd cheese

¾ oz cornstarch

1 Carefully wash the redcurrants, leave to drain, and remove the stems. Sift together the flour, the baking powder, and the yeast. Add ¼ cup sugar, 1½ tsp vanilla sugar, 1 pinch of salt, milk, and softened butter or margarine. Beat with the dough attachment of food mixer to make a smooth dough. Roll out onto a floured surface to make a 16 x 12 in rectangle. Roll up the pastry round a rolling-pin and unroll again onto a greased cookie sheet (16 x 12 in).

2 Beat together the eggs, bare 1 cup sugar, and the vanilla pulp with a hand-held mixer for 5 minutes until creamy. Stir in the curd cheese and cornstarch. Spread the mixture over the dough and sprinkle the redcurrants on top. Leave to stand for 5 minutes. Bake in the oven, preheated to 390 degrees (fan oven 355 degrees) on the second shelf from the bottom for 30–35 minutes. Leave to cool.

* **Preparation time:** 70 minutes (plus cooling time).
Per serving: 12 g P, 8 g F, 52 g C = 350 kcal (1466 kJ).

PREPARATION
The redcurrants can easily be removed from their stems by gently slipping the stems through the tines of a fork.

Treat your-self like an emperor

NO ONE KNOWS what the Emperor Augustus liked to eat, but he must have enjoyed all the good things in life. The month named after him offers all the fruit, vegetables, and salads you could wish for. You too will be able to eat like an emperor with all the recipes we have devised for you. Augustus himself could not have eaten better.

Caesar Sandwich

This snack was inspired by the classic Caesar salad: the salad is served on toast with broiled chicken. Delicious!

Serves 2:

3 oz mayonnaise

1 clove of garlic

2 tsp lemon juice

salt

black pepper

1 romaine lettuce heart

2 oz Parmesan in the piece

2 slices white bread

½ roast chicken (from a snack bar or supermarket)

1 Stir the crushed garlic, lemon juice, salt, and pepper into the mayonnaise.

2 Wash, dry, and prepare the salad. Grate the Parmesan using a potato peeler to make shavings.

3 Toast the bread in a toaster or under the preheated oven broiler. Stir half the cheese and lemon mayonnaise into the salad and arrange on the toast. Remove the chicken meat from the bones and pull into strips. Arrange on the salad.

4 Add the rest of the mayonnaise and sprinkle the remaining cheese on top.

* **Preparation time:** 25 minutes.
Per serving: 36 g P, 53 g F, 14 g C = 671 kcal (2812 kJ).

IF THERE IS ANY CHICKEN LEFT
use it in pasta salad or soup. You could also buy prepared chicken slices.

Lukewarm Tomato Salad

*Small but with substance: serve this sophisticated salad of
arugula, sorrel, and broiled tomatoes with a garnish of shrimp.*

Serves 4: 1 Cut 6 **tomatoes** in half. Place on a cookie sheet with the cut
surface facing upwards and season with salt and pepper. Sprinkle with
2 tbsp **olive oil** and 2 tbsp **sugar**. Broil under hot broiler on the second
shelf from the bottom for 7–8 minutes. **2** Meanwhile wash 2 oz each of
sorrel and **arugula**, and tear into bite-size pieces. Cut 1 **red onion** into
thin strips. **3** Fry 4 **shrimp** (2 oz each with head and shell) in 1 tbsp hot
oil for 3 minutes on each side. Season with salt and pepper. **4** Arrange
the tomatoes together with the onions, arugula, and sorrel on 4 plates.
Mix together 3 tbsp olive oil and 2 tbsp **lemon juice**. Season with salt and
pepper. Pour over the salad and serve with the shrimp.

* **Preparation time:** 30 minutes. **Per serving:** 11 g P, 16 g F, 15 g C = 254 kcal (1063 kJ).

Fresh Pea Stew

A modern classic: this stew, enhanced by lemon grass and basil, works green wonders.

Serves 2: 1 Bring 3½ cups **<u>vegetable stock</u>** to the boil with 1 crushed stem of **<u>lemon grass</u>** (or strips of the zest of 1 **<u>untreated lemon</u>**). **2** Cut 3½ oz **<u>carrots</u>**, 3½ oz **<u>celeriac</u>**, and 3½ oz **<u>leeks</u>** into ⅜ in cubes. Add to the vegetable stock and cook for 8 minutes. **3** Cut 9 oz **<u>smoked loin of pork</u>** into cubes and add to the vegetable stock and vegetables with 7 oz frozen peas, then cook for 3–4 minutes. **4** Thicken the soup with 3–4 tbsp **<u>mashed potatoes powder</u>**. Season with salt and pepper, and 1 tbsp minced **<u>basil</u>**.

* **Preparation time:** 25 minutes.
  Per serving: 33 g P, 6 g F, 23 g C = 286 kcal (1200 kJ).

Chanterelle Risotto

Food for the soul of those who miss their holidays: chanterelles, bacon, and arugula make a delicious dish that will satisfy your hunger for things Mediterranean.

Serves 2: 1 Cut 1 **shallot** into small cubes. Mince 1 **clove of garlic**. Heat 1 tbsp **oil** in a pan, add the shallots and garlic, and fry until transparent. Add ⅝ cup **short-grain rice** and fry for 1 minute. Now add ⅝ cup **white wine** and cook over medium heat until completely absorbed. **2** Cook the rice for another 20 minutes, stirring continuously, gradually adding 2½ cups hot **vegetable stock** to the rice. **3** Meanwhile cut 3 oz **bacon** into cubes, and wash and prepare 9 oz **chanterelles**. **4** Heat 1 tbsp oil in a pan, then add the bacon and fry until crisp. Add the chanterelles and fry for 3 minutes. Season with salt and pepper. **5** 2 minutes before the end of the risotto's cooking time, stir in the mushrooms, ¼ cup freshly grated **Parmesan** and 1 oz coarsely torn **arugula**.

* **Preparation time:** 40 minutes. **Per serving:** 20 g P, 29 g F, 62 g C = 607 kcal (2543 kJ).

Ginger-Turkey Steaks

It need not always be a turkey roast: served with cabbage and cherry tomatoes, these simple turkey steaks are transformed into a delicious light Sunday meal.

Serves 4: 1 Peel 1 oz raw **ginger** and grate finely and mix with 1 crushed **clove of garlic**, ½ tsp ground **black pepper**, and 4 tbsp **soy sauce**. Rub this mixture on the **turkey steaks** (13 oz each) and leave to marinate in the refrigerator for ½ hour. Wash and prepare 1 **cabbage** (about 18 oz), cut into quarters, and remove the hard stump. Cut the cabbage into strips of about ¼ in. Wash and wipe dry 5 oz **cherry tomatoes**. **2** Heat 3 tbsp **oil** in a non-stick pan. Dab the meat dry but keep the marinade. Briskly sear the meat for 1–2 minutes on each side and put in a baking dish. Bake in the oven, preheated to 355 degrees (fan oven 320 degrees) on the second shelf from the bottom for 12–17 minutes. Heat 2 tbsp in a pan, add the cabbage, and fry for 3–4 minutes while stirring. **3** Add the marinade and the tomatoes to the cabbage, and bring to the boil. Season with salt and pepper. Serve with the meat and 2 tbsp minced **cilantro** (or **flat-leaved parsley**).

* **Preparation time:** 30 minutes (plus marinating time).
  Per serving: 47 g P, 15 g F, 4 g C = 342 kcal (1429 kJ).

Thousand Island Salad

You may not be fortunate enough to enjoy life on an island but you can still enjoy this salad.

Serves 4: 1 Put 1 **egg** in boiling water and boil for 8 minutes. Remove from the boiling water, dip in cold water, and shell. **2** Cut 1 **red bell pepper** into quarters, remove the seeds and mince. Mince 1 **pickled gherkin** and 1 **red onion**. Mince the egg and 1 oz **green olives** (without pits). Put ⅓ of all ingredients to one side. **3** Put the remaining ⅔ of the ingredients in a bowl. Add 5 oz **mayonnaise**, 5 tbsp of the **pickled gherkin liquid**, and 5 tbsp **ketchup**, and mix well. Season with salt, pepper, and **Tabasco**. **4** Wash and prepare 1 **large green lettuce** and spin dry. Tear into bite-size pieces and arrange on a dish. **5** Pour the dressing over the salad and sprinkle the rest of the ingredients on top.

* **Preparation time:** 25 minutes.
  Per serving: 4 g P, 33 g F, 7 g C = 344 kcal (1443 kJ).

Tomato and Mozzarella Gratin

Break the sheets of lasagne into pieces. This is not only fun but it is also the creative foundation for this very quick gratin.

Serves 2:

5 oz light lasagne sheets

salt

4 tbsp olive oil

10 oz ripe vine tomatoes

1 ball Mozzarella (4½ oz)

pepper

½ bunch basil

1 Break the sheets of lasagne into pieces and cook in plenty of boiling salted water with 2 tbsp olive oil for 10 minutes. Stir frequently so that the pieces do not stick together. Drain, run under cold water, and drain thoroughly.

2 Cut the tomatoes into slices about ¾-in thick. Cut the Mozzarella into slices. Arrange half the pieces of lasagne in a greased gratin dish (about 10 x 8 in). Now arrange the tomatoes, Mozzarella, and the rest of the lasagne on top so that they overlap. Sprinkle with 2 tbsp olive oil and season with salt and pepper.

3 Brown lightly in the oven, preheated to 430 degrees (fan oven 390 degrees) on the middle shelf for 12–15 minutes. Tear some basil leaves into pieces and sprinkle on the gratin before serving.

* **Preparation time:** 30 minutes.
 Per serving: 22 g P, 24 g F, 55 g C = 537 kcal (2250 kJ).

SHARDS BRING LUCK
Break the lasagne sheets into shard-like pieces. Boil in plenty of boiling salted water with a dash of olive oil, stirring frequently to prevent the pasta from sticking together. You will relish it from the very first bite!

Cherry and Raspberry Dessert

In Denmark this dessert is called Rød Grød med Fløde and it is delicious served with mint-flavored cream.

Serves 4: 1 Wash and pit 10 oz **sour cherries**. Pick over 9 oz **raspberries**. From 1 cup **sour cherry drink**, take 6 tbsp and stir it together with ¾ oz **cornstarch**. Bring the rest of the juice to the boil, then stir in the cornstarch and cherry juice mixture as well as the fruit. Bring back to the boil. Pour into a bowl and leave to cool. **2** Mince 2 oz **mint chocolate**. Beat ⅞ cup **whipping cream** until stiff and stir in the minced chocolate. Serve the dessert with the whipped cream. Garnish with **mint leaves** if you like.

* **Preparation time:** 25 minutes (plus cooling time).
  Per serving: 3 g P, 17 g F, 33 g C = 306 kcal (1284 kJ).

Oreo Cheesecake

This cheesecake recipemade with Oreo cookies is deliciously different.

For 14–16 pieces: 1 Finely crumble 6 oz (16 pieces) **Oreo cookies**
in a freezer bag, using a rolling pin. Melt 4 tbsp **butter** (or **margarine**),
add to the cookies, and knead into a paste. Spread on the bottom
of a springform mold (9½ in diameter), using a spoon to press it down.
Line the sides of the mold with 14 **Oreo cookies halves**. **2** Beat together
1¾ lb **low-fat curd**, 10 oz **heavy cream fromage frais**, 2 packets
vanilla sugar, 1½ grated **orange zest (untreated)**, ½ cup **sugar**, and good
¾ cup **flour** using a hand-held mixer on a medium setting until creamy.
3 Stir in 3 medium **eggs**, one after the other, and incorporate well. Pour
this mixture into the springform mold and smooth it flat. **4** Decorate
the surface with Oreo cookies halves. Bake in the oven, preheated to
340 degrees (fan oven 300 degrees) on the second shelf from the bottom
for 40–50 minutes. Allow to cool at room temperature, then put in the
refrigerator for at least 5 hours (preferably overnight). **Tip:** the Oreo
cookies can be replaced by filbert sandwich cookies with cream filling.

* **Preparation time:** 1 hour (plus cooling time).
  Per serving (out of 16 portions): 13 g P, 12 g F, 28 g C = 273 kcal (1145 kJ).

Tomato Salad

There is no messing about with simple salad which only requires a few natural ingredients.

Serves 2: 1 Wash and prepare 14 oz ripe **tomatoes** and cut into slices. Cut the white and the green of 2 **scallions** into thin rings. To make the vinaigrette, stir together 2 tbsp **white balsamic vinegar**, a little salt, pepper, 1 pinch of **sugar**, 1 crushed **clove of garlic**, 8 tbsp **tomato juice**, and 4 tbsp **olive oil**. Add the scallions to the sauce. **2** Coarsely tear ½ bunch **flat-leaved parsley** and add to the tomatoes and the sauce.

* **Preparation time:** 20 minutes.
 Per serving: 2 g P, 20 g F, 13 g C = 247 kcal (1038 kJ).

Chanterelle Medallions

Try this dish before the end of the chanterelle season, it highlights the greatness of this small mushroom.

Serves 4: 1 Wash and prepare 18 oz **chanterelles** and dry thoroughly. Mince 1 **onion**. **2** Heat 2 tbsp **butter**, add the onion and fry until transparent. Stir in the chanterelles and fry for 4 minutes. Crush 2 tbsp **green peppercorns** (from a jar). Add together with 1–2 tbsp brine and ½ cup **white wine** to the pan and reduce the liquid to half. **3** Pour in ⅞ cup **whipping cream**, bring to the boil and thicken until the mixture becomes creamy. Season with salt and pepper and keep warm. **4** Sprinkle a little salt and pepper on 8 **beef tenderloin medallions** (3 oz each). Heat 1 tbsp oil in a second pan and fry the medallions for 3–4 minutes on each side. **5** Mince ½ bunch **chives** and add to the sauce. Arrange 2 medallions and the sauce on each plate.

* **Preparation time:** 35 minutes. **Per serving:** 35 g P, 29 g F, 2 g C = 418 kcal (1748 kJ).

Crêpe Wraps

A perfect snack for handicraft enthusiasts: people in a rush can obviously also use frozen ready-made crêpes.

Serves 6:

12 large frozen shrimp (defrosted, shelled, and without heads)

4 medium eggs

⅝ cup milk

2 tsp curry powder

salt

1 ½ cups flour

3 ½ oz snow peas

7 oz carrots

6 tsp oil

2 tbsp mayonnaise

1 tsp lime zest (from an untreated lime)

2 tbsp lime juice

5 oz full cream yoghourt

pepper

sugar

½ bunch green cilantro (or flat-leaved parsley)

1 Defrost the shrimp. Beat together the eggs, milk, curry, and 1 pinch salt. Add the flour, 1 tbsp at a time, while stirring, and leave the mixture to rest for 15 minutes. Cut the snow peas diagonally into thin strips. Peel the carrots and cut into thin 2 in long sticks. Cook the snow peas and carrots for 3 minutes in boiling salted water. Run under cold water and drain thoroughly.

2 Stir the batter thoroughly again. Put 1 tsp oil in a non-stick pan and cook the 6 crêpes one after the other, adding another 1 tsp oil between each one. Leave the crêpes to cool. Mix together the mayonnaise, lime zest, lime juice, and yoghourt. Season with salt, pepper, and 1 pinch of sugar.

3 Remove the cilantro from the stems, mince, and stir in. Spread the yoghourt mixture on the crêpes, leaving a ¾-in edge all around. Put the carrots and snow peas on top and put 2 shrimp in the middle. Roll up the crêpe, wrap in Saran wrap, put in the refrigerator for 30 minutes and cut in half.

* **Preparation time:** 1 hour (plus resting time).
  Per serving: 19 g P, 14 g F, 23 g C = 310 kcal (1297 kJ).

Bean Salad with Crostini

A salad made with green beans, kidney beans and wax beans.

Serves 2: 1 Wash and prepare 9 oz **green beans** and 9 oz **wax beans**, and cut into pieces 1 ½ in long. Cook in boiling salted water for about 8–10 minutes with 3 sprigs of **savory** (or ½ tsp **dried savory**). Run under cold water, drain well, and remove the savory. Rinse 1 can of **kidney beans** (14 oz drained weight) in a strainer and drain well. **2** Cut 5 oz **onions** into thin rings. In a small bowl, beat together 2 tbsp **white wine vinegar**, 1 tsp **prepared mustard**, 5 tbsp **sunflower oil**, a little salt, pepper, and 1 pinch of **sugar**, using a hand whisk. Pit 2 oz **ripe olives** and mince coarsely. Mix together the beans, olives, and onion, and stir in the vinaigrette.

For 2 portions of Crostini: Cut ½ baguette diagonally into slices, arrange on a cookie sheet and broil in the oven, preheated to 390 degrees (fan oven 355 degrees) on the second shelf from the top for 5–7 minutes. Cut 5 oz **goat's cheese** into slices. Put 1 slice on each slice of baguette and broil for another 8–10 minutes. Sprinkle with a little **dried oregano** and serve with the salad. **Tip:** instead of the Crostini, this can also be served with salmon steak.

*Preparation time: 25 minutes. Per serving: 28 g P, 59 g F, 60 g C = 882 kcal (3695 kJ).

Chicken and Vegetable Casserole

The simplest way ever to cook chicken: resting on a bed of vegetables, it is slowly cooked to perfection in the oven.

Serves 2: 1 Cut 9 oz **zucchinis**, 1 **green bell pepper**, 1 **red onion**, and 3 ½ oz **celery** into bite-size pieces. **2** Stir together 3–4 tbsp **olive oil**, salt, pepper, and 1 tbsp each of minced **parsley** and **basil** in a bowl. Crush 1 **clove of garlic**. Add the vegetables, mix well, and arrange in a casserole dish. **3** Rub salt, pepper, and 1 tsp oil into the **chicken breast** with bone (1 ½ lb) and place on top of the vegetables. **4** Cook in the oven, preheated to 390 degrees (fan oven 355 degrees) on the second shelf from the bottom for 45 minutes. After 20 minutes add ⅞ cup **vegetable stock**.

* Preparation time: 1 hour.
Per serving: 52 g P, 28 g F, 5 g C = 489 kcal (2047 kJ).

Corn on the Cob

Those who like exotic food can add some lime butter.
This classic variation is enhanced by the addition of garlic or herb butter.

Serves 4: 1 Heat together in a wide pan 4½ cups **milk**, 2¼ cups water, and 1 tsp **sugar**. Add 4 washed and prepared **corn cobs** and cook for 20 minutes over medium-high heat. Remove from the milk and drain thoroughly. **2** Using a potato peeler, thinly peel ½ **lime**. Mince the zest. Cut 1 **red chili pepper** in half, remove the seeds, and mince. Mix together 3 tbsp **butter** (at room temperature) with the lime zest, minced chili pepper, and a little salt. **3** Broil the corn cobs for 5–8 minutes. Remove from the broiler and serve each with ¼ of the lime butter. **Tip:** Only sprinkle the salt on the corn cobs at the end, otherwise they would become tough.

* **Preparation time:** 30 minutes.
  Per serving: 3 g P, 10 g F, 16 g C = 163 kcal (685 kJ).

Italian Pasta Salad

Who would not be reminded of sunshine and the sound of the sea by these ingredients?

Serves 4–6: 1 Cook 14 oz **short macaroni**, following the instructions on the packet. Remove from the water, run under cold water and drain thoroughly. Drain 7 oz **sun-dried tomatoes in oil** and cut into small pieces. Toast 6 tbsp **pine nuts** in a pan without fat until golden brown. Mince 2 **cloves of garlic** coarsely. **2** Finely puree half the sun-dried tomatoes, garlic, and 3 tbsp roasted pine nuts in a blender. Cut 18 oz **tomatoes** into quarters, then cut these quarters diagonally in half. Strip the leaves of 1 bunch **basil** and cut the large leaves in half. **3** Stir together 3 tbsp **olive oil**, 3 tbsp **white balsamic vinegar**, pureed tomatoes, 2 tbsp water, salt, pepper, 1 pinch of **sugar**, the rest of the sun-dried tomatoes, and garlic. Now mix together the pasta, tomatoes, pine nuts, basil, and vinaigrette.

* **Preparation time:** 20 minutes.
  Per serving (based on 6 servings): 12 g P, 15 g F, 54 g C = 399 kcal (1672 kJ).

Picnic Bread

Instead of salami you could also use canned tuna fish. Another delicious variation is salami and goat's cheese.

Serves 8:

1 round white country or crusty loaf (about generous 1 lb and 7 in diameter)

3 oz tomato pesto (from a jar)

3 ½ oz cucumber

salt

pepper

3 ½ oz Saint Albray or Camembert cheese

½ bunch basil

3 ½ oz roasted preserved red bell pepper (from a jar)

3 oz very thin salami slices

3 tbsp olive oil

1 Cut off the end of a loaf to make an opening large enough to remove the soft inside of the bread, leaving the crust ⅜-in thick (dry the soft inside and use as breadcrumbs for other purposes). Coat the inside of the bread with pesto. Grate unpeeled cucumber into paper-thin slices. Season with salt and pepper.

2 Cut the cheese into thin slices. Pull the basil leaves off the stems. Carefully dab the pepper dry. Layer half the pepper, cheese, half the basil, salami, half the cucumber, the rest of the pepper and basil in the bread. Sprinkle with olive oil.

3 Replace the "crusty lid" and wrap the bread tightly in aluminum foil. Keep in the refrigerator overnight, weighting it down with a can. Slice only when about to eat it.

* **Preparation time:** 45 minutes (plus cooling time).
Per serving: 7 g P, 12 g F, 19 g C = 217 kcal (910 kJ).

A NOURISHING SNACK

A delicious snack for eating during the journey. The evening before, generously coat the inside of the hollowed out bread with pesto. Then fill with the ingredients, pressing them down hard before adding the next layer so that there are no gaps. Keep in the refrigerator overnight, weighted down with a can. This will make it nicely compact.

Sweet Berry Vol-au-Vent

Choose any berry you like and serve in light puff pastry pie shells,
topped with whipped cream, flavored with coconut liqueur.

Serves 4: 1 Sprinkle 4 **puff pastry vol-au-vent shells** (1 oz each) with
2–3 tbsp **confectioners' sugar** and put on a cookie sheet. Bake in a hot
oven, preheated to 430 degrees (fan oven 390 degrees) on the second
shelf from the top for 8–10 minutes. Roast 3 tbsp **coconut flakes** in a pan
without fat. Wash and prepare 3 ½ oz **strawberries**, cut into quarters,
and mix with 3 ½ oz **raspberries**, 3 ½ oz **blueberries**, 2 tbsp **lime juice**,
and 2 tbsp confectioners' sugar. **2** Beat ⅞ cup **whipping cream** and 1 tbsp
confectioners' sugar until stiff. Add 3 ½ oz **coconut-flavored yoghourt**,
3 tbsp **coconut liqueur** or **syrup**, and the grated zest of 1 **lime**, and beat
again. Fill the puff pastry shells with this cream mixture and the berries.
Sprinkle with coconut flakes. Serve with the remaining cream mixture.

Preparation time: 20 minutes. **Per serving:** 7 g P, 38 g F, 40 g C = 538 kcal (2250 kJ).

Sangria Jelly

The Spanish national drink can now be enjoyed with a spoon.
Enjoy a breath of Majorca on your balcony.

Serves 6: 1 Soak 4 sheets of **white** and 2 of **red gelatin** in cold water.
Remove the seeds from 10 oz each of **honeydew melon**, **watermelon**,
and **Cantaloupe melon** each, and cut into small pieces. Bring 2¼ cups
red wine, 1 **cinnamon stick**, the peeled zest of ½ untreated **orange**,
1 tbsp **vanilla sugar**, and ⅓ cup **sugar** to the boil, and cook without a
lid to reduce the liquid to 1 cup. **2** Pour through a strainer into a bowl.
Squeeze the gelatin and dissolve into the hot liquid. Stir in 1 cup **orange
juice**. Put the pieces of melon in 6 glasses (with a capacity of 1 cup each)
and fill with the red wine mixture. Allow to set overnight in the refrigerator.
Delicious served with vanilla sauce.

* **Preparation time:** 30 minutes (plus cooling time).
  Per serving: 3 g P, 0 g F, 28 g C = 144 kcal (604 kJ).

Greek Country Salad

The best-seller at any barbecue party! It is also delicious served with rice.

Serves 4: 1 Peel 14 oz of **cucumbers**, cut in half, and then into large cubes. Cut 1 ¼ lb **tomatoes** into eight segments each. Cut 1 **onion** into rings. Wash and prepare 18 oz **yellow bell peppers** and cut into large strips. Crumble 9 oz **Feta** cheese coarsely. Strip the leaves of ¼ bunch of **oregano** (or **parsley**) and mince coarsely. **2** Put all the ingredients and 3 ½ oz **ripe olives** with pits in a bowl. Mince 2 **cloves of garlic** and mix together with 3 tbsp **lemon juice**, 6 tbsp **olive oil**, salt, 1 pinch **sugar**, and pepper. Pour the vinaigrette over the rest of the ingredients and mix well.

* **Preparation time:** 20 minutes.
  Per serving: 14 g P, 36 g F, 12 g C = 432 kcal (1811 kJ).

Spicy Ground Beef Kebabs

This spicy South-eastern European specialty is also widely known to many under the name Cevapcici.

Serves 4: 1 Finely dice 1 **onion**, 1 **clove of garlic**, and ⅞ oz **red bell peppers**. Add to 14 oz **ground beef** together with 1 **egg**, 3 tbsp **breadcrumbs**, and 1 tsp dried **thyme**, and knead the mixture until it becomes a smooth paste. Season generously with salt, pepper, and hot **paprika powder**. Make 8 small sausage-shaped rolls (about 3¼ in long) with slightly oiled hands. **2** Stick on 8 metal or wooden skewers and cook under a hot broiler for about 8–10 minutes. Cut 1 untreated lemon in segments. Broil briefly. Delicious with a green salad with chili vinaigrette.

* **Preparation time:** 25 minutes.
  Per serving: 23 g P, 26 g F, 8 g C = 263 kcal (1103 kJ).

Cold Tomato Sauce

Two reasons to try this sauce: rubbing the tomatoes on a grater is an excellent way to get rid of stress. And as a regards taste, it is a revelation.

Serves 4: 1 Rub generous 1 lb of firm ripe **vine tomatoes** on the coarse side of a grater until only the skin remains. It is best to stand the grater in a bowl to do this and to press hard on the tomato. Mince 1 **red onion**. Stir 8 tbsp **olive oil** and 2 tbsp **paprika paste** into the tomato mass. Season generously with salt and pepper. **2** Cook 14 oz **spaghetti** following the instructions on the packet. Tear the leaves of 1 bunch of **basil** into coarse pieces. Drain the spaghetti and immediately stir in the cold tomato sauce. Stir in the basil and sprinkle 1½ oz **Parmesan** on top.

* **Preparation time:** 30 minutes.
  Per serving: 17 g P, 27 g F, 73 g C = 606 kcal (2537 kJ).

Exotic Tomato Sauce

A sauce from the distant Far East: enriched with coconut milk, ginger and coriander, these gnocchi have acquired a deliciously exotic taste.

For 4 portions: 1 Cut 2 **onions** and 1 **clove of garlic** into small cubes. Cut generous 1 lb **tomatoes** into 2 in large cubes. Peel and finely grate 1 oz raw **ginger**. Heat 2 tbsp **oil**, add the onions and fry until light brown. Add the garlic and ginger and fry briefly. Stir 1 tsp each of ground **cumin**, **coriander**, and **paprika**, and ¼ tsp each of **turmeric** and **chili powder** (or replace all the spices with 3 tsp of **curry powder**), and fry briefly. **2** Add the tomatoes and 1¾ cups **coconut milk**, then season with salt. Cover and simmer over medium heat for 10 minutes. Cook 1 lb 12 oz fresh **gnocchi** following the instructions on the packet. Adjust the seasoning if necessary and stir into the gnocchi. Sprinkle with 2 tbsp **cilantro** (or **flat-leaved parsley**) and 1 oz roasted **peanuts**.

Preparation time: 25 minutes.
Per portion: 11 g P, 27 g F, 76 g C = 598 kcal (2512 kJ).

Black Forest Cherry Jelly

Treat yourself at breakfast with cherry jelly, enhanced by a delicate chocolate taste.

For about 5½ cups: 1 Wash and prepare 2⅔ lb **sour cherries** and pit. Weigh 2 lb 3 oz **cherries** and put in tall pan with 2¼ cups **preserving sugar** (2:1), and leave for 1 hour to draw the juice. Then puree half the fruit in the pan with a hand-blender [ask me]. Add the pulp of 1 **vanilla bean** as well as the pod. Bring to the boil over high heat while stirring with a wooden spoon. Allow to cook over high heat for 3 minutes starting from the time it began to make bubbles. **2** Stir in 4 tbsp clear **chocolate liqueur** (for instance Crème de Cacao). Rinse clean jars with chocolate liqueur and immediately fill with the hot jelly. Close the jars with screw-top lids and turn upside down for 5 minutes.

Preparation time: 30 minutes (plus drawing and cooling time).
Per tsp: 0 g P, 0 g F, 4 g C = 17 kcal (72 kJ).

Blackberry, Strawberry and Lime Jelly

A treat for breakfast: refreshing and fruity with a rich berry taste.

For about 5½ cups: 1 Thinly peel 1 **untreated lime** using a potato peeler and cut into thin strips. Mix some **pectin** or pectin sugar according to the instructions with 2¼ cups light **brown sugar**. Put in a pan, add lb 2 oz prepared **strawberries**, cut into quarters (about 1 lb 5 oz gross), 1 lb 2 oz **blackberries**, 5 tbsp **lime juice**, and the zest of a lime, and mix well. Leave to draw for 30 minutes. **2** Puree half the mass in the pan with a hand-held blender. Bring to the boil over high heat, while stirring with a wooden spoon. Cook over high heat for 3 minutes from the time the mixture started bubbling. Spoon immediately in clean jars. Close the jars with screw-top lids and turn upside down for 5 minutes.

* **Preparation time:** 20 minutes
  (plus drawing and cooling time).
  Per tsp: 0 g P, 0 g F, 3 g C = 15 kcal (63 kJ).

Bream in Foil

A refined gourmet dish for the calorie-conscious. Cooked in foil, this low-fat fish stays tender and juicy.

For 4 portions: 1 Grease 4 pieces of **aluminum foil** (16 x 16 in) with **olive oil**. Put 1 **fillet of bream** or **rosefish** (5 oz each) on each piece of aluminum foil. Season the fish with salt, pepper, and **lemon juice**. **2** Place 1 sprig of **basil** and **parsley** on the fish. Then garnish each fillet with 5 **cherry tomatoes** and 5 **green olives**. **3** Wrap in aluminum foil to make small parcels. Cook under the broiler at a medium-hot setting for 8–9 minutes without turning.

* **Preparation time:** 25 minutes.
  Per portion: 29 g P, 12 g F, 3 g C = 240 kcal (1008 kJ).

Turkey and Radish Salad

Quick and refreshing: tender turkey meat with green salad with radishes.

For 2 portions: 1 Mince 1 **onion**. Wash and prepare 1 **head of lettuce**, spin dry and tear the bigger leaves into large pieces. Wash and prepare 1 bunch of **pink radishes** and grate thinly or cut into thin slices. Peel 7 oz of **white radish** and grate or cut into thin slices. Strip the leaves off 4 sprigs of **chervil** and tear coarsely. **2** Cut 2 **turkey escalopes** (about 4 ¼ oz each) into three. Fry briskly in hot **oil** for 1–2 minutes on each side, season with salt and pepper. Remove from the pan, wrap in aluminum foil and put to one side. Fry the onions in the cooking juices with ¼ tsp **sugar**. Then add 2 tbsp **lemon juice**, 4 tbsp **vegetable stock**, 4 tbsp oil, and 2 tsp **creamed horseradish**. Stir in salt and pepper. **3** Carefully stir the sauce and chervil into the salad and arrange on the plates with the turkey escalopes.

* **Preparation time:** 30 minutes. **Per portion:** 32 g P, 33 g F, 8 g C = 463 kcal (1937 kJ).

Coconut Yoghourt Mousse

A heavenly coconut dessert with raspberries and nectarines:
pure delight and without any chocolate.

For 4 portions:

8 coconut balls
(coconut-covered wafer
with cream filling)

4 sheets clear gelatin

10 oz full fat yoghourt

grated zest of 1 lime

4 tbsp lime juice

4 tbsp confectioners' sugar

6 tbsp coconut syrup

⅝ cup whipping cream

2 nectarines

3 ½ oz raspberries

1 Mince the coconut balls. Soak the gelatin in cold water. Stir together the yoghourt, lime zest, 2 tbsp lime juice, and 2 tbsp confectioners' sugar. Heat 4 tbsp coconut syrup and dissolve the squeezed gelatin in it. Put this mixture in the refrigerator to set. As soon as it begins to set, beat the cream until stiff and add it to the coconut mixture together with the minced coconut balls.

2 Spoon this creamy coconut mixture into a bowl or 4 individual ramekins. Refrigerate for at least 3 hours. Wash the nectarines, cut in half, remove the pit, and cut into thin slices. Add 2 tbsp confectioners' sugar, 2 tbsp lime juice, 2 tbsp coconut syrup, and raspberries, and mix well.

3 Using a spoon dipped in hot water, scoop out dollops and garnish with the fruit.

* **Preparation time:** 25 minutes (plus cooling time).
 Per portion: 7 g P, 23 g F, 41 g C = 414 kcal (1734 kJ).

CONFECTIONER'S TIP
When is the mixture set enough
for the ingredients to be folded in?
Take a spatula and make a "road".
If it remains visible, it means
that the mixture is ready
for the whipped cream and
coconut balls to be added.

Stuffed Escalope Rolls

Veal which is rich in protein has a very delicate taste. If your supermarket does not have any veal, you can use turkey instead.

For 4 portions: 1 Cut the crust off 2 slices of **white bread** and crumble finely. Mince 1 **clove of garlic**. Mix together 3½ oz **herb fromage frais**, **crumbled bread**, the grated rind of ¼ **lemon (untreated)**, 2–3 tbsp minced **basil**, and garlic. Soak 24 **toothpicks** in water. **2** Put 4 thin **veal escalopes** (4½ oz each) between 2 sheets of Saran wrap and beat with a pan to make them thinner. Straighten slightly and cut in half. Season with salt and pepper. **3** Spread ⅛ of the fromage frais on each of the escalopes, leaving an edge of ⅝ in free all round. Fold the escalope inwards and secure tightly with the toothpicks. Brush with **oil** and broil for about 10–12 minutes. **Tip:** It is even easier to use a mallet to flatten the escalopes.

* **Preparation time:** 30 minutes. **Per portion:** 30 g P, 13 g F, 8 g C = 275 kcal (1148 kJ).

Quesadillas

Quesadillas can be prepared ahead in the morning: covered with Saran wrap, they will remain fresh for several hours in the refrigerator.

For 4 portions: 1 Mix together 4½ oz grated **Edam cheese** and 4½ oz **mature Gouda**. Cut 2 **green sweet peppers** into rings. Mince 2 **Jalapeños** or other **green chili peppers** (from a jar). **2** Put 4 **wheat tortillas** (about 7 in in diameter) on the work top. Divide the cheese, peppers, chili peppers, and 2 tbsp **minced onion** between them. **3** Cover with 4 more tortillas and press down. 4 Broil under a medium-hot broiler for 3–4 minutes on each side.

* **Preparation time:** 25 minutes.
  Per portion: 22 g P, 22 g F, 42 g C = 454 kcal (1904 kJ).

Pork Medallions with Apricot Mustard

Mustard may be used to season all kinds of dishes: sweet apricots for instance. The sauce is also an ideal accompaniment to white fish.

For 2 portions:

7 oz ripe apricots

1 onion

2 tbsp oil

2 tsp sugar

1–2 tbsp white wine vinegar

2 oz hot mustard

2 oz prepared mustard

6 pork medallions
(2 oz each)

salt

coarsely ground black pepper

1 clove of garlic

2 sprigs rosemary

1 Cut the apricots in half, remove the pits and mince coarsely. Mince the onion. Heat 1 tbsp oil in a pan and fry the onion over medium heat until transparent.

2 Add the apricots and sprinkle with sugar. Add the vinegar and cook for 4–5 minutes.

3 Leave to cool, then stir in the two kinds of mustard.

4 Season the medallions with salt and pepper. Heat 1 tbsp oil in a pan and fry the meat, the whole clove of garlic and rosemary over medium heat for 3–4 minutes on each side and serve with the apricot mustard.

* **Preparation time:** 40 minutes (plus cooling time).
  Per portion: 37 g P, 15 g F, 19 g C = 365 kcal (1531 kJ).

A SWEETENER FOR A SPICY ACCOMPANIMENT
Stored in a well-sealed jar the apricot mustard will keep for about ten days in the refrigerator. What else can it be served with? With Spanish Manchego cheese, roast pork or salami. There should be no limit to your culinary imagination!

The agony of choice

ON THE CALENDAR, this is the month when autumn starts. But from a culinary point of view, things are not so clear-cut, because we are in a wonderful transitional stage: on the one hand there are still plenty of summery delights, but there are also some delicious autumn foods. In fact, as far as food goes we can choose between summer and autumn!

Pasta Patchwork

A symphony of green and red vegetables and crispy bacon!
A delicious pasta dish without any cream.

For 4 portions:

1 red and 1 yellow sweet pepper

2 onions

3½ oz bacon (thinly sliced)

14 oz pasta
(for instance, tagliatelle)

salt

4 tbsp oil

2 tbsp butter

⅝ cup vegetable stock

3 oz Comté cheese1 bunch chives

pepper

rose paprika powder

1 Wash and prepare the peppers and mince coarsely. Mince the onions and cut the bacon into wide strips. Break the pasta into pieces and cook in plenty of boiling salted water, following the instructions on the packet.

2 Meanwhile, heat 2 tbsp oil in a non-stick pan, add the bacon and fry until crisp. Remove from the pan. Now add 2 tbsp oil and butter in the pan, add the peppers and onions and fry for 2 minutes. Add the stock and simmer without a lid for 3–4 minutes. Grate or cut the cheese very thinly. Cut the chives into small rings. Season generously with salt, pepper, and paprika powder.

3 Drain the pasta and stir in the chives, bacon, and peppers. Sprinkle the Comté cheese on top.

* **Preparation time:** 30 minutes.
  Per portion: 23 g P, 32 g F, 71 g C = 676 kcal (2832 kJ).

BREAKING THE PASTA
You can use many kinds of pasta for this dish: from wide tagliatelle to lasagne sheets. Just break the pasta into large pieces and cook al dente in plenty of water.

Oatcakes with a Creamy Topping

Simple but delicious: cook bread dough in a pan and enjoy this crispy crêpe with a creamy onion topping.

For 4 portions: 1 Make the bread dough using 9 oz **wheat and rye bread dough** mixture, following the instructions on the packet. Leave to rise in a warm place for about 30 minutes. Stir together 9 oz **whipping cream** with 2 tbsp minced **chives**, salt, pepper, and 1 pinch of **sweet paprika** until smooth. Cut the white and the green of 4 **scallions** into thin rings. **2** Knead the dough again and make 4 balls of similar size. Roll out on a floured surface to make thin round crêpes (about 9 ¼ in in diameter). Heat a non-stick pan and cook the crêpes, one after the other, over medium heat for 3–4 minutes on each side. After turning the crêpe, spread ¼ of the cream on each crêpe. Sprinkle scallions on top and cut the crêpes into bite-sized pieces.

* **Preparation time:** 45 minutes (plus rising time).
Per portion: 8 g P, 15 g F, 49 g C = 372 kcal (1568 kJ).

Bread and Peppers Gratin

This dish will bring color to your dining table. And it is very easy to make!

For 2 portions: 1 Cut 1 **red** and 1 **yellow bell pepper** into eight and remove the seeds. Cut 10 ½ oz **stale bread** into slices. Mix together in a bowl with 1 tbsp minced **parsley**, 1 tsp minced **rosemary** and 2 thinly sliced **scallions**. **2** Rub an oven-proof dish with 1 peeled **clove of garlic** and grease. Mince the garlic, add to the bread and put everything in the gratin dish. Stir well so that all the ingredients are well distributed. **3** Beat 3 **eggs** into 1 cup **milk**, and ½ cup **whipping cream**. Season with salt and pepper. Pour over the bread mixture. **4** Bake in the hot oven, preheated to 375 degrees (fan oven not recommended) on the second shelf from the bottom for 30–35 minutes. Delicious served with green salad.

Preparation time: 45 minutes.
Per portion: 30 g P, 39 g F, 87 g C = 826 kcal (3463 kJ).

Breaded Chicken Breast Strips

Cooked in a tasty, crisp breadcrumb coating, the chicken remains beautifully juicy.

For 2 portions: 1 Mix together 2½ oz **breadcrumbs**, 1 tsp of each minced **parsley**, minced **thyme**, **rosemary**, and **sage**. Beat 1 **egg**. **2** Cut 14 oz **chicken breast** without skin or bones into strips. Season with salt and coat in **flour**, then dip into the egg and roll into the breadcrumbs. Fry in plenty of hot **oil** over medium to high heat until golden brown all round.

Preparation time: 25 minutes. Per portion: 55 g P, 36 g F, 32 g C = 668 kcal (2797 kJ).

317

Shallots with Balsamic Vinegar

A little sweet, a little sour, a little sharp – these shallots soon become quite addictive.

For 2 portions: 1 Peel 10½ oz very small **shallots**. Then put the shallots in a small pan with 5 tsp **brown sugar**, ⅞ cup **balsamic vinegar**, and ½ cup **vegetable stock**, and bring to the boil and reduce over high heat for 8–10 minutes. Stir occasionally. **2** Remove from the heat, season with salt and pepper and sprinkle with **fresh thyme** if desired.

* **Preparation time:** 20 minutes.
  Per portion: 2 g P, 0 g F, 55 g C = 232 kcal (974 kJ).

Roast Eggplants

No antipasto menu is complete without eggplant. Combined with
zucchinis and roasted in the oven, it is easy to make and very tasty.

For 2 portions: 1 Wash and prepare 1 small **eggplant** and cut lengthways
into slices ⅛-in thick, sprinkle with salt and leave to stand for 10 minutes. Rinse thoroughly and dab dry. Wash and prepare 2 medium-sized
zucchinis and cut lengthways into ⅛-in thick slices. Mince 2–3 **cloves
of garlic**. **2** Sprinkle a cookie sheet with 2–3 tbsp **olive oil** and scatter
2 tsp dried **oregano**. Arrange the slices of eggplant and zucchini next
to each on the tray. Sprinkle with 1 tbsp olive oil. **3** Bake in the oven, preheated to 430 degrees (fan oven not recommended) on the second shelf
from the top for 15–20 minutes. Sprinkle with 2 tbsp **lemon juice** and
2 tbsp olive oil. Season with freshly ground pepper and salt, if necessary.
Serve with salami if you like.

* **Preparation time:** 35 minutes. **Per portion:** 4 g P, 26 g F, 9 g C = 283 kcal (1189 kJ).

Spinach Pouches

Crispy because of the puff pastry, soft because of the spinach and Feta, delicious because of our recipe.

For 2 portions: 1 Defrost 14 oz **<u>frozen spinach</u>** and squeeze out as water as possible. Defrost 1 lb **<u>frozen puff pastry</u>**, following the instructions of the packet, and roll out on a lightly floured surface to make 2 rectangles 16 x 8 in each. Crumble 7 oz **<u>Feta</u>** and mix together with 1 tbsp **<u>olive oil</u>** and 1 tsp **<u>dried oregano</u>**. Mince 1 medium **<u>onion</u>** and 1 **<u>clove of garlic</u>**. **2** Heat 2 tbsp olive oil in a pan, add the onion and garlic and fry for 1 minute over high heat. Add the spinach and fry for 2–3 minutes. Add the 2 medium **<u>eggs</u>** and Feta. Season with salt, pepper, and **<u>nutmeg</u>**. **3** Spoon the spinach mixture on one half of the puff pastry rectangles, leaving an edge ¾ in free all round. Brush the edges with beaten egg and fold the other half on top of the filling. Press the edges down with a fork, make a hole in the puff pastry and brush over with **<u>egg yolk</u>**. **4** Put on a tray lined with waxed paper and bake in the oven, preheated to 390 degrees (fan oven 355 degrees) on the second shelf from the bottom for 20 minutes.

* **Preparation time:** 45 minutes. Per portion: 46 g P, 96 g F, 82 g C = 1373 kcal (5753 kJ).

Mushrooms with Basil and Zucchinis with Mint

The herbs add a refreshing note to mushrooms while the mint transform the zucchinis into a sophisticated dish.

Serves 2 – mushrooms with basil: 1 Mince 1 small **onion**. Cut 1 **clove of garlic** in half. Wash and prepare 7 oz **mushrooms** and cut the larger ones in half. Heat 2 tbsp **olive oil** in a pan, add mushrooms and fry briefly. Season with salt, pepper, and 1 pinch of **sugar**. Add 1 tbsp minced **rosemary**, 8 tbsp **vegetable stock**, and 2 tbsp **balsamic vinegar**. **2** Cover and simmer for 10 minutes over low heat. Then stir in 2 tbsp olive oil and adjust the seasoning if necessary. Leave to stand for at least 3 hours. Sprinkle with 2 tbsp **basil leaves**.

Serves 2 – zucchinis with mint: 1 Cut 2 small **zucchinis** into slices ⅛-in thick. Heat 2 tbsp **olive oil** in a pan and fry the zucchinis until golden brown. Add 7 tbsp **white wine** and reduce to thicken. Remove the zucchinis from the heat. Season with salt and pepper. **2** Strip the leaves off 2–3 stems of **mint** and cut into thin strips. Stir into the zucchinis and serve warm.

✳ **Preparation time:** 25 minutes (plus marinating time).
  Per serving (mushrooms with basil): 3 g P, 20 g F, 5 g C = 210 kcal (881 kJ).
  Per serving (zucchinis with mint): 2 g P, 10 g F, 4 g C = 123 kcal (517 kJ).

Spanish-Style Rabbit

Hasta luego, rabbit: seasoned with saffron and sherry and cooked with chickpeas and white raisins, this dish is a real delicacy.

For 4 portions: 1 Season 4 **rabbit legs** (about 9 oz) with salt and pepper and fry briskly in a 2 tbsp **oil** in a pan. Meanwhile cut 2 **onions** and 2 **cloves of garlic** into thin slices. Add to the pan with the rabbit and fry for another 2 minutes. **2** Now add 2 **bay leaves**, 2 tsp **sweet paprika**, and 2 pinches **saffron** and stir in ½ cup **dry sherry**. Pour in ⅞ cup **vegetable stock** and add 1 ¾ oz white **raisins**. Bring to the boil, cover and braise over medium heat for 55 minutes. **3** Drain and rinse 1 can of **chickpeas** (15 oz drained weight) in a strainer and add 10 minutes before the end of the cooking time. **4** After cooking, season with salt and pepper, and sprinkle generously with minced **flat-leaved parsley**.

* **Preparation time:** 1 hour 10 minutes.
  Per portion: 43 g P, 10 g F, 21 g C = 372 kcal (1557 kJ).

Country Soup

*You will be richly rewarded for all the time spent preparing the vegetables:
this soup has all the taste and fragrance of the south.*

For 2–4 portions: **1** Mince 2 **onions** and 2 **cloves of garlic**. Remove the
stringy fibers from 3½ oz **celery** and dice very finely. Heat 2 tbsp **olive oil**
in a pan, add the onions and garlic and cook for 5–6 minutes while stirring. **2** Add 2 tins **minced tomatoes** (each 14 oz drained weight) and
3½ cups **vegetable stock**. Cover and cook for 25 minutes. Season with
salt, pepper and 1–2 tbsp **sugar**. **3** Meanwhile wash and prepare 7 oz
green beans and cook for 9 minutes in salted water. Drain and run under
cold water. **4** At the end of the cooking time, drain 1 can **artichoke hearts**
(15 oz drained weight) and cut into quarters. Add to the soup with the
green beans and 1 tsp minced **thyme** and cook for about 1 minute. Serve
with bread.

Preparation time: 40 minutes.
Per portion (out of 4 portions): 6 g P, 5 g F, 16 g C = 146 kcal (616 kJ).

Layered Blueberry Dessert

There is no better way to enjoy blueberries: with creamy curd and crisp nutty-flavored almond cookies.

For 2 portions: 1 Stir together 9 oz **creamy curd**, the grated rind of ½ **orange (untreated)**, 4–5 tbsp **orange juice**, 1 tbsp **vanilla sugar**, and 1 tbsp **sugar**. Beat 125 g 4½ oz **whipping cream** until stiff and fold into the curd. **2** Select 4½ oz **blueberries**. Put 1¾ oz **Cantuccini** or other Italian almond cookies in a freezer bag and crumble coarsely using a wooden rolling-pin. **3** Now arrange layers of creamy curd, crushed cookies, and blueberries in a bowl. The last layer should be curd, garnished with a few blueberries.

Preparation time: 10 minutes. **Per portion:** 15 g P, 32 g F, 39 g C = 508 kcal (2129 kJ).

Strawberry Ice Cream on a Stick

This is the perfect solution when you have a lot of strawberries which are no longer good enough for cakes and pastries. You can also use other fruit in this recipe.

For 6 portions: **1** Wash and prepare 10 ½ oz **strawberries**, mince coarsely, and put in a tall container. Add **strawberry syrup** (or **raspberry syrup**) and puree with a hand-held blender until very smooth. **2** Put this mixture in 6 ice cream molds (4 tbsp) and freeze for at least 3 hours in the freezer compartment. Warm the molds briefly in your hands and remove the ice cream from the mold.

* **Preparation time:** 10 minutes (plus cooling time).
Per portion: 0 g P, 0 g F, 14 g C = 64 kcal (266 kJ).

White Wine Soup

A frothy soup with crisp croutons and masses of parsley which will be enjoyed by all.

For 4–6 portions: 1 Bring 3½ cups <u>**vegetable stock**</u> to the boil and add 1¾ cups <u>**white wine**</u> (Sauvignon Blanc) and ⅞ cup <u>**whipping cream**</u>. Bring back to the boil and reduce for 10 minutes over high heat without a lid. **2** Cut 2¾ oz of <u>**baguette**</u> into very thin slices and put on a cookie sheet. Toast in the oven, preheated to 390 degrees (fan oven 355 degrees) on the second shelf from the top for 6–8 minutes until gold-brown. Remove the leaves from ½ bunch <u>**parsley**</u> and mince. **3** Put 6 <u>**egg yolks**</u> in a large bowl and add the soup gradually while stirring. Return the soup to the pan and beat continuously over medium heat to thicken. (Careful: do not allow the soup to boil because it may curdle). **4** Season the soup with salt, pepper, <u>**nutmeg**</u>, and <u>**sugar**</u>. Serve in bowls, garnished with croutons and parsley.

Preparation time: 40 minutes.
Per portion: 24 g P, 37 g F, 9 g C = 460 kcal (1930 kJ).

Duck Breast with Pears

Even in the kitchen there are romances and marriages made in heaven. For instance, duck and pears.

For 4 portions: 1 Wash and spin-dry 5 oz **corn salad**. **2** Slash the skin of 2 **duck breasts** (7 oz each) in a diamond-shaped pattern, using a sharp knife. Place the duck breasts with skin down in a cold pan and fry over medium heat for 7–8 minutes. Season with salt and pepper. Only then turn the breasts and fry for 1 more minute. Wrap in aluminum foil and allow to rest. **3** Pour the fat out of the pan until there is only 1 tbsp left. Cut 2 **pears** into slices, core and fry the slices in the hot fat until light brown. Add 1 ½ oz minced **walnuts**. Season with salt and pepper. **4** For the vinaigrette, stir together 3 tbsp **raspberry vinegar** and 5–6 tbsp **walnut oil** and pour over the salad. Cut the duck breasts into slices and arrange on plates with the salad and sliced pears. Sprinkle 2 ½ oz crumbled **Roquefort** or other blue cheese on top.

Preparation time: 40 minutes. **Per portion:** 24 g P, 37 g F, 9 g C = 460 kcal (1930 kJ).

Flat Bread Pizza

A very quick, very delicious variation on the classic Margherita pizza.

For 2 portions: 1 Coarsely mince 3½ oz **dried tomatoes** and 2 **cloves of garlic**, and put in a tall container. Add 3 crushed **juniper berries** and 6 tbsp **olive oil** and puree everything with a blender. Season with salt and pepper. Cut 3 **tomatoes** into slices. Drain 4½ oz **Mozzarella**, wipe dry and cut into slices. **2** Cut 1 round **flat bread** (about 8 in) crosswise into half. Place the two halves on a cookie sheet with the cut surface facing upward. Spread the pureed tomatoes on top and garnish with the sliced tomatoes and cheese. Bake in the oven preheated to 390 degrees (fan oven 355 degrees) on the second shelf from the bottom for 5–8 minutes. Strip the leaves of 3 sprigs of **basil** and sprinkle on the pizza just before serving. **Tip:** If you want a more substantial meal, you can replace the Mozzarella by Feta.

* **Preparation time:** 20 minutes. **Per portion:** 22 g P, 48 g F, 68 g C = 800 kcal (3347 kJ).

Pasta and Nut Salad

The aristocrat among salads: it would difficult to improve on this salad which owes its elegance and original flavor to the addition of nuts and maple syrup.

For 2 portions: 1 Cook 5 oz **pasta** (for instance mini-penne) in plenty of salted water, following the instructions on the packet. Mince 3 tbsp **walnuts** and toast together with 2 tbsp each of **pine nuts** and minced **filberts** in a pan without fat. Stir together 4 tbsp **lemon juice**, salt, pepper, and tsp **maple syrup** (or **honey**). Gradually beat in 4 tbsp **olive oil** and 2 tbsp **walnut oil** (or more olive oil). **2** Cut the white and pale green of 3 **scallions** into thin rings. Mince the leaves of 4 stems of flat-leaved parsley and cut the **cress** from 1 box. Drain the pasta thoroughly and add to the lemon sauce. Add the nuts, herbs, and scallions, and adjust the seasoning if necessary.

* **Preparation time:** 25 minutes.
  Per portion: 15 g P, 52 g F, 67 g C = 807 kcal (3380 kJ).

Grated Apple and Potato Crêpe

A very successful combination: the delicate smoky taste of salmon and the sweet acidity of apples with the slight sharpness of horseradish.

For 2 portions: 1 Peel 1 <u>onion</u> and grate on a hand-grater. Put in a bowl. Peel and wash 10½ oz **potatoes** and grate coarsely on the grater. Wash 1 <u>apple</u> (5 oz) and grate coarsely as far as the core. **2** Put both in the bowl with the onion and stir in 1 <u>egg</u>, 2 tbsp <u>flour</u>, 1 tsp minced <u>parsley</u>, salt and pepper. **3** Heat 3 tbsp oil in a non-stick pan and fry the 6 flat crêpes (about 3–4 minutes on each side). **4** Put 5 oz <u>smoked salmon</u> on the crêpes and garnish with 1 tbsp creamy <u>horseradish</u> and a little <u>dill</u>.

* **Preparation time:** 45 minutes. **Per portion:** 24 g P, 39 g F, 40 g C = 610 kcal (2553 kJ).

Cubed Smoked Loin of Pork

This salted pork is delicious with crisp green beans cooked in white wine.

For 2 portions: 1 Wash and prepare 3½ oz **green beans** and cut in half diagonally. Cook for 6 minutes in boiling saltwater, drain and run under cold water. **2** Cut 9 oz **smoked saddle of pork** without bone into cubes. Mince 2 **onions**. **3** Heat 1 tbsp **oil** in a pan and fry the cubed pork briskly all round over high heat. Remove from the pan. Pour 1 tbsp oil into the pan, add the onions and fry briefly over medium heat, add the beans, ½ cup **white wine**, cover and cook for 2–3 minutes. Return the meat to the pan, Season with salt and pepper. Sprinkle **lemon balm** on top before serving.

* **Preparation time:** 20 minutes. **Per portion:** 25 g P, 16 g F, 5 g C = 272 kcal (1142 kJ).

Melon Granita

Make your own dessert: with very little trouble and a lot of cooling time, it is without doubt one of the most refreshing ice desserts.

For 4 portions: 1 Bring ¼ cup **sugar** and ½ cup water to the boil, stirring occasionally. Put to one side and leave to cool a little. Peel 1 **watermelon**, remove the seeds and cut into large pieces. **2** Put the pieces of melon, 3–4 tbsp **lemon juice**, and the sugar syrup in a tall container, and puree finely with a hand blender. Strip the leaves off 1–2 stems of mint and cut into thin strips. Add the **mint** to the pureed melon and transfer to a shallow dish. Put in the freezer. **3** After 1 hour prick about with a fork. Then repeat every 3–4 hours. Loosen the granita again with the fork before serving it in cooled glasses.

* **Preparation time:** 15 minutes (plus freezing time).
  Per portion: 0 g P, 0 g F, 18 g C = 77 kcal (321 kJ).

Ice Cream Sandwich

Who says that ice cream should always be served in a bowl? It looks much prettier as a cold sandwich, served with a sauce of mixed berries.

For 2 portions: 1 Take 5 oz <u>vanilla ice cream</u> and divide into 4 scoops. Put 1 scoop on 1 <u>petit-beurre cookie</u> and cover with 1 other cookie. Make 3 more sandwiches in the same way. Keep the sandwiches in the freezer until serving. **2** Bring to the boil 7 oz <u>mixed berries</u> (<u>raspberries and blueberries</u>), 2–3 tbsp <u>Amaretto</u>, 1 tbsp <u>vanilla sugar</u>, and ¼ cup <u>sugar</u>. Stir 1 level tbsp <u>cornstarch</u> into 2 tbsp <u>lemon juice</u> and add this to the berries. Bring to the boil and remove from the heat. Allow to cool completely, stirring occasionally. **3** Take the ice cream sandwiches out of the freezer shortly before serving and garnish with the berries compote. **Tip:** when berries are out of season, you can use frozen berries.

* **Preparation time:** 10 minutes (plus freezing time).
  Per portion: 12 g P, 27 g F, 97 g C = 702 kcal (2941 kJ).

Redcurrant Crumble Meringue

It crackles quite irresistibly: puff pastry with meringue and redcurrants.

For 8 pieces: 1 Defrost 9 oz **frozen puff pastry**. Mix ½ cup **flour**, ½ tsp **cinnamon**, 2 tbsp softened **butter**, and 2 tbsp **sugar** together to a crumble consistency. Wash and prepare 7 oz **redcurrants**. Moisten the sheets of puff pastry with a little water, put on top of each other and roll out on a floured surface to make a rectangle 16 x 8 in. Cut into 8 4-in squares. Prick several times with a fork and put on a cookie sheet lined with waxed paper. **2** Bake in the oven, preheated to 390 degrees (fan oven not recommended) on the lowest shelf for 10 minutes (fan oven). Beat 2 **egg whites** stiff with a pinch of salt, carefully add ¼ cup sugar and beat for another 2 minutes. Spread 3½ oz **redcurrant jelly** on the hot puff pastry and sprinkle the redcurrants on top. Cover with the meringue and sprinkle the crumble on top. Bake for another 20–25 minutes.

* **Preparation time: 1 hour. Per portion:** 4 g P, 11 g F, 38 g C = 265 kcal (1108 kJ).

Sweet and Sharp Crunchy Nuts

Careful: this can be addictive! No one can resist these nibbles with beer or wine.

For 2 portions: 1 Put 5 oz **cashew nuts** and 5 oz **almonds** in a bowl. Crumble 1 dried **chili pod**, mix with 1–2 tbsp liquid **honey** and 1 tbsp **oil** and pour over the nuts. **2** Season with salt, pepper, and 1 tsp **hot paprika**, and mix well. **3** Put on a cookie sheet, lined with waxed paper. Bake in the oven, preheated to 430 degrees (fan oven 390 degrees) for 9–12 minutes, turning the nuts over several times. Remove from the oven and leave to cool.

Preparation time: 20 minutes. **Per portion:** 9 g P, 26 g F, 10 g C = 307 kcal (1284 kJ).

Green Beans with Almonds and Chili Peppers

*Often it is the addition of unimportant ingredients
that transform an ordinary vegetable into a sophisticated dish.*

For 2 portions: 1 Wash and prepare 14 oz **green beans** and cook for
7 minutes in boiling salted water. **2** Meanwhile, toast 1 oz **flaked almonds**
in a pan without fat. Cut 1 **red bell pepper** lengthways in half, remove
the seeds and cut lengthways into strips. **3** Heat 2 tbsp **olive oil** in a
pan, add the pepper, and fry over low heat. Drain the beans and add to
the pan. Now add the flaked almonds and season with salt and pepper.
Sprinkle with 1 tbsp minced **parsley** and serve.

Preparation time: 25 minutes. **Per portion:** 7 g P, 18 g F, 6 g C = 218 kcal (916 kJ).

Fried Döner Kebab

You do not need an expensive roasting spit for your döner kebab. A pan will do just as well! In addition, you can stuff it with the most delicious chicken!

For 2 portions: 1 Peel ½ **cucumber**, cut into quarters, and then into ⅕-in thick slices. Mix together the cucumber, 2 tbsp **dill**, 4 tbsp **flat-leaved parsley**, 1 tbsp **olive oil**, and 1 tbsp **lemon juice**. Season with salt and pepper. Mince 1 **clove of garlic**. Mix together the minced garlic, 5 oz **creamy yoghourt**, ½ tsp crushed dried **chili peppers**, and 1 pinch of salt. **2** Wash 2 medium-sized **tomatoes**, cut into quarters, remove the seeds and mince coarsely. Wash and prepare ½ **yellow bell pepper** and mince coarsely. Toast one round **flat loaf** (about 8 in diameter) in a pan without fat for 2–3 minutes on each side. Remove from the pan and cut so as to make 2 pouches. **3** Season the **thin slices of chicken** with ½ tsp **sweet paprika**, salt and pepper. Heat 2 tbsp olive oil, add the chicken and fry over a high heat for 2–3 minutes until golden brown. Add the tomatoes and pepper and fry for 1 more minute. Fill the pouches with alternate layers of cucumber, yoghourt, and chicken mixture and serve.

* **Preparation time:** 25 minutes. **Per portion:** 49 g P, 16 g F, 70 g C = 627 kcal (2626 kJ).

Damson and Poppyseed Cake

The perfect cake: the classic damson cake which is popular with young and old.

For 20 pieces:

2⅔ lb damsons

1 cup 2 tbsp butter or margarine

1 cup sugar

salt

3 medium eggs

4 cups flour

2 tsp baking powder

½ cup milk

½ cup whipped cream

8 tbsp ground poppy seeds

1 tbsp vanilla sugar

3 oz redcurrant jelly

1 tbsp confectioners' sugar

1 Wash and prepare the damsons, cut in half and remove the pits. Beat together the softened butter or margarine, bare 1 cup sugar, and 1 pinch of salt with the whisk attachment of the hand-held mixer for 8 minutes until very creamy. Beat in the eggs one after the other, whisking for ½ minute each time. Sift the flour and baking powder and stir in the milk and cream alternately. Quickly incorporate the poppy seeds.

2 Spread the pastry mixture in deep greased cookie sheet (16 x 12 in) and arrange the damsons on top. Mix together the vanilla sugar and 2 tbsp sugar and sprinkle over the damsons. Bake in the oven, preheated to 375 degrees (fan oven 170 degrees) on the second shelf from the bottom for 35 minutes. Warm up the jelly and spread over the hot damsons, then let the cake to cool a little. Sprinkle with confectioners' sugar.

* **Preparation time:** 1 hour (plus cooling time).
Per portion: 4 g P, 15 g F, 36 g C = 306 kcal (1280 kJ).

GRIND THE POPPY SEEDS YOURSELF

If you cannot find ready-ground poppy seeds (normally available in health food shops) you can buy poppy seeds and grind them yourself. Place the amount indicated in the list of ingredients in the freezer for 1 hour and then grind finely in the blender. This prevents the poppy seeds from becoming bitter and helps them develop their intense aroma.

Provençal Risotto

Neither the cook nor the rice should be hurried. even if your risotto arm gets tired from continuous stirring.

For 2 portions: 1 Bring 3 cups <u>**vegetable stock**</u> to the boil. Mince 1 <u>**onion**</u>.
2 Heat 2 tbsp <u>**oil**</u> in a medium-sized pan, add the onion and fry over medium heat until transparent. Now add ⅞ cup <u>**short-grain rice**</u>, 3 tsp <u>**herbs of Provence**</u>, and ½ tsp <u>**sweet paprika**</u>, and fry briefly. Add ½ cup <u>**white wine**</u> and reduce. Add ⅓ of the vegetable stock to pan. Cook without a lid over low heat for 20–25 minutes until the rice is *al dente*, stirring frequently and adding the rest of the vegetable stock little by little.
3 Wash and prepare 1 small <u>**red bell pepper**</u> (about 5 oz); wash and prepare 3½ oz <u>**zucchinis**</u> and cut into small cubes. Add to the risotto about 10 minutes before the end of the cooking time and stir in 2 tbsp grated <u>**Parmesan**</u>.

* **Preparation time:** 35–40 minutes. **Per portion:** 8 g P, 12 g F, 71 g C = 442 kcal (1850 kJ).

Baked Potatoes with Chanterelles

An ideal combination on the plate:
mushrooms and potatoes – and so easy to make.

For 2 portions: **1** Prick 4 **large potatoes** (each 6 oz) several times with a fork and rub with **olive oil**. Wrap 2 potatoes, 1 sprig **thyme**, and 1 stem of **rosemary** in waxed paper, and tie the ends like a sweet; repeat with the other 2 potatoes. Bake in a hot oven, preheated to 390 degrees (fan oven 355 degrees) on the second shelf from the bottom for 45 minutes. **2** Peel 1 small **onion** and mince. Mince 1¾ oz smoked **bacon**. Wash and prepare 9 oz **chanterelles**. Mix together 3½ oz **crème fraîche** with 1 tbsp **minced chives** and season with salt and pepper. **3** Shortly before the end of the cooking time, fry the onions and bacon together in a pan until crisp. Remove from the pan and wipe the pan. Heat 1 tbsp **oil**, add the chanterelles and fry over high heat. Return the onion-bacon mixture to the pan and season with salt and pepper. **4** Take the potatoes out of the oven and cut open. Stuff the chanterelles inside and serve with the crème fraîche.

* **Preparation time**: 1 hour. **Per portion**: 13 g P, 30 g F, 44 g C = 506 kcal (2122 kJ).

Plum Tomatoes with Arugula

A concentration of sun and aroma.

For 2 portions: 1 Cut 10 <u>plum tomatoes</u> in half. Put in a bowl with 1 tsp minced <u>rosemary</u>, 1 tsp minced <u>thyme</u>, 2 minced <u>cloves of garlic</u>, salt, pepper, 2 tbsp <u>olive oil</u>, and 1 tbsp <u>balsamic vinegar</u>. **2** Now arrange in a cookie sheet with the cut surfaces upward and cook in the oven, preheated to 355 degrees (fan oven 320 degrees) on the second shelf from the bottom for 15–20 minutes. Wash 1 ¾ oz <u>arugula</u> and spin dry. **3** Mix the arugula with the tomatoes after they are cooked.

* **Preparation time:** 30 minutes.
   Per portion: 4 g P, 11 g F, 13 g C = 166 kcal (702 kJ).

Plum Tomatoes with Mozzarella and Basil

A variation on this classic salad: it is broiled in the oven.

For 2 portions: 1 Cut 6 <u>plum tomatoes</u> into half. Put in bowl with 1 tbsp <u>dried basil</u>, 2 minced <u>cloves of garlic</u>, salt and pepper, 2 tbsp <u>olive oil</u>, and 1 tbsp <u>balsamic vinegar</u> and mix well. **2** Arrange the tomatoes on a cookie sheet with the cut surface facing upward. Drain 5 oz <u>Mozzarella</u> and mince. Distribute on the tomatoes. Bake in the oven, preheated to 375 degrees (fan oven 170 degrees) on the second shelf from the bottom for 15 minutes. **3** Strip the leaves off 2 stems <u>basil</u> and sprinkle over the tomatoes.

Preparation time: 25 minutes.
Per portion: 17 g P, 25 g F, 9 g C = 333 kcal (1398 kJ).

343

Turkish Bread Soufflé

A simple but absolutely delicious dish which tastes delicious not only on the shores of the Black Sea: unleavened bread, ground beef, and tomatoes, baked in the oven.

For 2 portions:

7 oz ground beef

3 medium eggs

2 tbsp breadcrumbs

2 tbsp minced oregano (or ½ tsp dried oregano)

salt

pepper

¼ tsp rose paprika powder

1 onion

2 cloves garlic

3 tbsp olive oil

5 oz flat bread

9 oz creamy Greek Yoghurt

¼ tsp chili powder

8 cherry tomatoes

1 Knead together the ground beef, 1 egg yolk, the breadcrumbs, 1 tbsp oregano, salt, pepper, and paprika. Mince the onion and add to the ground beef mixture with 1 crushed clove of garlic. With wet hands, shape 10 meatballs of similar size. Heat 3 tbsp oil in a pan add the meatballs and fry for 10 minutes.

2 Rub the oven-proof dish (10 x 6 in) with the cut surface of 1 halved clove of garlic. Break the flat bread into coarse chunks and put in the dish. Toast under the hot oven broiler on the middle shelf for about 4 minutes.

3 For the sauce, stir together the yoghourt with 2 egg yolks, 1–2 tbsp olive oil, salt, pepper, and chili flakes.

4 Cut the cherry tomatoes in half and add to unleavened bread together with the meatballs. Pour the yoghourt mixture on top. Bake in the oven, preheated to 355 degrees (fan oven 320 degrees) on the second shelf from the bottom for 15–20 minutes. Garnish with 1 tbsp oregano.

* **Preparation time:** 50 minutes.
  Per portion: 36 g P, 62 g F, 51 g C = 913 kcal (3826 kJ).

THE BEST CREAMINESS
Greek yoghourt is particularly food for this dish because of its firm, creamy consistency.

The laughing pumpkin

THE best time of the year for those who love cooking and especially for those who love eating. A walk to the market or even wandering through the vegetable aisle in the supermarket will fire our culinary imagination. There are mushrooms galore, pears, and apples in abundance – as well as a selection of magnificent pumpkins. Save this magnificent fruit from being dismembered and living a sad existence in a preserving jar.

Stuffed Pumpkin

A dish bursting with delicious goodness: every bit of this Hokkaido pumpkin, stuffed with spinach and ricotta, can be eaten, even the skin.

For 2 portions:

1 pumpkin (about 2¼ lb)

7 oz frozen leaf spinach (thawed and squeezed dry)

10½ oz ricotta

2 egg yolks

1 oz breadcrumbs

salt

pepper

nutmeg

1 cup vegetable stock

15 cherry tomatoes

REMOVING THE SEEDS
Cut off the top of the pumpkin and use a spoon to remove the seeds. Now you can stuff the pumpkin.

1 Cut the top off the pumpkin and remove the seeds and fibers (see photograph below).

2 Mince the spinach coarsely and add to the ricotta, egg yolk, and breadcrumbs. Season with salt, pepper, and nutmeg.

3 Season the inside of the hollowed-out pumpkin with salt and pepper. Put the stuffing in the pumpkin. Place the pumpkin in an oven-proof dish and put the pumpkin lid next to it. Pour in the stock. Bake in the oven, preheated to 375 degrees (fan oven 170 degrees) on the lowest shelf for 40 minutes.

4 10 minutes before the end of the cooking time, add the cherry tomatoes to the pan.

5 Take the pumpkin out and put the lid on, season the juices with salt and pepper, and serve separately.

* Preparation time: 1 hour 10 minutes.
 Per portion: 19 g P, 22 g F, 28 g C = 390 kcal (1633 kJ).

Fried Herb Sausages

A brilliant idea: how to create a favorite dish with the simplest ingredients in a very short time.

For 2 portions: 1 Cut 5 oz **onions** lengthways into thin slices. Cut 1 apple lengthways into quarters, core, and cut into 12 segments. Strip the leaves off 5 stems of **marjoram**. **2** Cut 10½ oz **herb-flavored sausages** into 6 pieces of similar size. Heat 3 tbsp **oil**, add the sausages, and fry for 2–3 minutes until golden brown. Remove from the pan. Add 1½ tbsp **butter** to the pan and fry the onion and apple slices until golden brown. Add the sausages and ⅔ marjoram and cook for ½ minute. Sprinkle with the rest of the marjoram and serve. Delicious with mashed potatoes.

* **Preparation time:** 20 minutes. Per portion: 22 g P, 61 g F, 16 g C = 703 kcal (2920 kJ).

Corn salad with Pears

This is and will always be one of the best salads: a winning combination of walnuts and pears.

For 2 portions: 1 Coarsely mince 2 tbsp **walnuts** and toast in a pan without fat. Cut 1 **red pear** into quarters, core and cut into long segments. Immediately sprinkle with 1 tbsp **lemon juice**. Wash and prepare 5 oz **corn salad** and spin-dry. **2** Beat together 2 tbsp lemon juice, 2 tsp **honey**, a little salt, pepper, and 4 tbsp **walnut oil** (or vegetable oil). Pour the vinaigrette over the lettuce and pear segments. Sprinkle with walnuts.

* **Preparation time:** 15 minutes. **Per portion:** 3 g P, 27 g F, 16 g C = 313 kcal (1311 kJ).

Fig Gratin

Light and fruity: gratin of figs in creamy curd.

For 2 portions: 1 Stir together
3½ oz **curd**, 1 **egg yolk** (medium),
2 tbsp **butter**, 1 packet of **vanilla
sugar**, 1 tbsp **sugar**, 1 tsp
cornstarch, and the **grated rind**
of ½ **orange (untreated)** until
creamy. Beat 1 **egg white** stiff
with 1 pinch of salt. Stir in 1 tbsp
sugar and beat for another
1–2 minutes. Carefully fold into
the curd. **2** Wash 4 **figs**, cut
into four and arrange in a deep,
oven-proof dish or in a small
baking dish. Using a teaspoon,
distribute the curd mixture over
the figs. **3** Put on a cold cookie
sheet in the oven, preheated
to 430 degrees (fan oven
not recommended) on the
second shelf from the top
for 10–15 minutes. Serve as
soon as the gratin has turned
a beautiful brown.

* **Preparation time:** 20 minutes.
 Per portion: 12 g P, 15 g F, 43 g C =
 356 kcal (1490 kJ).

Gorgonzola Tagliatelle

Childishly simple and yet an experience out of this world: tender pasta, creamy cheese sauce, and crisp walnuts.

For 2 portions: 1 Coarsely mince 4 **walnuts**. Coarsely crumble 7 oz **gorgonzola**. Cook 1 cup **whipping cream** with ⅔ cheese over low heat. Season with salt and pepper. **2** Cook 7 oz **green tagliatelle** in boiling salted water until *al dente*, following the instructions on the packet. Drain briefly. Bring the sauce back to the boil. Add 1 tbsp minced **parsley** to the sauce and toss the tagliatelle in it. Sprinkle with the rest of the cheese and walnuts.

* **Preparation time:** 25 minutes. **Per portion:** 36 g P, 75 g F, 73 g C = 1102 kcal (4617 kJ).

Swiss Chard and Chili Peppers

It need not always be spinach when you fancy something green.
Just try our Swiss Chard recipe.

For 2 portions: 1 Wash and prepare 1 **<u>Swiss Chard</u>** (about 1 lb 5 oz). Cut the stems into very thin strips and the leaves into ¾-in strips. Remove the seeds of 1 **<u>red chili pepper</u>** and mince. Mince 1 **<u>onion</u>**. Heat 2 tbsp **<u>oil</u>** in a pan, add the onion, chili pepper, Swiss chard stems, and 1 crushed **<u>clove of garlic</u>**, and fry over medium heat for 2–3 minutes while stirring. **2** Now add the leaves and ⅝ cup **<u>vegetable stock</u>**. Season with salt, 1 pinch of **<u>sugar</u>**, and 1–2 tsp **<u>lemon juice</u>**. Cover and cook for 10 minutes over medium heat. Adjust the seasoning if necessary and sprinkle with 2 tbsp roasted **<u>pine nuts</u>** before serving.

* **Preparation time:** 20 minutes.
  Per portion: 8 g P, 16 g F, 12 g C = 232 kcal (963 kJ).

Potato Soup with Shrimp

Nothing can beat this classic soup. An excellent choice for a Sunday lunch.

For 2 portions: 1 Peel 7 oz **carrots**, cut lengthways into half and cut into pieces of ⅛–⅓ in. Peel 14 oz **potatoes** and cut into pieces of similar size. Add both to 3½ cups **vegetable stock**, cover, and cook for 10–12 minutes over medium heat. **2** Meanwhile wash and prepare ½ **leek** and cut the white and light green parts into ¼-in rings. After 5 minutes, add to the potatoes and continue cooking until they are done. Season the soup with salt and pepper. Heat 3½ oz **shrimp** in the soup and sprinkle with 2 tbsp minced **dill**.

* **Preparation time:** 35 minutes. **Per portion:** 16 g P, 2 g F, 30 g C = 204 kcal (853 kJ).

Lamb with Lentils

If all low-calorie dishes were as delicious, no one would have any weight problems. Unless we ate twice as much ...

For 2 portions: 1 Put 2 oz large **<u>lentils</u>** in 1 ¼ cups boiling **<u>vegetable stock</u>**, cover, bring to the boil, and cook over low heat for 10–12 minutes until *al dente*. Drain the lentils in a strainer and keep the cooking liquid. Strip the leaves off 6 sprigs of **<u>thyme</u>**. Wipe 7 oz **<u>saddle of lamb fillet</u>** dry, season with salt and pepper. Heat 2 tbsp **<u>oil</u>** in a non-stick pan. Add the thyme and the meat to the pan and fry the meat briskly for 2 minutes on each side. Wrap the meat in aluminum foil and keep in the oven, heated to 180 degrees. **2** Put the reserved cooking liquid from the lentils, 5 tbsp **<u>apple juice</u>**, and 1 crushed **<u>clove of garlic</u>** in the pan and bring to the boil. Season with 1 tbsp **<u>lemon juice</u>** and 1 tsp **<u>honey</u>**, salt and pepper. Heat the lentils in the sauce. Sort and wash ½–1 bunch **<u>arugula</u>** and spin dry. Stir into the lentils. Cut the meat diagonally into slices ¾-in thick and serve with the lentils. Delicious with boiled potatoes.

* **Preparation time:** 35 minutes. **Per portion:** 28 g P, 4 g F, 23 g C = 305 kcal (1278 kJ).

Pears in Nightgowns

Almost even nicer than the similar apple dessert, thanks to the marzipan, nut praliné and coriander.

For 4 portions: 1 Defrost 1 lb **frozen puff pastry** following the instructions of the packet. Coarsely grate 2 oz **marzipan**. Stir together 3 tbsp **milk**, the marzipan, 1 tsp **confectioners' sugar**, and ½ tsp **ground coriander** until creamy. Crumble ¾ oz **sweet cookies** (about 4 pieces) and stir into the marzipan mixture together with 2 tbsp **nut praliné**. Put in a throw-away pastry bag with a large nozzle. **2** Put the sheets of puff pastry on top of each other and roll out to make a square 16 x 16 in. Cut into 4 squares. Peel 4 small ripe **pears** (5 oz), core with an apple corer and rub all over with 2 tbsp **lemon juice**. Pipe the filling into the pears. Stir together 1 **egg yolk** and 2 tbsp **whipping cream** and coat the puff pastry with half of it. **3** Put the pears on the coated side of the puff pastry. Fold the corners together to cover the pear and twist at the top to close. Spread the rest of the egg yolk and cream mixture on the outside of the puff pastry. Bake in the oven, preheated to 375 degrees (fan oven 170 degrees) on the second shelf from the bottom for 25–30 minutes. Serve warm with **vanilla custard**.

* **Preparation time:** 40 minutes. **Per portion:** 11 g P, 38 g F, 71 g C = 663 kcal (2775 kJ).

Semolina Mousse with Damsons

This classic dessert has been ennobled: lighter and more delicate, it has been transformed into an irresistible mousse, served with damson compote.

For 4 portions: 1 Bring to the boil 2¼ cups **milk**, the pulp of 1 **vanilla bean**, and ¼ cup **sugar**. Add 3½ oz **semolina**, bring to the boil again and allow to thicken on the turned off heat for 3–5 minutes while stirring. Add 2 **egg yolks** (medium). **2** Beat 2 **egg whites** stiff with 1 pinch of salt and ¼ cup sugar and fold into the semolina together with 3½ oz **low-fat curd**. Put in 4 ramekins (¾ cup capacity), rinse under cold water and refrigerate for at least 4 hours. **3** Remove the pits of 1 lb 2 oz **damsons** and cut into segments. Bring to the boil with ¼ cup sugar, 4 tbsp **red wine** (or **orange juice**), and 1 **cinnamon stick**. Cover and cook over low heat for 3–5 minutes. Allow to cool down. Loosen the mousse along the edges with the tip of a knife, turn out, and serve with the damson compote.

* Preparation time: 25 minutes. **Per portion:** 14 g P, 8 g F, 70 g C = 423 kcal (1775 kJ).

Artichokes

The easiest of all artichoke recipes. All you need to do is dip the leaves and hearts in the lemon butter and enjoy it.

For 4 portions: 1 Break off the stem of 4 large **artichokes** (12 oz each). Cut off the top third of the artichoke and rub immediately with half a **lemon (untreated)**. Simmer the artichokes with the half lemon in boiling salted water for 35–40 minutes. **2** To make the lemon **butter**, melt 4 tbsp butter and stir in the juice of 1 lemon. Season with pepper and serve with ciabatta.

* **Preparation time:** 50 minutes. **Per portion:** 4 g P, 13 g F, 8 g C = 164 kcal (685 kJ).

Lentil Stew

An ordinary lentil stew can be transformed into a sophisticated dish by introducing a couple of minor but elegant changes.

For 2–4 portions: 1 Cook 9 oz **brown lentils** in 5½ cups **meat stock** for 30 minutes over low heat. **2** Mix together 2 tbsp minced **cilantro**, ½ tsp grated **lemon rind (untreated)**, 1 crushed **clove of garlic** and 1 tbsp **tomato paste**. Peel 7 oz **carrots** and cut into thin slices. Add the carrots and herb mixture to the lentils after 20 minutes cooking time. Add 1 bunch of **scallions**, cut into rings, after 25 minutes. **3** Add 3½ oz **spiced sausages**, cut into slices. Season with 2 tbsp **lemon juice** and pepper. Fry 4 **giant shrimp** without their shells in 2 tbsp **oil**. Season with salt and pepper and add to the stew. Sprinkle with **cilantro**. Delicious with a baguette.

* Preparation time: 45 minutes.
Per portion (out of 4 portions): 27 g P, 14 g F, 39 g C = 395 kcal (1654 kJ).

Spicy-Fried Escalope

Very spicy, very crisp, and very quick; an American-inspired escalope.

For 2 portions: 1 Cut 3 **pork escalopes** (3½ oz each) in half. Pour ⅔ cup **buttermilk** over the meat and leave to stand for 30 minutes at room temperature. Mix together 2½ oz **breadcrumbs** with 2 tsp **hot paprika**, 1 tsp **dried oregano**, and ½ tsp each salt and pepper. **2** Heat ⅔ cup oil in a pan. Remove the escalopes from the buttermilk, dip in the spicy breadcrumbs, press them in firmly and tap off excess breadcrumbs. Put the meat in the hot oil and fry for 2–3 minutes on each side until golden brown. Drain on kitchen paper and garnish with **lemon segments (untreated)**.

* Preparation time: 15 minutes (plus standing time).
  Per portion: 37 g P, 29 g F, 29 g C = 524 kcal (2195 kJ).

Yellow Bell Pepper Soup

A delicious appetizer: the intense yellow color is perfectly reflected in the extraordinarily intense taste of the soup.

For 4 portions: 1 Mince 2 **onions** and 2 **cloves of garlic**. Cut 2¼ lb **yellow bell peppers**, remove the seeds, and cut into large pieces. **2** Heat 2 tbsp **olive oil**, add the onions, garlic, and peppers, and fry until golden. Add 3½ cups **vegetable stock** and ⅞ cup **whipping cream**. Cook over medium heat for 20–25 minutes. Finely puree with a hand-held mixer, pour through a strainer, bring back to the boil and season with salt and pepper. Put the soup in the bowls and drizzle 4 tbsp olive oil on top. Sprinkle with 4 tbsp **Feta cheese** and **marjoram leaves**.

* **Preparation time:** 1 hour. **Per portion:** 7 g P, 34 g F, 10 g C = 370 kcal (1550 kJ).

Buttermilk Crêpes

*The perfect accompaniment for anything with a lot of sauce,
from a salad to a fricassée. But it is equally delicious on its own.*

For 2 portions: 1 Mince 4 tbsp **sun-dried tomatoes**. Strip the leaves off
8 sprigs of **parsley** and mince. Mix together ½ cup **flour**, ⅝ cup **buttermilk**,
2 **egg yolks**, 1 tsp **baking powder**, a little salt and pepper and stir well.
Add the parsley. **2** Heat 1 tbsp **oil** in a non-stick pan. Put 2 tbsp batter in
the oil per crêpe. Sprinkle a few minced tomatoes on each crêpe and cook
on each for 2–3 minutes until golden brown. Bake the rest of the crêpes
in the same way.

* **Preparation time:** 20 minutes. **Per portion:** 9 g P, 19 g F, 24 g C = 298 kcal (1247 kJ).

Mixed Salad with Orange

A mixed salad is delightful with any meal. Here is a fruity variation.

For 2 portions: 1 Peel 1 __orange__ so that the white pith is completely removed. Cut the orange in thin slices. Squeeze 5 tbsp juice from 1 orange. **2** Shake or mix together the orange juice, 2 tbsp __white wine vinegar__, a little salt and pepper, 1 pinch of __sugar__, and 4 tbsp __oil__. Pour the vinaigrette over 5 oz __prepared mixed green salad__ and the sliced orange and serve.

* **Preparation time:** 1 hour. **Per portion:** 7 g P, 12 g F, 50 g C = 341 kcal (1428 kJ).

Grape Muffins

A delicious pastry and perfect snack when you feel peckish and feel like something sweet. These mouth-watering muffins are quite irresistible.

For 12 pieces: 1 Cut in half 5 oz each **black** and **green grapes** and remove the seeds. Mix together 5 cups **flour**, ¾ cup **sugar**, 3 tsp **baking powder**, and ¼ tsp **salt**. Line a muffin pan (12 hollows) with paper molds. **2** Stir together 3 medium **eggs**, 1¼ cups **buttermilk**, and ½ cup **oil**. Stir in the flour mixture and fold in the grapes. **3** Put the pastry mixture in the paper molds and sprinkle with 1 oz minced **almonds** and 1 tbsp **vanilla sugar**. Bake in the oven, preheated to 390 degrees (fan oven 355 degrees) on the second shelf from the bottom for 30 minutes.

* **Preparation time:** 15 minutes. **Per portion:** 2 g P, 20 g F, 12 g C = 240 kcal (1006 kJ).

Baileys Chocolate Mousse

Invest 30 minutes of your time – the fridge will do the rest.

For 4 portions: 1 Mince 2¾ oz **plain cooking chocolate**. Bring 1 cup **whipping cream** to the boil. Remove from the heat and melt the cooking chocolate in the hot cream while stirring. Stir in 5 tbsp **whiskey and cream liqueur** (for instance Baileys) and mix with the hand-mixer. Put the cream mixture in the refrigerator overnight. **2** Beat the cream mixture until stiff with the whisk attachment of the hand-held mixer. Cut 6 filbert balls (filbert-covered wafer with cream filling) sweets into quarters and fold into the cream mousses. Pour into dessert bowls or champagne glasses. Lightly beat ⅝ cup **whipping cream** and spoon onto the mousse. Decorate with more filbert balls if you like.

* **Preparation time:** 20 minutes (plus cooling time).
  Per portion: 6 g P, 38 g F, 23 g C = 467 kcal (1955 kJ).

Stuffed Roast Beef Rolls

A party without ham or sausages used to be unthinkable in the past. It is high time to revive this classic dish.

For 4 portions: 1 Hard-boil 1 **egg**, run under water, shell, and mince. Drain 1 can of **tuna fish in oil** (4 oz drained weight) and separate the fish into flakes. Cut 7 oz **tomatoes** into four, remove the seeds, and mince. Mix together the egg, tuna fish, tomatoes, 1 tbsp **mayonnaise**, 1¾ oz **creamy yoghourt**, 1 tsp grated **lemon rind (untreated)**, and 1 tbsp **lemon juice**. Season with salt, pepper, and a dash of **Worcester sauce**. **2** Wash and prepare 2 oz **arugula** and spin dry. Put 8 slices of cold **roast beef** (about 7 oz) on a surface. Put some tuna salad and 2–3 arugula leaves on each slice and roll up. Garnish with the rest of the arugula.

Preparation time: 25 minutes.
Per portion: 24 g P, 12 g F, 4 g C = 224 kcal (941 kJ).

Winegrower's Salad

*Whether as a appetizer or side dish: the combination of grapes,
cheese, and green salad is always a success.*

For 4 portions: 1 Wash and prepare 5 oz of each **green** and **black seedless grapes**, and cut in half. Wash and prepare 14 oz **green salad** (for
instance, oak-leaf salad, corn salad or lollo bianco), and spin dry. Cut
5 oz **Cambozola** into large cubes. Put 3 tbsp **white wine vinegar**, 6 tbsp
apple juice, a little salt and pepper, and 5 tbsp in a screw-top jar and
shake well. **2** Cut 2 slices of **currant bread** into ¾-in cubes and fry in
2 tbsp melted **butter** until golden brown. Pour the dressing over the
salad and grapes, garnish with the cheese and fried bread cubes and
serve immediately.

Preparation time: 25 minutes. Per portion: 8 g P, 33 g F, 20 g C = 415 kcal (1727 kJ).

Mashed Pumpkin

It would be better to make double portions to be on the safe side: people tend to find it irresistible.

For 2 portions: 1 Remove the seeds of a 1 lb 2 oz **Hokkaido pumpkin** and peel. Mince coarsely and fry in 1 tbsp melted **butter** until transparent. Season with salt, pepper, and **nutmeg**. Add 5 tbsp **whipping cream**, cover, and cook for 15 minutes over low heat, stirring occasionally. **2** Then mash with a potato masher and adjust the seasoning if necessary. Sprinkle with 2 tbsp **roasted pumpkin seeds** before serving.

* **Preparation time:** 25 minutes. **Per portion:** 6 g P, 21 g F, 10 g C = 250 kcal (1040 kJ).

Cabbage Roulade

A famous traditional dish, tried and tested, which has been updated and made easier for you.

For 2 portions: 1 Blanch 4 large **pointed cabbages** in boiling water, run under cold water, and dab dry. **2** Mince 1 **onion**. Coarsely mince a small handful of **chervil**. Add to 7 oz raw ground **veal** and mix with 1 **egg**, 1 soaked and squeezed slice of **white bread**, **hot paprika**, salt, and pepper. Knead into a smooth mixture. **3** For each portion, arrange 2 **cabbage leaves** in such a way that they overlap. Put the veal mixture in the middle. Fold the cabbage leaves over the veal mixture and roll up. Fry in 3 tbsp hot **oil**. Add ⅜ cup **stock** and 1 tsp **caraway**. Cover and braise over low heat for 30 minutes. Cut 1 **apple** into four, core, cut into large chunks. Add to the pan after 25 minutes. Stir 1 tsp **cornstarch** in 5 tbsp cold water and thicken the cooking juices with it.

* **Preparation time:** 1 hour. **Per portion:** 19 g P, 46 g F, 22 g C = 575 kcal (2406 kJ).

Spicy Meat Loaf

A meat loaf is a very special dish: tender and fairly spicy,
it is ideal for Sundays and special occasions.

For 4 portions:

2 ½ oz peppers (bottled)

9 oz shallots

2 cloves of garlic

1 bunch flat-leaved parsley

1 ¾ oz dried tomatoes

2 tbsp oil

2 medium eggs

3 ½ oz breadcrumbs

½ tsp rated lemon zest
(from an untreated lemon)

2 lb 3 oz mixed ground meat

2–4 tbsp Tabasco sauce

salt

pepper

1 Drain the peppers, remove the stems, and mince. Mince the shallots and garlic. Strip the parsley leaves off the stems and mince coarsely. Mince the tomatoes finely.

2 Fry the peppers, shallots, and garlic in hot oil over medium heat for 2–4 minutes. Allow to cool down. Add the parsley, tomatoes, eggs, breadcrumbs, and lemon rind to the mixed ground meat. Knead until you have a smooth mixture. Season Tabasco, salt, and pepper.

3 Put the mixture in a terrine (capacity 5 ½ cups). Cook in the oven, preheated to 320 degrees (fan oven not recommended) on the second shelf from the bottom for 50 minutes.

* Preparation time: 1 hour 30 minutes.
Per portion: 54 g P, 54 g F, 25 g C = 798 kcal (3344 kJ).

PRACTICAL While your spicy meat loaf is cooking in the oven, you can already relax with the appetizer. Like that you will not miss out!

Ice Cream with Chocolate-Chili pepper Sauce

Nowadays it is the trend to flavor ice cream with herbs and spices.
Here is a very successful combination: vanilla ice cream with a spicy sauce.

For 2 portions: 1 Mince 1 ¾ oz **dark chocolate** and slowly melt in 1 tbsp melted **butter** and 5 tbsp **milk** over low heat while stirring constantly. When the mixture has become smooth, stir in 1–2 tsp **rum**, and season lightly with some ground **chili peppers**. If the sauce is too thick, stir in a little milk. **2** Put 3 scoops of **vanilla ice cream** each in two bowls. Pour a little of the sauce in top. Sprinkle with ground chili peppers and serve with the rest of the sauce and ice cream wafers.

* **Preparation time:** 10 minutes. **Per portion:** 6 g P, 28 g F, 46 g C = 464 kcal (1943 kJ).

White Chocolate Cake

You cannot see the white chocolate but you can taste it.
Almonds and orange further complete this delicious cake.

For 16 pieces: 1 Mince 2½ oz **white chocolate**. Beat together ¾ cup **butter** (or margarine), ⅔ cup **sugar**, 1 packet **vanilla sugar**, and 1 tsp **grated orange zest** (untreated) with the whisk attachment of the hand-held mixer for 5 minutes at least until creamy. Stir in 3 medium **eggs**, one after the other, only adding the next when the previous one has been completely incorporated. Stir in 2¼ cups **flour**, 2½ oz finely **ground almonds**, 2 level tsp **baking powder**, and the chocolate. **2** Stir half the flour mixture into the butter mass. Gradually stir in 8 tbsp **milk**. Now stir in the rest of the flour mixture and another 8 tbsp milk. Line a rectangular pan (12 x 4¾ in) with waxed paper. Put the dough in the pan and smooth flat. **3** Bake in the oven, preheated to 355 degrees (fan oven 320 degrees) on the second shelf from the bottom for 55–60 minutes. Leave the cake to cool in the pan on a rack and then turn out of the pan. Melt 2 tsp butter. Stir together ¾ cup **confectioners' sugar** with 2 tbsp **orange juice** until smooth. Stir in the butter. Decorate the cooled cake with the confectioners' sugar.

* **Preparation time:** 1 hour 20 minutes (plus cooling time).
  Per portion: 4 g P, 15 g F, 28 g C = 268 kcal (1123 kJ).

373

Pears, Beans and Bacon

A classic North German dish, a nourishing and delicious meal which everyone will enjoy!

For 2 portions: 1 Cut 2 **onions** into strips. Put into 2½ cups **vegetable stock** together with a 5 oz piece of **smoked bacon**, bring to the boil, and simmer for 15 minutes. **2** Meanwhile wash and prepare 11½ oz **green beans** and cut into bite-size pieces. Add the beans to the bacon and cook for another 5 minutes. **3** Cut 2 **pears** (each 5 oz) into eight and core. Add the pear segments with 1 tsp minced **savory** to the beans and bacon, then simmer for another 5 minutes. Season with salt and pepper. Remove the bacon and cut into pieces. Return the bacon to the pan. **4** Stir 1–2 tsp **cornstarch** into cold water and thicken the cooking juices. Serve with boiled potatoes.

* **Preparation time:** 45 minutes. **Per portion:** 17 g P, 23 g F, 24 g C = 365 kcal (1530 kJ).

Quick Mushroom Soup

A sophisticated start to almost any menu but also a delight in its own right.

For 4 portions: 1 Soak ⅓ oz **dried ceps** in ⅞ cup hot water for 10 minutes. Wash and prepare 10½ oz **mixed mushrooms** (for instance mushrooms and ceps). Melt 2 tbsp **butter**, add the mixed mushrooms and **crushed garlic**, and fry. Season with salt and pepper. Add the soaking water and 2¼ cups **vegetable stock** to the mushrooms. Bring to the boil, cover, and cook for 10 minutes. Now add 3 tbsp minced **parsley** and puree finely with a hand-held mixer. **2** Add ⅝ cup **whipped cream** to the mushrooms and bring back to the boil. Season with salt, pepper, 1–2 tsp **lemon juice**, and **nutmeg**. Cut 3½ oz washed and prepared **ceps** (or **mushrooms**). Sprinkle with the sliced mushrooms and 2 tbsp minced parsley before serving.

* **Preparation time:** 30 minutes. **Per portion:** 5 g P, 18 g F, 3 g C = 192 kcal (806 kJ).

Braised Fennel

Fennel is a relatively uncommon vegetable here but it is easy to prepare and absolutely delicious.

For 2 portions: 1 Cut 3½ oz **shallots** into thin strips. Peel ¼ of 1 **untreated orange** and cut the rind into thin strips. Then squeeze 6 tbsp **juice**. Wash and prepare 1 **fennel bulb** (about 10½ oz) and put the green parts to one side. Cut the bulb into quarters, remove the hard stem ends, and cut each quarter into 4. Drain 4 canned **artichoke hearts** (3½ oz drained weight) and cut into quarters. **2** Fry the fennel and shallots in 3 tbsp **olive oil**. Season with salt, pepper, and 1 pinch of **sugar**. Add the orange rind, orange juice, artichokes, ½ cup **vegetable stock**, and 2 tsp **capers**. Cover and cook over medium heat for 12–14 minutes. Stir in the minced fennel leaves and adjust the seasoning if necessary.

* **Preparation time:** 30 minutes. **Per portion:** 5 g P, 16 g F, 12 g C = 210 kcal (878 kJ).

Fried Cod

The uncomplicated cod which is so popular with everyone.
And thanks to the pepper and lime this is also a delicious dish.

For 2 portions: 1 Roll 4 **cod fillets** in 2 tbsp **coarsely-ground pepper**
and press it in firmly. Fry the fillets in 2 tbsp hot **oil** over high heat on
the meat side for 2 minutes. Add 1 halved **lime (untreated)** with the cut
surface downward in the pan with the fish. Reduce the heat and add
1 ½ tbsp **butter** and 2 minced **cloves of garlic**. Turn the fish and cook for
another 2 minutes. Sprinkle with 2 tbsp **soy sauce**.

* **Preparation time:** 20 minutes. **Per portion:** 32 g P, 20 g F, 2 g C = 314 kcal (1315 kJ).

Flavored Curd

It tastes as refreshing as it easy to make: your own personal spicy curd. It is delicious with French bread or pretzels.

For 1 portion: 1 Mince 1¾ oz **pickled gherkin** and ½ **red bell pepper**. Beat 2 tbsp softened **butter** until smooth and stir in 5 oz **low-fat curd**, 1 tsp **mustard**, and ½ **hot paprika**. Add the gherkins and peppers. Season generously with salt and pepper. **2** Cut the **cress** of 1 box of mustard cress and stir into the curd mixture. Serve with a **baguette**.

* **Preparation time:** 15 minutes. **Per portion:** 13 g P, 36 g F, 74 g C = 680 kcal (2847 kJ).

Autumn Fruit Salad

Made with grapes, pears, and apples, it is particularly delicious with sharp apple varieties such as Granny Smith.

For 2 portions: 1 Bring to the boil 5 tbsp **orange juice** with 2 tbsp **honey** and cook for 2–3 minutes. Remove from the heat and stir 1 tbsp **orange liqueur**. **2** Wash 7 oz **seedless black grapes**, remove from the stems and cut in half. Peel ½ **apple** and ½ **pear**, core and cut into thin slices. Immediately sprinkle with 1–2 tbsp **lemon juice** and mix well. Wash 1 **fig** and cut into eight. Coarsely mince 1¾ oz **walnuts**. Stir the sauce into the fruit with the nuts. **3** Stir 5 oz **creamy yoghourt** until smooth and serve with the fruit salad.

* **Preparation time:** 15 minutes. **Per portion:** 8 g P, 24 g F, 48 g C = 450 kcal (1884 kJ).

A month full of delights

OF ALL THE MONTHS of the year, November probably has the worst reputation. This is very unfair. It has many qualities: we can sit by the fire with a clear conscience, listening to music and drinking wine; some of us are no longer obsessed by the concerns about vitamins which characterizes the summer months. Let us see what culinary delights this month has to offer!

Pork Tenderloin Wrapped in Bacon

This delicious, tender pork fillet can be prepared in no time at all and it is an excellent dish for a celebration.

For 4 portions:

5 sprigs thyme

2 pork tenderloins
(12 oz each)

salt

black pepper

10 oz bacon

2 tbsp oil

⅞ cup dry white wine

3–4 bay leaves

1 Mince the leaves of 2 sprigs of thyme. Season the fillets lightly with salt and pepper and sprinkle with the minced thyme.

2 Arrange half the bacon slices so that they overlap and wrap round the fillet. Do the same with the rest of the bacon and the second fillet.

3 Heat the oil in a large pan, add the fillets and fry briskly all over on a high heat. Remove from the pan and put in a roasting tray. Add white wine to the cooking fat in the pan. Add the bay leaves and 3 sprigs of thyme. Transfer the contents of the pan to the roasting pan with the pork tenderloin.

4 Bake in the oven, preheated to 390 degrees (fan oven 355 degrees) on the second shelf from the bottom for 15–17 minutes. Remove the pork tenderloins from the roasting pan, wrap in aluminum foil and allow to rest for 5 minutes.

5 Pour the cooking through a strainer and bring to the boil. Cut the pork tenderloins into slices and serve with the cooking juices.

WRAPPING PROPERLY
Arrange the bacon slices on the Saran wrap so that they overlap. Put the fillets on the overlapping bacon slices and use the Saran wrap to roll it into a tight roll.

* **Preparation time:** 40 minutes.
  Per portion: 50 g P, 28 g F, 0 g C = 461 kcal (1930 kJ).

Greek Rice

A highly flavored excellent accompaniment to any Mediterranean-style dish.

For 2 portions: 1 Cut 1 <u>**clove of garlic**</u> into thin strips. Mince 1 <u>**onion**</u>. Cut 1 <u>**red bell pepper**</u> into quarters, remove the seeds, and mince. Remove the seeds of 1 <u>**beef tomato**</u> and mince. **2** Heat 2 tbsp <u>**olive oil**</u> in a pan, add the garlic and onions and fry until transparent while stirring. Add the strips of pepper and minced tomato, fry for 1 more minute. Add ⅝ cup <u>**long-grain rice**</u>. Sprinkle with 1–2 tsp <u>**gyros spice**</u> (Greek kebab spice). **3** Add 1¼ cups <u>**chicken stock**</u>, bring to the boil, cover and cook for 20 minutes over low heat. Stir in 2 tbsp minced <u>**flat-leaved parsley**</u>.

Preparation time: 35 minutes. **Per portion:** 7 g P, 11 g F, 57 g C = 345 kcal (1441 kJ).

Roast Potato Segments

*You do not even need to peel the potatoes – yet they make
a sensational side dish.*

For 2 portions: 1 Thoroughly wash 1 lb 2 oz firm boiling **<u>potatoes</u>** and
cut into segments without peeling. In a bowl, mix together 2 tbsp **<u>lemon
juice</u>**, 2 tbsp **<u>olive oil</u>**, 1 pinch **<u>cayenne pepper</u>**, 1 tsp minced **<u>thyme</u>**
leaves, and a little salt. Add the potato segments and stir well. Put
the potatoes on a lightly oiled cookie sheet and spread out. **2** Bake in
the oven, preheated to 430 degrees (fan oven 390 degrees) on the
second shelf from the bottom for 35–40 minutes, turning once. When
done, sprinkle with coarsely ground **<u>pepper</u>**.

* **Preparation time:** 50 minutes. **Per portion:** 4 g P, 10 g F, 32 g C = 240 kcal (1008 kJ).

Broccoli

Plain broccoli benefits greatly from being fried with chili peppers in a pan after boiling.

For 2 portions: 1 Wash and prepare 10 ½ oz **<u>broccoli</u>**, divide into florets. Peel the stem, cut in half and then in ⅓ in long pieces. Cook in boiling water for 3–5 minutes and run under cold water. Drain thoroughly.
2 Cut 2 **<u>red bell peppers</u>** in half lengthways, remove the seeds and cut across into thin strips. Heat 4 tbsp **<u>olive oil</u>** in a pan, add the broccoli and chili peppers, and fry over medium heat for 5 minutes. Season with salt and pepper.

* **Preparation time:** 30 minutes. **Per portion:** 3 g P, 20 g F, 2 g C = 202 kcal (848 kJ).

Pear and Ricotta Soufflé

No trouble to make and an undiluted pleasure to eat.
Although there are 6 portions, three people would quickly finish it!

For 4–6 portions: 1 Mix together 750 g **ricotta**, 3 medium **egg yolks**, 1 tbsp **vanilla sugar**, 1 pinch of **salt**, and 2 tsp grated **lime rind (untreated)**. Spread this mixture in a greased soufflé dish (8 in diameter). **2** Peel 1 lb 2 oz **ripe pears**, cut into quarters, core, and sprinkle with 2 tbsp **lime juice**. Arrange the pears with the rounded surface upward and press down lightly. Beat together 1 egg yolk and 1 tbsp **milk** and spread over the pears and ricotta mixture. **3** Bake in the oven, preheated to 355 degrees (fan oven 320 degrees) on the second shelf from the bottom for 50–60 minutes. Sprinkle with 4 tbsp **liquid honey** and 1 tbsp **minced pistachios** and serve warm or cold.

* **Preparation time:** 1 hour 15 minutes.
  Per portion (out of 6 portions): 10 g P, 23 g F, 27 g C = 355 kcal (1488 kJ).

Red Wine Cake

A surprisingly successful combination: chocolate and red wine brought together in a colorful cake.

For 14 pieces: 1 Beat together 1 cup 2 tbsp **butter** at room temperature, bare 1 cup **sugar**, 1 tbsp **vanilla sugar**, 1 tsp ground **cinnamon**, and 1 pinch of **salt** with the whisk attachment of the hand-held mixer for 6 minutes until creamy. Stir in 4 medium **eggs**, one by one, only adding the next one when the previous one is well incorporated and beat until the mixture is very creamy. Sift together 2½ cups **flour**, 1 tbsp **cocoa**, and 1 tsp of **baking powder**, and stir in ½ cup **red wine**. Fold in 1¾ oz **crumbled chocolate** and 1¾ oz dried **cranberries** (or **raisins**). **2** Put the dough in a greased, floured tube pan. Bake in the oven, preheated to 340 degrees (fan oven 300 degrees) on the second shelf from the bottom for 45–50 minutes. Leave in the pan for 10 minutes, then turn out on a rack and leave to cool. Mix ⅚ cup **confectioners' sugar** and 2–3 tbsp red wine until the mixture is smooth. Pour over the cake and sprinkle with 2 tbsp dried cranberries or raisins.

* **Preparation time:** 1 hour 15 minutes. **Per portion:** 5 g P, 18 g F, 43 g C = 356 kcal (1490 kJ).

Belgian Endive Salad

The bitter and the sweet, Belgian endive and orange, combined with the most delicious chicken breast. The result: a culinary masterpiece in no time at all!

For 2 portions: 1 Season 10½ oz **chicken breast** with salt and pepper and fry in 2 tbsp hot **oil** for 5–6 minutes on each side until golden brown. Wrap in aluminum foil and leave to rest. Peel the rind and remove the white pith of 2 **oranges (untreated)**. Then remove the membranes surrounding the segments. Wash and prepare 7 oz **Belgian endive** and cut into slices. **2** Stir 3½ oz **creamy yoghourt** with 3 tbsp **orange juice**, 1 tsp grated **orange rind** (untreated), salt, pepper, 1 pinch of **sugar**, and 1 tbsp **olive oil**. Cut the chicken into slices and add to the oranges and Belgian endive. Pour the dressing over the salad and sprinkle with 1 tbsp **dill** before serving.

* **Preparation time:** 20 minutes. **Per portion:** 40 g P, 16 g F, 21 g C = 399 kcal (1672 kJ).

Penne with Spicy Breadcrumbs

It need not always be "arrabbiata" with penne: our recipe is no less spicy but equally easy to prepare.

For 2 portions: 1 Mince 3 **onions**. Mince 2 **cloves of garlic**. Remove the seeds of 1 **chili pod** and mince. Boil 9 oz **penne** in plenty of boiling salted water, following the instructions on the packet. **2** Meanwhile, heat 2 tbsp **oil** in a pan, add 4½ oz **cherry tomatoes** and fry all over on a high heat for 1 minute. Remove from the pan. Now add the onions, garlic, and chili pod to the pan and brown over medium heat while stirring. Stir in 1 tbsp **breadcrumbs**, 3 tbsp **butter**, 1 tsp minced **thyme leaves**. Keep warm in the pan with the tomatoes. **3** Drain the pasta, add to the pan and mix well. Season with salt and pepper and serve.

Preparation time: 20 minutes. Per portion: 17 g P, 30 g F, 94 g C – 721 kcal (3021 kJ).

Beet Soup

A perfect soup for Sunday lunch and not only because of its attractive color.

For 4 portions: 1 Mince 2 **onions**. Peel 14 oz **beet** and mince coarsely. Wash 5 oz **potatoes**, peel and cut into cubes. Heat 2 tbsp **butter** in a pan, add the onions, beet and potatoes and fry for 5 minutes over medium heat. **2** Add 4½ cups **vegetable stock**, bring to the boil and cook over medium heat for 40 minutes. Puree finely with a hand-held mixer and season with salt and pepper. **3** Pour through a strainer, add ½ cup **whipping cream** and bring to the boil again. Put the soup in 4 bowls and garnish each bowl with 1 tsp creamy **horseradish** and minced **chives**.

* **Preparation time:** 50 minutes. **Per portion:** 4 g P, 14 g F, 14 g C = 198 kcal (825 kJ).

Mozzarella in a Toasted Sandwich

A classic dish – French toast with Mozzarella.

Serves 2: 1 Cut the crusts of 4 slices of white **toasting bread**. Drain 1 **Mozzarella** (6 oz) and cut into slices ⅛ in thick. Put the sliced Mozzarella on 2 slices of bread but leave a narrow edge free all round. Season with salt, pepper, and tsp **dried oregano**. Place the other 2 slices of bread on top. Beat together 2 **eggs**, 2 tbsp **milk**, and a little salt and pepper. Dip the sandwiches with the edges in the egg mixture and press together firmly. **2** Place the bread in a shallow bowl and pour the egg mixture over the top, allowing the bread to absorb it and turning the slices over occasionally. Mix together 4 tbsp **flour** and 2 tbsp **Parmesan** and dip the bread into this mixture. Heat 8 tbsp **olive oil** in a pan and fry the bread over medium heat for about 4 minutes on each side. Be very carefully when turning the bread. Serve with lettuce, cherry tomatoes, basil, and a herb vinaigrette dressing (ready-made).

* **Preparation time:** 20 minutes.
  Per serving: 36 g P, 49 g F, 70 g C =
  864 kcal (3620 kJ).

Spaghetti Carbonara

A great classic dish when made properly. As we are describing it here!

Serves 2: 1 Mince 3½ oz **bacon** (or **pancetta**) and fry in a pan in 1 tbsp **oil** until crisp. Keep warm in the pan. **2** Cook 7 oz **spaghetti** in plenty of boiling salted water until *al dente*, following the instructions on the packet. Meanwhile mix together 2½ oz freshly-grated **Parmesan**, 2½ oz **whipping cream**, and 1 **egg** in a bowl. **3** Drain the spaghetti and mix briefly with the bacon in the pan. Add the cheese and cream mixture, stir vigorously and serve immediately. Season generously with freshly ground black pepper.

⁕ **Preparation time:** 45 minutes. **Per serving:** 20 g P, 15 g F, 58 g C = 472 kcal (1977 kJ).

Lentil Bolognese

To make a good bolognese you not necessarily need meat.
Just try it with lentils!

Serves 4: 1 Wash and prepare 1 bunch of **soup vegetables** (about 14 oz), and dice into pieces of about ⅛ in. Mince 7 oz **onions**. Fry everything in 4 tbsp hot **olive oil**. Season generously with salt, pepper, and a little **sugar**. Add 5 tbsp **red bell pepper paste** and 1 tsp **dried oregano**, and fry briefly. Add ½ cup **red wine** and allow to reduce almost completely. **2** Add 4½ oz **Beluga lentils** (or other lentils) and 2¼ cups **vegetable stock**. Bring to the boil, cover, and cook for 20–25 minutes over medium heat, stirring occasionally. Cook 7 oz **tagliatelle** in boiling salted water, following the instructions on the packet, Adjust the seasoning if necessary. Drain the pasta and stir into the sauce. Sprinkle with 1 oz **Parmesan** shavings and 1 tbsp minced **parsley**.

* **Preparation time:** 1 hour 45 minutes. **Per serving:** 50 g P, 10 g F, 31 g C = 429 kcal (1792 kJ).

Braised Fillet End of a Leg of Veal

A roast that never fails to delight, whether it is eaten by guests or just the family.

Serves 4:

6 oz shalotts

12 cloves of garlic

14 oz carrots

1 veal knuckle

salt

pepper

2 tbsp oil

1 ½ cups dry hard cider

2 sprigs thyme

4 firm apples

1 Blanch the shallots and cloves of garlic together in boiling water for 1 minutes. Drain, run under cold water and peel. Peel the carrots and cut in half lengthways.

2 Season the roast with salt and pepper. Heat the oil in a pan, add the veal, and fry briskly on all sides over high heat, then remove from the pan. Add the shallots and garlic and fry briefly. Pour in the hard cider. Add the carrots and thyme, and bring everything to the boil.

3 Return the veal to the pan, cover, and braise in the oven, preheated to 375 degrees (fan oven 170 degrees) on the second shelf from the bottom for 70 minutes. Turn once.

4 Cut the apple into quarters, core, and peel. Add to the pan and braise for another 15 minutes. Season the sauce with salt and pepper, and serve with the roast. Delicious with Savoy cabbage.

* **Preparation time:** 30 minutes.
 Per serving: 40 g P, 46 g F, 16 g C = 653 kcal (2733 kJ).

DELICIOUS LEFT-OVERS
f by any chance some of the roast is left over, you can make a delicious fry-up: boil a few potatoes, peel, and cut into segments. Fry in 2 tbsp clarified butter together with 1 red onion cut into strips. Cut the veal into narrow strips and add 1 tbsp pumpkin seeds. Fry for 1 more minute and sprinkle with parsley before serving.

Veal Escalopes with Pears

Bring a little variation to the usual veal escalope: pears and rosemary work wonders.

Serves 2: 1 Cut 1 **pear** into quarters and core. Peel 2 **onions** and cut into strips. Remove the seeds of ½ red **chili pod** and mince. Season 12 oz **veal escalopes** with salt and pepper. Fry briskly on both sides in hot **oil** in a pan. Then remove from the pan and keep warm. **2** Add 2 tbsp **butter** and the onions to the pan and fry for 2 minutes. Now add the pear, minced chili pod, and ⅜ cup **white wine**. Cover and cook for another minute. **3** Add ⅝ cup **whipping cream** and 1 tbsp **minced rosemary** to the pan and cook for 2 more minutes. Season with salt and pepper. Reheat the escalopes briefly in the pan.

* **Preparation time:** 30 minutes. **Per serving:** 40 g P, 46 g F, 16 g C = 653 kcal (2733 kJ).

Turkey Curry

Mildly exotic but very easy to prepare.

Serves 2: 1 Mince 1 **shallot**. Cut 1 **apple** into quarters, core, and cut into segments. Cut 14 oz **turkey escalopes** into thin strips and season with salt and pepper. **2** Heat 2 tbsp **oil** in a pan, add the turkey, fry briskly all over and remove. Now add the shallots and apples in the pan and fry for 1 minute. Sprinkle 1 tbsp **curry powder** in the pan and add ⅞ cup **whipping cream**. **3** Cook for 2 minutes. Add 3½ oz **frozen peas** and 2 tbsp **mango chutney** (from a jar), and cook for 1 more minute. **4** Return the meat to the pan, season with salt and pepper. Delicious served with rice with roasted almonds.

Preparation time: 25 minutes.
Per serving: 54 g P, 44 g F, 27 g C = 724 kcal (3024 kJ).

Pollock with Salsa

A quick and easy meal – fish fillets with a strong Mexican association.

Serves 2: 1 Drain 1 can of **sweet corn** and rinse under cold water. Mince 1 small red **onion**. Remove the seeds of 5 oz **cucumber** and 1 **tomato**, and mince both. Remove the seeds of 1 **red chili pod** and mince. Mix all the ingredients together with 2 tbsp **lime juice** and 3 tbsp **oil**. Stir in 1 tsp minced **cilantro** (or parsley). **2** Season 2 **pollock fillets** (6 oz each) with salt, pepper, and 1 tbsp **lemon juice**, coat in **flour** and fry in 2 tbsp oil for 2–3 minutes on each side. Serve with the salsa.

* **Preparation time:** 35 minutes.
 Per serving: 37 g P, 27 g F, 22 g C = 487 kcal (2036 kJ).

Duck Escalope

Duck breast is transformed into a sophisticated eastern dish by the addition of chili peppers, soy, garlic, and peanuts.

Serves 2: 1 Remove the skin from 2 **duck breasts** (7 oz each) and cut the meat into very thin strips. Remove the seeds of 1 **red chili pod** and mince. Mince 2 **cloves of garlic**. Cut 1 **red** and 1 **green bell pepper** into quarters, remove the seeds and cut into thin strips. Cut 2 **scallions** into thin slices. **2** Heat the **oil** in a pan. Season the meat with salt and pepper and fry briefly in the very hot oil. Take out of the pan. Add the vegetables to the pan and cook for 3 minutes while stirring. **3** Add 4 tbsp **soy sauce** and 4 tbsp water. Bring to the boil and season with pepper and 2–3 tsp **sugar**. **4** Add the meat with the scallions, 1 tbsp **minced peanuts**, 1 tbsp minced **basil**, and tbsp minced **cilantro**, and reheat.

Preparation time: 25 minutes. **Per serving:** 52 g P, 33 g F, 14 g C = 570 kcal (2389 kJ).

Onion Tart

The "pizza of the North" would be a perfect description of our very easy variation of the onion tart.

Serves 8: 1 Cut 14 oz **onions** into quarters, then into thin strips. Heat 1 tbsp **oil** in a large pan, add 1¾ oz **diced bacon** and fry until crisp. Remove from the pan. Add 2 tbsp **butter** and the onions to the bacon fat and fry for 15 minutes over medium heat until golden brown. Season with salt, pepper, and **caraway**. Allow to cool. **2** Defrost 10½ oz **frozen pastry**. Mix together 5 oz **whipping cream**, 1 medium **egg yolk**, a little salt, pepper, and 4 tbsp minced **parsley**, and add to the onions. Roll out the dough to make rectangle 14 x 10 in, put on a cookie sheet lined with waxed paper and spread the onion mixture on top. **3** Bake in the oven, preheated to 430 degrees (fan oven 390 degrees) on the lowest shelf for 20–25 minutes. Sprinkle with 1 tbsp **parsley** and bacon.

* **Preparation time:** 55 minutes (plus cooling time).
  Per serving: 6 g P, 15 g F, 20 g C = 240 kcal (1010 kJ).

Pear Coleslaw

A perfect snack to satisfy hunger pangs between meals or ideal as a main meal for anyone dieting.

Serves 2: 1 Wash and prepare 10½ oz **white cabbage**, remove the stem and cut into thin strips. Put in a bowl and stir in ½ tsp salt. Peel 1 medium **carrot** and grate coarsely. Wash 1 **pear**, peel, cut into quarters, core, mince coarsely, and stir in 1 tbsp **lemon juice**. **2** Stir 5 oz **creamy yoghourt** until smooth. Pour over the cabbage, carrots, pears, and yoghourt, and mix well. Season with salt, pepper, and lemon juice. Sprinkle with 1 tbsp **walnuts**.

* **Preparation time:** 15 minutes. **Per serving:** 6 g P, 13 g F, 20 g C = 224 kcal (942 kJ).

Guacamole with Peas

Mild, slightly spicy, a touch exotic and rather sumptuous: pure pleasure.

Serves 2: 1 Cook 7 oz <u>**frozen peas**</u> in boiling salted water for 5 minutes and drain. Remove the seeds of 1 <u>**red bell pepper**</u> and mince. Cut 1 <u>**avocado**</u> in half, take out the pit and scoop out the flesh. Add salt, pepper, and 2 tbsp <u>**lemon juice**</u> and puree with 3 ½ oz peas. **2** Mince 1 bunch of <u>**cilantro**</u> and stir in the rest of the peas, and the minced pepper. Put on the guacamole as a garnish. Delicious served with taco chips.

* **Preparation time:** 15 minutes. **Per serving:** 9 g P, 20 g F, 16 g C = 285 kcal (1193 kJ).

Curd Soufflé

Quite sensational as a sweet main course: a light soufflé with a lot fruit and a hint of caramel!

Serves 4: 1 Soak 1 tbsp <u>**raisins**</u> in 1 tbsp <u>**rum**</u>. Beat together 2 medium <u>**egg yolks**</u>, 2 heaping tbsp <u>**sugar**</u>, 1 tbsp of <u>**vanilla sugar**</u>, 1 pinch of salt, and the grated rind of ½ <u>**lemon (untreated)**</u> for 3 minutes with the whisk attachment of the hand-held mixer until creamy. Stir in 9 oz low-fat curd and 1¾ oz <u>**semolina**</u>. **2** Beat 2 <u>**egg whites**</u> with 1 pinch salt until stiff. Add 2 tbsp sugar and beat for another 2–3 minutes. Carefully fold the stiffly beaten egg whites and raisins soaked in rum into the curd mixture. Put this mixture into a greased soufflé dish (diameter 12 in, or 12 x 8 in). **3** Drain the <u>**mango**</u> (canned, scant 1 lb drained weight), cut into thin slices, and arrange on the curd mixture. Bake in the oven, preheated to 390 degrees (fan oven 355 degrees) on the middle shelf for 25–30 minutes.

* **Preparation time: 40 minutes. Per serving:** 14 g P, 4 g F, 54 g C = 316 kcal (1333 kJ).

Spicy Pork tenderloin

The quickest and easiest way to prepare pork tenderloin: poached with apple horseradish.

Serves 2: 1 Wash and prepare 3½ oz **carrots** and **celeriac**, and mince. Bring 1½ cups **vegetable stock** to the boil and add the vegetables. Put the 2 **pork tenderloins** (6 oz each) into the stock, bring to the boil and poach for 10 minutes over medium heat. **2** Mix together 1–2 tbsp freshly grated **horseradish**, 5 oz **apple compote**, 1 tbsp **minced chives**, and 1 tsp **lemon juice**. Season with salt and pepper. **3** Remove the fillets from the stock, pour away half the liquid, add ⅜ cup **whipping cream** and bring to the boil. Cut 2 **scallions** into slices, add to the pan and thicken with **gravy granules**. Cut the meat into slices and serve with the apple horseradish and the sauce.

* **Preparation time: 30 minutes. Per serving:** 42 g P, 16 g F, 26 g C = 413 kcal (1735 kJ).

Chicken Stroganoff

It need not always be beef, it is also delicious made with chicken breasts.

Serves 2: 1 Drain 3½ oz **cocktail onions** (from a jar). Wash and prepare 5 oz **mushrooms**. **2** Season 2 **chicken breasts** (6 oz without the skin) with salt and pepper. Heat the **oil** in a pan; add the chicken breasts and fry for 2 minutes on each side. Add the mushrooms and fry for a further 3 minutes, stirring the mixture. Now add the cocktail onions, 1 tbsp **tomato paste** and 1 tsp minced **thyme**. Then add ⅝ cup **whipping cream**. **3** Cook for 3 minutes, turning once. Season with salt and pepper.

* **Preparation time:** 20 minutes. **Per serving:** 43 g P, 40 g F, 7 g C = 563 kcal (2346 kJ).

Oven-Baked "French Fries"

At last, "French fries" which are not fried and yet are made from raw potatoes.

Serves 2: 1 Wash generous 1 lb firm boiling **potatoes**, peel and cut into sticks about ⅜-in thick. Put in a bowl with 3–4 tbsp **oil** and mix well to ensure they are all coated in oil. **2** Spread on a cookie sheet. Bake in the oven, preheated to 430 degrees (fan oven 390 degrees) on the second shelf from the bottom for about 35 minutes, turning halfway through. **3** Remove from the oven and sprinkle with coarse salt.

*Preparation time: 45 minutes. **Per serving:** 4 g P, 15 g F, 30 g C = 280 kcal (1180 kJ).

Thyme-Flavored Polenta

Makes everything which is served with a hot spicy sauce taste even better.

Serves 2: 1 Put 2 ½ cups **vegetable stock** and 4 ½ oz **polenta** in a pan and stir vigorously with a whisk. Bring the polenta to the boil over high heat, reduce the heat to the lowest setting and simmer while stirring for 5–8 minutes. Remove from the heat, cover, and leave to stand for 10 minutes. **2** Add 1 oz grated **Parmesan**, 2–3 coarsely minced **thyme** (or 1–1 ½ tsp **dried thyme**), and 2 tbsp butter to the polenta.

* **Preparation time:** 25 minutes. **Per serving:** 12 g P, 18 g F, 41 g C = 374 kcal (1568 kJ).

Chocolate and Cherry Cake

Easy and delicious! Made in a cake pan with sour cherries, chocolate and yoghourt.

For 10–12 pieces: 1 Sift together 3 cups <u>flour</u>, 2½ tsp <u>baking powder</u>, and 1 pinch of salt in large bowl. Mince 3½ oz <u>dark chocolate</u>. Thoroughly drain ½ jar (1½ lb drained weight) <u>sour cherries</u>. **2** Whisk together 2 medium <u>eggs</u>, 7 oz <u>full cream yoghourt</u>, ⅔ cup <u>sugar</u>, and 1 tbsp <u>vanilla sugar</u>. Stir in 7 tbsp melted <u>butter</u>. Add the cherries and minced chocolate to the flour mixture and fold in with a spatula. **3** Put the dough in a cake pan (10 in) lined with waxed paper and smooth flat. Bake in the oven, preheated to 340 degrees (fan oven 300 degrees) on the second shelf from the bottom for 60–65 minutes. Allow to cool in the pan on a rack for 5 minutes before turning the cake out. **4** Beat 9 oz whipping cream, 1 packet vanilla sugar, and 1 tbsp rum until stiff. Serve the cake with rum-flavored whipping cream.

* **Preparation time:** 1 hour 15 minutes.
Per serving 9 out of 12 portions): 6 g P, 18 g F, 42 g C = 354 kcal (1485 kJ).

Apple and Sponge Dessert

As easy as crêpes but so much more delicious.

Serves 2: 1 Cut 1 **red apple** into quarters, core, cut into thin slices, and stir in 1 tbsp **lemon juice**. Beat 2 medium **egg whites** with 1 pinch of salt and 1 tbsp **sugar** until stiff. Beat 2 medium **egg yolks** and ½ tbsp sugar with a hand-held mixer until creamy. Stir in ½ cup **flour** and ½ cup **whipping cream**, then fold in the stiffly beaten egg whites. **2** Grease a non-stick pan (9½ in diameter) with 1 tbsp butter and add the egg mixture and the apple slices. Sprinkle with 1 tbsp sugar. Bake in the oven, pre-heated to 390 degrees (fan oven 355 degrees) on the second shelf from the bottom for 15 minutes (wrap the handle with aluminum foil). Break up the mixture into pieces. Serve with **cinnamon sugar**.

Preparation time: 30 minutes. **Per serving:** 12 g P, 31 g F, 60 g C = 566 kcal (2369 kJ).

Meatballs in Mustard Sauce

This variation on the famous Königsberger meatballs is quicker and tastes even better.

Serves 2: 1 Cut the crusts off 1 slice of **white toasting bread** and mince. Mix thoroughly 14 oz **mixed ground meat**, 1 **egg**, and 2 tbsp **whipping cream** in a bowl, season with salt and pepper. **2** Make 6 meatballs, using moist hands. Bring 2½ cups **chicken stock** to the boil, add the meatballs and simmer over low heat for 20 minutes. **3** Pour 1¾ cups of the **stock** through a strainer and bring to the boil. Dilute 3 tsp of cornstarch in a little cold water and add to the stock. Now add 6 tbsp whipping cream, 2 tbsp hot **mustard**, and 2 **pickled gherkins** to the stock. Remove the meatballs from the stock, arrange on a dish, and pour the sauce on top. Delicious with boiled potatoes.

* **Preparation time:** 40 minutes. **Per serving:** 46 g P, 58 g F, 17 g C = 771 kcal (3230 kJ).

Leek Gratin

Anyone who believes that vegetarian dishes are less satisfying is quite mistaken. This leek gratin proves the point.

Serves 2: 1 Peel 9 oz **potatoes**, peel and cut into slices. Wash and prepare 9 oz **leeks** and cut into rings. Pre-cook the potatoes and leeks for 3 minutes in boiling water. Drain and put in a greased soufflé dish. Cut 3½ oz smoked **turkey breast** into strips and arrange over the vegetables. Add 3 tbsp **white wine** to 1 carton (9 oz) of **cream cheese** and season with, salt, pepper and **nutmeg**. Pour over the gratin and sprinkle with ⅓ cup grated **Emmental** or other semi-hard cheese. Bake in the oven, preheated to 200 degrees (fan oven 180 degrees) on the second shelf from the bottom for 25 minutes.

Preparation time: 50 minutes. Per serving: 27 g P, 45 g F, 22 g C = 616 kcal (2574 kJ).

Pears in Mulled Wine

You need not wait for winter to enjoy this exquisite dessert.
You can enjoy pears in mulled wine at any time!

Serves 2:

2 ripe pears

1 tbsp lemon juice

1 quart dry red wine

½ cup orange juice

1 small cinnamon stick

3–4 allspice
(or 2–3 whole cloves)

1 star anise

pulp of ½ vanilla bean

bare ½ cup sugar

3 slices of 1 untreated
orange

1 Cut the base of the pears off flat, then peel very carefully but leave the stem. With a melon-baller (or a small knife), remove the core from the base of the pears. Put the pears in a tall container, add the lemon juice and fill with water until the pears are covered.

2 Put the red wine, orange juice, cinnamon stick, allspice, star anise, vanilla pulp, and sugar in a tall pan, and bring to the boil. Remove the pears from the lemon water and add to the wine. Cut the orange slices in half.

3 Simmer the pears for about 20 minutes over low heat. Add the orange slices after 15 minutes. When the pears are cooked, allow them to cool in the pan (overnight is best). Serve the pears with vanilla custard or vanilla ice cream.

Tip: You can heat up the cooking liquid again and enjoy it as mulled wine.

* **Preparation time:** 30 minutes.
Per serving: 1 g P, 0 g F, 25 g C = 109 kcal (464 kJ).

SCOOPING OUT
A melon-baller is best for scooping out the bottom of the pears. But a small knife and a spoon will also do to the job of removing the core.

At the end of the year

CHRISTMAS without cookies would be like Easter without eggs. And Christmas Day without Christmas dinner does not bear thinking about. December is undoubtedly the month when we consume the most food. This is the party season after all, and our recipes will help you with this!

Almond and Chocolate Crescent Cookies

These classic cookies, which you can buy, are even nicer when you make them yourself!

For 16 cookies:

7 oz marzipan

½ cup confectioners' sugar

1 medium egg white

3 drops almond essence

7 oz slivered almonds

1¾ oz bitter chocolate

1 tbsp butter

1 Coarsely grate the marzipan, mix with the confectioners' sugar, egg white, and almond essence, and knead to a smooth mixture with the hook attachment of a mixer. Sprinkle 2½ oz almonds each on 2 cookie sheets lined with waxed paper. Put the marzipan mixture in a pastry bag with a large nozzle. Pipe the marzipan mixture onto the almonds to make 16 cookies. Sprinkle with the rest of the almonds and press down lightly.

2 Bake the cookies in the oven, preheated to 355 degrees (fan oven 320 degrees) on the second shelf from the bottom for 15–17 minutes until golden brown. Allow them to cool on the cookie sheet. You can use any almonds left over on the cookie sheets in other desserts.

3 Mince the cooking chocolate and melt it with the butter in a hot bain-marie. Dip one edge of each cookie into the chocolate mixture, drain well and leave to dry.

* **Preparation time:** 1 hour (plus cooling time).
Per serving: 4 g P, 13 g F, 15 g C = 193 kcal (810 kJ).

IN THE PAN
Different types of cookies should be stored separately in well-sealed metal boxes (do not use plastic boxes because the cookies go soft in them). Put waxed paper between each layer of cookies so that they do not stick together. Add a few slices of apple to cookies that are intended to remain soft, such as macaroons or gingerbread. The apple slices should be replaced after a few days.

Coconut Macaroons

Soft structures made of stiffly beaten eggs, sugar, and coconut flakes: the best way to use egg white.

For 50 macaroons: 1 Beat 4 medium **egg whites** and 1 pinch salt with the whisk attachment of the hand-held mixer until stiff. Add 1 packet **vanilla sugar**, ⅓ cup **sugar**, and ⅔ cup **confectioners' sugar** and beat for another 3 minutes until very stiff. **2** Stir in 3 tbsp **lime juice**. Mix together 9 oz **coconut flakes**, 2 tsp grated **lemon rind** with 1 heaping tsp **cornstarch** and add to the stiffly beaten egg in 2 portions. Cover a cookie sheet with **wafers** (2 in in diameter) and put a dollop of macaroon on each wafer, using 2 teaspoons. **3** Bake in the oven, preheated to 340 degrees (fan oven 300 degrees) on the second shelf from the bottom for 14–16 minutes until they begin to go brown. Remove from the oven and put them on a rack, using a spatula and leave to cool.

* **Preparation time:** 40 minutes.
Per serving: 1 g P, 3 g F, 4 g C = 47 kcal
(197 kJ).

Almond and Chocolate Cookies

Chocolate and almonds are combined in a very high concentration here – this is how they like their cookies on the other side of the Atlantic.

For 35 cookies: 1 Mince 8 ½ oz **plain cooking chocolate**. Melt the chocolate and 4 tbsp **butter** in a hot bain-marie over medium heat, stirring occasionally. As soon as the chocolate is liquid, put to one side and leave to cool a little. **2** Beat together ⅔ cup **sugar**, 1 tbsp **vanilla sugar** and 3 medium **eggs** with a hand-held mixer for 3 minutes until foamy. Add the soft chocolate-butter mixture. Now stir in 4 ¼ oz finely **ground almonds**, ½ cup **flour**, ½ tsp **baking powder**, 2 oz **minced almonds** and 1 ¾ oz minced **milk chocolate** and add to the chocolate mixture, stirring it in only briefly. **3** Spoon dollops of the mixture onto a cookie sheet lined with waxed paper. Bake in the oven, preheated to 340 degrees (fan oven 300 degrees) on the second shelf from the bottom for 10–12 minutes. Put the cookies, still on the waxed paper, on a rack to cool. Then remove with a spatula.

* **Preparation time:** 1 hour.
  Per serving: 3 g P, 6 g F,
  11 g C = 108 kcal (450 kJ).

Filbert Double-Decker

A decorative addition to any plate of cakes: crisp filbert cookies with a redcurrant jelly filling, sprinkled with a thick layer of confectioners' sugar.

For 40–45 pieces: 1 Roast 3½ oz **ground filberts** in a pan without fat until golden brown. Leave to cool. Mix together ⅞ cup **butter** (softened at room temperature), ¾ cup **sugar**, 1 tbsp **vanilla sugar**, and 1 pinch of salt with a hand-held mixer until smooth. Add 1 **egg** (medium). **2** Add 3 cups **flour** and filberts and knead to a smooth dough with a hand-held mixer. Shape the dough into a ball and wrap in aluminum foil. Refrigerate for 1 hour. Roll out the dough on a floured work top to a thickness of ⅛ in and cut out your favorite shapes such as fir trees or stars (size 2–2¾ in). **3** Put the cookies on a cookie sheet lined with waxed paper. Bake in the oven, preheated to 340 degrees (fan oven 300 degrees) on the second shelf from the bottom for 13–15 minutes until golden brown. **4** Heat 7 oz **raspberry and redcurrant jelly** (or redcurrant jelly) while stirring. Allow to cool until it sets, then spread on half the cookies. Put with the remaining cookies on top to make a "sandwich" and press lightly. Sprinkle a thick layer of **confectioners' sugar** on all the cookies.

Preparation time: 1 hour 30 minutes.
Per piece (based on 45 pieces): 1 g P, 5 g F, 12 g C = 102 kcal (428 kJ).

ORANGE-ALMOND SLICES

VANILLA
CRESCENTS

Vanilla Crescents

A must during the Christmas period:
crumbly vanilla crescents!

For 35 crescents: 1 Roast 4 ¼ oz finely **ground almonds**
in a pan without fat, leave to cool. Mix together ½ cup
butter (softened at room temperature), ⅔ cup **confectioners'**
sugar, the pulp of 1 **vanilla bean**, 2 tbsp **vanilla sugar**, and
1 pinch of salt. Stir until smooth and then stir in 2 medium **egg yolks**.
Incorporate the almonds and 3 cups **flour**. Shape the resulting dough
into 2 rolls ¼ in in diameter, wrap in Saran wrap, and refrigerate for
2 hours. **2** Cut the rolls in slices ⅝ in thick. Shape into crescents and put
on a cookie sheet, lined with waxed paper. Bake in the oven preheated
to 355 degrees (fan oven 320 degrees) on the second shelf from the bottom
for 14–15 minutes. **3** Mix together bare ¾ cup confectioners' sugar, the
pulp of 1 vanilla bean, and 1 tbsp of vanilla sugar. Coat the hot crescent
cookies immediately in the sugar and leave to cool on a rack. Sprinkle
with the rest of the sugar.

* **Preparation time:** 1 hour (plus cooling time). **Per crescent:** 2 g P, 7 g F, 11 g C = 116 kcal (485 kJ).

Orange-Almond Slices

A delicious almond filling between the crisp short pastry.

For 40 slices: 1 Mix together ⅝ cup **butter** (softened at room temperature),
⅓ cup **sugar**, 1 tbsp **vanilla sugar**, and 1 tsp grated **orange rind** until
smooth. Briskly stir in 3 medium **egg yolks**, then incorporate 2 ½ cups **flour**,
and 1 tsp **baking powder**. **2** Roast 7 oz finely **ground almonds** in a pan
without fat, then leave to cool. Mix together ½ cup sugar, 2 tsp grated
orange rind, ⅝ cup **orange juice**, and 2 tbsp **orange liqueur**, and leave to
stand for 20 minutes. **3** Divide the dough in two equal pieces. Roll out
one piece on lightly floured waxed paper to make a square 10 x 10 in and
put on a cookie sheet together with the waxed paper. Spread the almond
paste on the pastry mix, leaving a ⅜ in edge free all round. **4** Roll out the
other half of the dough in the same way and place over the almond paste
with the paper facing upward. Now remove the paper and press the edges
of the pastry together. Prick the surface several times with a fork. Bake
in the oven, preheated to 390 degrees (fan oven 355 degrees) on the second
shelf from the bottom for 25 minutes. **5** Mix together ⅝ cup **confectioners'**
sugar with 2 tbsp orange juice. Spread this mixture on the hot pastry, leave
to cool and cut into 2 x 1 ¼ in slices.

* **Preparation time:** 55 minutes (plus cooling time). **Per slice:** 2 g P, 6 g F, 12 g C = 115 kcal (480 kJ).

Toffee Brownies

Very sophisticated: caramel toffees in a delicious chocolate pastry.

For 35 brownies: 1 Mince 4 oz **chocolate caramel toffees** with a heavy knife. Mix together 1½ cups **flour** and pinch of salt and put to one side. Mince 4 oz **dark chocolate** and melt slowly with 1 cup **butter** over a hot bain-marie. Slowly stir in ½ cup **sugar** and leave the mixture to cool. **2** Beat 4 medium **eggs** with ½ cup sugar using a hand-held mixer for 8–10 minutes until very creamy. Slowly stir in the chocolate mixture. Now sift the flour over this mixture and incorporate it. Spread the pastry mixture in a deep cookie sheet lined with waxed paper (11 x 8 in) or a large cookie sheet lined with aluminum foil to make a rectangle of the same size with raised edges. Sprinkle the chocolate caramel toffees and 5 oz **mixed nuts** and **almonds** on top. **3** Bake in the oven, preheated to 355 degrees (fan oven 320 degrees) on the second shelf from the bottom for 35 minutes. Leave to cool. Put in the refrigerator for 2 hours and cut in 1½ in squares. Store in a box in the refrigerator.

Preparation time: 55 minutes (plus cooling time).
Per serving: 2 g P, 10 g F, 13 g C = 157 kcal (658 kJ).

Stollen Muffins

The smallest kind of stollen and the quickest way to make it – and being muffin-shaped it is also pleasantly unusual.

For 12 muffins: 1 Mix together in a bowl 3½ oz **mixed dried fruit**, 2 tsp **stollen spices**, and 2 tbsp **rum**. Leave to draw for 20 minutes. **2** Stir together 7 tbsp melted **butter**, 2 medium **eggs**, ¼ cup **sugar**, 5 oz **honey**, and ½ cup **milk**. Sift into this mixture 3½ cups **flour**, 2 tsp **baking powder**, and 1 pinch of salt and stir to make a smooth mixture. Spoon the mixture in a muffin pan lined with paper molds and bake in the oven, preheated to 390 degrees (fan oven 355 degrees) on the second shelf from the bottom for 20 minutes. Leave to cool on a rack and sprinkle with **confectioners' sugar**.

* **Preparation time:** 45 minutes. **Per serving:** 4 g P, 9 g F, 41 g C = 365 kcal (1108 kJ).

Stuffed Duck à l'Orange

A very sophisticated dish: a strongly aromatic variation of duck à l'orange with a crispy skin.

Serves 4:

2 untreated oranges

7 oz onions

4 sprigs thyme

salt

pepper

1 duck (4½ lb oven-ready)

1¼ cups chicken
or duck stock

⅝ cup white wine

2 tbsp liquid honey

¾ cup orange juice

2 star anise

1 Cut the oranges with the skin into eight. Cut the onions into thin strips. Mince the thyme. Mix everything together and season with salt and pepper.

2 Rinse the duck under cold water, pat dry and season with salt inside and out. Put the stuffing inside the duck and close the opening with cooking string (see photograph below).

3 Put the duck in a roasting pan and cook in the oven, preheated to 375 degrees (fan oven 170 degrees) on the second shelf from the bottom for 1¾ hours. After 20 minutes add the chicken stock and white wine.

4 Bring the honey, orange juice, and star anise to the boil in a pan. Brush the duck with this mixture repeatedly at brief intervals during the last 10 minutes of its cooking time.

5 Take the duck out of the roasting pan and allow to rest briefly. Degrease the roasting juices and stir the remaining honey and orange mixture. Bring to the boil, pour through a strainer and season generously with pepper. Serve the duck with the sauce.

* **Preparation time:** 2 hours.
Per serving: 65 g P, 45 g F, 9 g C = 702 kcal (2940 kJ).

THE ART OF SEWING
Impressive but simple: close the opening with cocktail sticks and tie these with yarn.

Red Cabbage and Quince

Red cabbage as you have never tasted before – with quince and white wine, it is transformed into a delicate, refined dish.

Serves 4: 1 Mince 2 **onions**. Peel 1 **quince**, cut into quarters and core. Cut into ⅜-in cubes. Fry the onions and quince in 2 tbsp **butter** for 2 minutes over medium heat. Add ⅝ cup **white wine**, put the lid on loosely and braise until the liquid has evaporated. **2** Add 1 jar **red cabbage** (1 lb 8 oz drained weight) and cook over medium heat for 10 minutes. Season with salt, pepper, and **sugar**.

* **Preparation time:** 25 minutes. **Per serving:** 3 g P, 1 g F, 12 g C = 79 kcal (329 kJ).

Chestnut Potatoes

The chestnuts come from a pack and therefore do not require any work!
They make a delicious addition to the potatoes.

Serves 2: 1 Cook 10½ oz small **firm boiling potatoes** in their skins in
salted water, run under cold water, wait until they stop steaming and
peel. Heat 3 tbsp **oil** in a non-stick pan, add the potatoes and fry over
medium heat until golden brown. Only turn the potatoes when the under-
side is brown. **2** Mince 1 **onion** and add with the 5 oz **chestnuts** (vacuum-
packed or from a pan, drained) and 1 tbsp **butter** to the potatoes in the
pan and fry for another 2 minutes. Sprinkle 1 tsp **sugar** and melt briefly.
Season the potatoes with salt and pepper and sprinkle with 2 tbsp **parsley**.

Preparation time: 45 minutes. **Per serving:** 4 g P, 23 g F, 45 g C = 403 kcal (1687 kJ).

Orange Pannacotta

*The addition of orange to this sophisticated Italian dessert adds
a refreshing touch while the cinnamon adds a note of Christmas.*

Serves 4: 1 Soak 3 leaves of **<u>gelatin</u>** in cold water. Bring 2¼ cups
<u>whipping cream</u>, 3 tbsp **<u>sugar</u>**, 1 packet **<u>vanilla sugar</u>** with 1 **<u>cinnamon
stick</u>** to the boil and simmer for 5 minutes over low heat. **2** Remove
from the heat, squeeze the gelatin to remove as much water as possible
and dissolve in the hot cream. Pour through a strainer. Stir in 1 ½ tsp
grated **<u>orange rind</u>** and pour into 4 ramekins (⅝ cup content). Refrigerate
for at least 5 hours (even better overnight). **3** Peel 2 **<u>oranges</u>** with a
sharp knife in such a way that all white pith is removed. Cut the orange
in quarters and then in slices. Stir together 1 tbsp **<u>honey</u>** and 2 tsp
<u>orange juice</u>. **4** Dip the ramekins briefly in hot water and turn out on a
plate. Orange the slices of orange round the Pannacotta and sprinkle
with the honey sauce.

Preparation time: 15 minutes (plus cooling time).
Per serving: 5 g P, 38 g F, 24 g C = 450 kcal (1889 kJ).

Christmas Trifle

Fruity, creamy, chocolaty: alternate layers of berry compote, chocolate cake, and yoghourt have been combined to create a gourmet dessert.

Serves 4–6: 1 Stir 1 heaping tsp **cornstarch** into 2 tbsp **red wine**. Bring to the boil 1 lb **frozen mixed berries**, 2 heaping tbsp **sugar**, 1 tbsp **vanilla sugar**, ½ cup **red wine** with 2 pinches of **ground cinnamon**. Stir in the cornstarch and bring to the boil again. Put to one side and leave to cool. **2** Coarsely crumble 5 oz **chocolate cake** (bought ready-made). Stir together 10½ oz **yoghourt** until creamy. **3** Spoon 1 thin layer of compote into individual glasses or bowls. Cover with half the crumbled chocolate cake and then half the yoghourt. Repeat the layers. Finally garnish the trifle with a little berry compote.

* **Preparation time:** 15 minutes (plus cooling time).
  Per serving (based on 6 servings): 4 g P, 7 g F, 32 g C = 224 kcal (937 kJ).

otato Salad with Scampi

Potato salad with scampi make a delicious appetizer for a festive occasion.

Serves 4: 1 Wash 1¾ lb small <u>**firm boiling potatoes**</u> and boil with their skins for 20–25 minutes. Drain and leave to cool. Then peel and cut into slices. **2** Cut 1¾ oz <u>**sun-dried tomatoes**</u> (without the oil) into thin strips. Mince 3½ oz <u>**celery ribs**</u> having first removed the stringy fibers. Mince 2 <u>**shallots**</u>. **3** Fry the celery and shallots in 2 tbsp oil until transparent. Add 1 cup <u>**vegetable stock**</u>, 3 tbsp <u>**tarragon**</u> or <u>**white wine vinegar**</u>, and the tomatoes, bring to the boil, and pour over the potatoes. Season with salt and pepper and stir in 1 tbsp minced <u>**tarragon**</u> and 2 tsp <u>**Dijon mustard**</u>. **4** Shell 12 large <u>**scampi**</u> (about 14 oz), cut lengthways along the back and remove the intestines. Fry the scampi in 1 tbsp <u>**olive oil**</u> over medium heat. Sprinkle with <u>**paprika powder**</u> and 1 tbsp <u>**lemon juice**</u>. Season with salt and pepper.

* **Preparation time:** 50 minutes. Per serving: 21 g P, 10 g F, 21 g C = 268 kcal (1122 kJ).

Turkey Involtini

These rolls look so exquisitely delicate that to describe them as a roulade seems a little crude.

Serves 2: 1 Flatten 4 small **turkey escalopes** (2¾ oz each) between Saran wrap using a steak bat. Season lightly with salt and pepper. Put 1 slice of **air-dried ham** on each escalope and sprinkle each one with 1 tbsp **Gouda**. Roll up the meat and secure with cocktail sticks. **2** Heat 2 tbsp **oil** and 1½ tbsp **butter**, add the involtini and fry on all sides over medium heat for 3–4 minutes until golden- brown. Add ½ cup **chicken stock** and 10 **cherry tomatoes** and cook for another 2 minutes.

Preparation time: 30 minutes. Per serving: 49 g P, 22 g F, 1 g C = 404 kcal (1689 kJ).

Fried Onion Roast Beef

A delicious meal in a trice: the mere smell of the golden-brown onions will put you in a good mood.

Serves 2: 1 Cut 14 oz **onions** into thin slices and fry in 2 tbsp hot **butter** until golden brown. Season with salt and pepper. **2** Grease a griddle with 1 tbsp **oil** and fry 4 **slices of roast beef** (3½ oz each) over high heat for 1 minute on each side. Season with salt and pepper. Serve with the fried onions on top.

* **Preparation time:** 25 minutes. **Per serving:** 47 g P, 27 g F, 9 g C = 467 kcal (1956 kJ).

Creamed Savoy Cabbage

You like Savoy cabbage? You like potatoes? Then this will appeal to you: we have combined both ingredients and created a superb dish of creamed Savoy cabbage and potatoes.

Serves 2: 1 Wash and prepare generous 1 lb **Savoy cabbage** and remove the stem. Cut the Savoy cabbage into thin strips and cook in boiling salted water for 4 minutes. Drain and run under cold water. **2** Mince 1 **onion** and fry in 2 tbsp **butter** until transparent. Add ½ cup **whipping cream** and ½ cup **milk**, bring to the boil and season with salt, pepper, and **nutmeg**. Add the cabbage, cook for 1 minute and thicken with a little **mashed potato powder**. **3** Lightly brown 4 tbsp butter in a small pan. Add 1 oz **filberts** and serve with the creamed cabbage.

Preparation time: 25 minutes. **Per serving:** 11 g P, 58 g F, 18 g C = 639 kcal (2670 kJ).

Cod in Puff Pastry

Baking fish in pastry has two advantages: it remains very moist while cooking beautifully in a delicious crisp pastry.

Serves 4–6:

3 ½ oz sun-dried tomatoes (in oil)

2 sprigs basil

4 cod fillets with skin (7 oz each)

salt

pepper

8 sheets frozen puff pastry

1 egg yolk

5 tbsp whipping cream

7 oz sour cream

1 tbsp minced chives

1 tbsp lemon juice

1 ¾ oz minced mushroom caviar

BEAUTIFUL SCALES
Make the scales by carefully pressing kitchen scissors into the pastry and seal the ends by pressing them together with a fork. The fish-like appearance is now complete!

1 Drain the tomatoes and puree coarsely with 1 tbsp tomato oil. Mince the basil and add to the tomatoes. Season the fish lightly with salt and pepper, then spread the tomato mixture on top. Put 2 fillets with their meaty side together, repeat with the other 2 fillets and put in the refrigerator.

2 Put 4 sheets of puff pastry on top of each other and roll out to make a rectangle 12 x 10 in; repeat to make a second rectangle. Cut 2 fish shapes out of the dough, slightly larger than the fish fillets. Beat together the egg yolk and cream.

3 Place each double fillet on a fish-shaped piece of pastry. Brush the edges with the egg mixture and put the other fish-shaped pastry on top. Press the edges of the pastry together. Make a fish-scale pattern on the top of each one. Brush the pastry with the rest of the egg mixture.

4 Put the fish on a cookie sheet, lined with waxed paper and bake in the oven, preheated to 430 degrees (fan oven 390 degrees) on the second shelf from the bottom for 25–30 minutes until golden-brown.

5 Stir chives, lemon juice, salt, and pepper into the sour cream. Take the fish out of the oven and leave to rest for 3–4 minutes. Stir the mushroom caviar into the sauce and serve with the fish.

* **Preparation time:** 1 hour 30 minutes.
  Per serving (based on 6 servings):
  32 g P, 28 g F, 31 g C = 510 kcal (2138 kJ).

Potato and Morel Soup

As refined as it is exquisite: the morels develop their powerful aroma in the light foam of the potato soup.

Serves 4: 1 Soak ⅓ oz dried **morels** in hot water. Peel 14 oz **potatoes** and cut into cubes. Cut 1 **onion** into thin strips. Add both to 3½ cups **vegetable stock** together with ½ tsp **dried marjoram** and cook for 15 minutes. Puree with a mixer until smooth and stir in ½ cup semi-beaten **whipping cream**. Season with salt and pepper. **2** Mince the morels and fry with 1 minced **shallot** in 2 tbsp butter. Season with salt and pepper and add 1 tbsp **Madeira** or **sherry**. **3** Serve the hot soup in bowls and serve with the morels and **minced chives**.

* Preparation time: 40 minutes. Per serving: 4 g P, 15 g F, 14 g C = 210 kcal (880 kJ).

Shrimp in Aspic

The perfect appetizer for a stress-free party menu:
aspic is very quick and easy to make and tastes absolutely delicious.

Serves 4: 1 Soak 3 leaves of white **gelatin** in cold water. Cut 1 **onion** into rings and bring to the boil with ⅝ cup **white wine**, 1 cup **fish stock**, 2 tbsp **white wine vinegar**, and sprig of **dill**. Remove from the heat and dissolve the squeezed gelatin in it. Allow to stand for 20 minutes. Season generously with salt, pepper, and **sugar**. Pour through a strainer and leave to cool to room temperature. **2** Stir a little salt, pepper, and 1–2 tsp minced dill into 9 oz **shrimp** and put into 4 ramekins (⅝ cup capacity). Now pour the stock on the shrimp and refrigerate for 4 hours. **3** Mix together 3½ oz **crème fraîche**, 2 tbsp **lemon juice**, 1 tbsp **tomato paste**, salt, and pepper. Remove the aspic from the molds and serve with the dip and a little salad.

* Preparation time: 30 minutes (plus cooling time).
Per serving: 15 g P, 8 g F, 5 g C = 185 kcal (773 kJ).

Almond Cookie Parfait

Without ice cream machine and without much trouble:
an ice cream dessert that will delight every one.

Serves 8–10: 1 Allow 2 cups **vanilla ice cream** to thaw a little for
15 minutes. Coarsely mince 3½ oz **almond cookies**. Mince 3½ oz **dark
chocolate**. Grate the rind of 1 **orange** (untreated). Beat ⅝ cup **whipping
cream** until stiff. Line a baking pan (8 in long) with waxed paper. **2** Stir
the ice cream thoroughly. Quickly fold in the cream, cookies, chocolate
and orange rind. Put the mixture in the mold. Return to the freezer
and keep overnight. Take out of the mold. Cut into slices and serve with
½ cup **raspberry sauce** (from a bottle)

Preparation time: 30 minutes (plus freezing time).
Per serving (based on 10 servings): 3 g P, 16 g F, 17 g C = 224 kcal (940 kJ).

Honey Cake

Even better with butter and marmalade.

For 20 slices: 1 Heat up ⅝ cup **milk**, 3½ oz **black molasses** (or **corn syrup**), 3½ oz **acacia honey** and bare ½ cup **brown sugar** until the sugar has dissolved, then leave to cool down. Mince 1¾ oz **candied ginger** and 2½ oz **candied orange peel** very finely. Sift 5 cups **flour**, 1 tbsp **baking powder**, and ½ oz **gingerbread spice** with 1 packet **vanilla sugar** and 1 pinch of salt.
2 Add the cold honey milk, 2 medium **eggs**, and 7 tbsp cold **butter**, and beat with the hook attachment of the hand-held mixer until smooth. Transfer the dough to a cake pan, lined with waxed paper (12 in long). Bake in the oven, preheated to 340 degrees (fan oven 300 degrees) on the second shelf from the bottom for 60–65 minutes. Take out of the pan and allow to cool.
3 Stir ⅞ cup **confectioners' sugar** into 3 tbsp **orange juice** and pour over the cake. Garnish with candied orange peel.

Preparation time: 1 hour 30 minutes (plus cooling time).
Per slice: 4 g P, 5 g F, 45 g C = 235 kcal (992 kJ).

Steak Tartare Meatballs

These meatballs are low in calories and very tasty, made with steak mince they are quite irresistible.

Serves 2: 1 Mix together 7 oz **ground beef steak** with 2¾ oz drained **low-fat curd** and 1 tsp **mustard**. Season with salt and pepper. Mince 2 **scallions** and stir into the mince with 2 tbsp minced **parsley**. Shape 2 flat meatballs from the ground beef. Grease the griddle with 1 tbsp **oil** and broil the meatballs for 2 minutes on each. **2** Stir 2¾ oz low-fat curd with 4 tbsp **milk**, 1 tsp mustard, 1 minced **red bell pepper**, and 1 tbsp minced parsley until smooth. Cut 2 tomatoes into slices. Cut 1 **roll** in half and spread each half with some curd, put 1 meatball on top and garnish with the tomatoes, 1 **salad leaf**, the rest of the low-fat curd, and 1 sprig of parsley.

* **Preparation time: 35 minutes. Per serving:** 36 g P, 6 g F, 21 g C = 289 kcal (1212 kJ).

Fried Bread Dumplings

A brilliant way to use dumplings left over from the day before. The dumplings taste even better!

Serves 2: 1 Cook 4 **bread dumplings**, following the instructions on the packet. Allow to cool. **2** Cut the dumplings into ⅜-in slices. Heat 3 tbsp **butter** with 2 tbsp **pumpkin seeds**, and 1 tsp coarse **black pepper** in a large non-stick pan. Add the dumpling slices and cook for 2–4 minutes on each side until golden brown. Season with salt.

Preparation time: 20 minutes. **Per serving:** 13 g P, 29 g F, 33 g C = 440 kcal (1844 kJ).

441

Creole Pasta

Oranges, curry, raisins, and cilantro give the pasta a pleasing sweet, fruity taste, and a touch of the exotic.

Serves 2: 1 Wash and prepare 5 oz **celery** and remove the stringy fibers. Cut into thin slices. Cut 2 **cloves of garlic** and 2 small **onions** into thin slices. Peel 2 **oranges** in such a way that the white pith is completely removed. Remove the membranes that surround the segments and catch the juice. **2** Cook 9 oz **rigatoni** in plenty of boiling salted water with 1 tsp **curry powder**, following the instructions on the packet. **3** Meanwhile heat 2 tbsp **olive oil** in a pan, add the celery, garlic, and onions, and fry over medium heat. Add 1¾ oz **raisins** and sprinkle with 1 tsp curry powder. Add the orange segments with the juice. **4** Drain the pasta and transfer to the pan. Stir in 1 tbsp minced **cilantro**.

* **Preparation time:** 25 minutes. **Per serving:** 18 g P, 14 g F, 114 g C = 668 kcal (2797 kJ).

Winter Ratatouille

Treat yourself to the aromatic charms of this variation on a Mediterranean dish. Even in winter there are still enough colorful vegetables.

Serves 2: 1 Cut 7 oz **onions** lengthways into quarters and then cut across into slices ⅛-in thick. Peel 3 ½ oz **carrots** and cut into thin slices. Wash and prepare 3 ½ oz **celery** and cut into ¾ in chunks. Cut 7 oz **zucchinis** lengthways and cut into ⅜ in large cubes. **2** Heat 4 tbsp **olive oil** in a pan, add the onions and the carrots and fry over medium heat for 3 minutes. Add the celery and zucchinis and fry for another 3 minutes. Season with salt and pepper. **3** Add a 14 oz **can of tomatoes** with the juice to the pan with ½ tsp **herbs of Provence**. Bring to the boil and simmer for 3 minutes over low heat. Serve immediately.

* **Preparation time:** 40 minutes. **Per serving:** 5 g P, 21 g F, 12 g C = 256 kcal (1073 kJ).

Maldive Salad

These paradise islands may be far away, but you can enjoy its spirit from afar with this exquisitely delicious salad.

Serves 2: 1 Wash ½ **cucumber**, peel, and cut in half lengthways. Remove the seeds and cut into ⅛ in thick slices. Wash 1 **romaine lettuce heart**, spin-dry and tear into pieces. Wash 1 **red apple**, cut into quarters, core and cut into slices. Cut 1 **avocado** in half, remove the pit, peel, and cut lengthways into slices. **2** Peel the rind of 1 **lemon** thinly with a potato peeler and cut into thin strips with a knife. Put 3–4 tbsp **lemon juice**, 1 tsp **honey**, 4 tbsp **sunflower oil**, salt, and pepper in a jar with a screw-top lid. Close and shake vigorously. **3** Arrange the romaine lettuce, cucumber, apple, and avocado on a dish, pour the vinaigrette over the salad and sprinkle with **lemon rind**.

* **Preparation time:** 15 minutes. **Per serving:** 2 g P, 34 g F, 14 g C = 368 kcal (1540 kJ).

Carrot and Orange Soup

Stuffed with vitamins and aroma, a perfect dish for all seasons: carrots, oranges, and scallions combine to make an exquisite soup.

Serves 2: 1 Peel 1 lb 2 oz **carrots** and cut diagonally into slices. Cut 1 bunch of **scallions** diagonally into rings. Fry the white of the onions and the carrots in 2 tbsp **butter**. **2** Add 1 ¼ cups **vegetable stock**, cover and simmer for 12–15 minutes. Remove about ¼ of the carrots with a skimming ladle and finely puree the rest of the carrots with a hand-held mixer in the pan. While doing so, gradually add ½ cup **orange juice**. **3** Bring the soup to the boil again and season with salt, pepper and 1 pinch of **sugar**. Remove the seeds of 1 **red bell pepper**, cut into thin slices and heat the soup again with the carrots and scallion rings. Serve with 2 tbsp **crème fraîche**.

* Preparation time: 30 minutes. **Per serving:** 4 g P, 21 g F, 23 g C = 297 kcal (1244 kJ).

Spaghetti a l'Amatriciana

One of the simplest and therefore probably one of the most popular of all Roman pasta dishes.

Serves 2: 1 Mince 5 oz **pancetta** (or **bacon**). Cut 1 **onion** into small cubes. Heat 2 tbsp **olive oil** in a pan. Add the pancetta and onions and fry over medium heat until brown, stirring all the while. **2** Add 1 can of **minced tomatoes** (14 oz drained weight) and cook for 15 minutes over low heat while stirring. Season with salt, pepper, and a little dried **chili pepper**. Cook 9 oz **spaghetti**, following the instructions on the packet, and drain. **3** Stir 1 tbsp flat-leaved **parsley** into the sauce and serve with the spaghetti.

Preparation time: 35 minutes. Per serving: 30 g P, 36 g F, 94 g C = 824 kcal (3450 kJ).

Sauerkraut Gnocchi

A delicious way of serving gnocchi: in German style with bacon and sauerkraut.

Serves 2: 1 Heat 2 tbsp **oil** in a pan. Add 1¾ oz **diced bacon** and 1 minced **onion** and fry together for 3–4 minutes until brown. **2** Add 1 can of **sauerkraut** (10½ oz drained weight) and fry for another 2 minutes. Add ½ cup **white wine**, cover and simmer for 10 minutes. Five minutes before the end of the cooking time, add 3½ oz **cherry tomatoes**. **3** Cook 14 oz fresh **gnocchi**, following the instructions of the packet, drain and serve with the sauerkraut.

* **Preparation time:** 25 minutes. **Per serving:** 13 g P, 19 g F, 72 g C = 530 kcal (2233 kJ).

Quick Curd Stollen

Quick to make because it uses baking powder rather than yeast, and moist because it is stuffed with apricots and almonds.

For 20 pieces:

14 oz dried soft apricots

⅞ cup orange juice

2 tbsp lemon juice

⅔ cup sugar

3½ oz almonds

5 cups flour

3½ oz whipping cream

1 tbsp baking powder

3 medium eggs

salt

12 oz curd

1 cup 2 tbsp butter

¼ cup confectioners' sugar

BAKING STOLLEN WITHOUT A STOLLEN MOLD

If you do not have a special stollen mold you can proceed as follows. Roll out the dough, spread the filling all over the dough and roll up one third of the way towards the middle. Then from the other side, roll up to two thirds of the way, to meet the other side. Place the stollen upside down on a cookie sheet, lined with waxed paper, and bake as described in the recipe.

1 Mince the apricots, add to the orange juice, lemon juice, and ¼ cup oz sugar. Bring to the boil. Cook over medium heat for 5 minutes without a lid until the juice is almost completely absorbed, stirring occasionally. Put the fruit mixture in a bowl, puree briefly with a mixer, and leave to cool down. Roast the almonds in a pan without fat and leave to cool.

2 Sift the flour, cornstarch, and baking powder in a bowl. Add bare ½ cup sugar, eggs, ¼ tsp salt, and curd, and mix with the hook attachment of a hand-held mixer. Cut ⅞ cup butter in small pieces and incorporate into the flour and curd mixture. Roll the dough out on a floured surface to make a 16 x 16 in square. Spread the apricot mixture evenly all over the dough. Sprinkle with almonds. Roll up tightly starting from a long side.

3 Put in a greased stollen mold (15¼ in long) with the "seam side" upwards. Turn over onto on a cookie sheet lined with waxed paper and press down the stollen mold. Bake in the oven, preheated to 390 degrees (fan oven 355 degrees) on the second shelf from the bottom for 50 minutes. Lift the mold up and bake for another 10 minutes. Melt 1½ tbsp butter, brush over the stollen and sprinkle with confectioners' sugar. Leave to cool.

* Preparation time: 1 hour 30 minutes (plus cooling time).
Per serving: 7 g P, 15 g F, 42 g C = 332 kcal (1404 kJ).